Rape Culture and Religious Studies

Feminist Studies and Sacred Texts Series

Series Editor
Susanne Scholz (sscholz@mail.smu.edu)

Advisory Board
Naomi Appleton, Tamara Cohn Eskenazi,
Lynn Huber, Sa'diyya Shaikh, and Sharada Sugirtharajah

Feminist Studies and Sacred Texts makes available innovative and provocative research on the interface of feminist studies and sacred texts. Books in the series are grounded in religious studies perspectives, theories, and methodologies, while engaging with the wide spectrum of feminist studies, including women's studies, gender studies, sexuality studies, masculinity studies, and queer studies. They embrace intersectional discourses such as postcolonialism, ecology, disability, class, race, and ethnicity studies. Furthermore, they are inclusive of religious texts from both established and new religious traditions and movements, and they experiment with inter- and cross-religious perspectives. The series publishes monographs and edited collections that critically locate feminist studies and sacred texts within the historical, cultural, sociological, anthropological, comparative, political, and religious contexts in which they were produced, read, and continue to shape present practices and discourses.

Titles in Series

Rape Culture and Religious Studies: Critical and Pedagogical Engagements, edited by
    Rhiannon Graybill, Meredith Minister, and Beatrice Lawrence
Jewish Feminism: Framed and Reframed, by Esther Fuchs
Feminist Theory and the Bible: Interrogating the Sources, by Esther Fuchs
Unraveling and Reweaving Sacred Canon in Africana Womanhood, edited by Rosetta E.
    Ross and Rose Mary Amenga-Etego

Rape Culture and Religious Studies

Critical and Pedagogical Engagements

Edited by Rhiannon Graybill,
Meredith Minister,
and Beatrice Lawrence

LEXINGTON BOOKS
Lanham • Boulder • New York • London

Published by Lexington Books
An imprint of The Rowman & Littlefield Publishing Group, Inc.
4501 Forbes Boulevard, Suite 200, Lanham, Maryland 20706
www.rowman.com

6 Tinworth Street, London SE11 5AL, United Kingdom

Copyright © 2019 by The Rowman & Littlefield Publishing Group, Inc.

All rights reserved. No part of this book may be reproduced in any form or by any electronic or mechanical means, including information storage and retrieval systems, without written permission from the publisher, except by a reviewer who may quote passages in a review.

British Library Cataloguing in Publication Information Available

Library of Congress Cataloging-in-Publication Data

Names: Graybill, Rhiannon, 1984- editor.
Title: Rape culture and religious studies : critical and pedagogical engagements / edited by Rhiannon Graybill, Meredith Minister, and Beatrice Lawrence.
Description: Lanham : Lexington Books, 2019. | Series: Feminist studies and sacred texts series | Includes bibliographical references and index.
Identifiers: LCCN 2019012143 (print) | LCCN 2019013926 (ebook) | ISBN 9781498562850 (electronic) | ISBN 9781498562843 (cloth)
Subjects: LCSH: Rape--Religious aspects.
Classification: LCC HV6558 (ebook) | LCC HV6558 .R3533 2019 (print) | DDC 364.15/32071--dc23
LC record available at https://lccn.loc.gov/2019012143

Contents

Acknowledgments		vii
Introduction: Engaging Rape Culture, Reimagining Religious Studies *Rhiannon Graybill, Meredith Minister, and Beatrice Lawrence*		1
1	Reading Biblical Rape Texts beyond a Cop-Out Hermeneutics in the Trump Era *Susanne Scholz*	21
2	Constructions of Hindu Mythology after the Rape of Jyoti Singh Pandey: Coupling Activism with Pedagogy *T. Nicole Goulet*	37
3	Teaching Rape, Slavery, and Genocide in Bible and Culture *Gwynn Kessler*	55
4	On #MosqueMeToo: Lessons for Nuancing and Better Implementing the Goals of #MeToo *Kirsten Boles*	73
5	Judges 19 and Non-Con: Sado-Kantian Aesthetics of Violence in the Tale of an Unnamed Woman *Minenhle Nomalungelo Khumalo*	93
6	To Confess the Fundamental Marian Dogma: Postulating the Doctrine of Mary's Reproductive Justice *Jeremy Posadas*	113
7	Rape Culture and the Rabbinic Construction of Gender *Beatrice Lawrence*	137

| 8 | Sex and Alien Encounter: Rethinking Consent as a Rape Prevention Strategy
Meredith Minister | 157 |
| 9 | Good Intentions are Not Enough
Rhiannon Graybill | 175 |

| Index | 195 |
| About the Contributors | 205 |

Acknowledgments

The Wabash Center for Teaching and Learning in Theology and Religion brought us together and supported early stages of our work with summer grant funding. We are grateful to our Wabash cohort, especially those who helped us plan a preliminary workshop on sexual violence: Meghan Clark, Shannon Dunn, and Caleb Iyer Elfenbein. We would also like to thank the other members of our cohort: Spencer Dew, Joseph Tucker Edmonds, Jenna Gray-Hildenbrand, Erik Hammerstrom, Leah Kalmanson, Nanette Spina, and SherAli Tareen, as well as our Wabash leaders Richard Ascough, Trina Janiec Jones, Nami Kim, Carolyn Medine, and Tom Pearson. Tom also supported our research by including an article we co-authored in the journal *Teaching Theology and Religion*; we are grateful to him and the anonymous reviewers. We would also like to thank Elizabeth Pritchard, Susan M. Woolever, and the *Journal of Feminist Studies in Religion* for publishing a roundtable we curated on teaching and sexual violence as well as the contributors to that roundtable: Susanne Scholz, Caleb Iyer Elfenbein, Jeremy Posadas, and Mary A. Nyangweso. Several of the papers in this volume were originally presented at the 2016 Annual Joint Meeting of the Society of Biblical Literature and American Academy of Religion; we would like to thank AAR's Feminist Theory and Religious Reflection Group (FTRR) and SBL's Gender, Sexuality, and the Bible for co-sponsoring the session.

At Lexington Books, we have been lucky to work with editors Sarah Craig, Michael Gibson, and Mikayla Mislak. We also express our thanks to Susanne Scholz for including the volume in the series Feminist Studies and Sacred Texts.

Rhiannon Graybill would like to thank her colleagues in the Gender and Sexuality Studies program at Rhodes College, including Judith Haas, Rebecca Tuvel, Leslie Petty, Evie Perry, and Zandria Robinson, who participated in a panel on sexual violence on campus that was an early incubator for many of the ideas around gender and violence in this volume. The Department of Religious Studies has also provided consistent support. In addition, she would like to thank Kurt Beals, Jessica Crist, Raphael Graybill, Turner Graybill, Emily Regier, Lena Salaymeh, and Krista Spiller.

Beatrice Lawrence would like to thank her colleagues and friends at Seattle University, who have demonstrated unwavering support for her work in both teaching and scholarship, as well as the University's Dean's Office, which provided a fellowship for research during the summer of 2017. In addition, she is grateful for the support of her community of friends and scholars, in Seattle and elsewhere, for creating a safe space to discuss matters as difficult as these. Most of all, she thanks her daughters, Elana and Abigail, who make this work all the more urgent. The W. J. Millard Professor fund provided financial support for indexing.

Meredith Minister would like to thank all of the students that taught her about the problem of sexual violence on campus both at Kentucky Wesleyan College and at Shenandoah University and the colleagues that have supported her at both institutions, especially those that have given platforms for her research on and teaching about sexual violence including Amy Sarch and Petra Schweitzer. She would also like to thank the two people who most consistently push her to make her written arguments better: Kevin Minister and Sarah Bloesch. During the summer of 2017, Meredith had the opportunity to attend an institute at Elon University on "Diverse Philosophical Approaches to Sexual Violence" developed by Ann Cahill and sponsored by the National Endowment for the Humanities. This institute brought together an incredible group of scholars working on sexual violence and helped me to consider some key arguments in this book. Many thanks to the institute leaders, Ann Cahill, Susan Brison, Louise du Toit, Nicola Gavey, Renée Herbele, Debra Bergoffen, and Sarah Clark Miller and to my small group, Michael Deckard, Zenon Culverhouse, and Jennifer Collins-Elliott. Thanks also to everyone who got me through cancer treatment, including Bea and Rhiannon (who sent clever and fun care packages from faraway places), my partner, Kevin Minister, friends who drove me to chemo when Kevin was out of town, Andrea Smith and Dana Baxter, my parents, grandmother, and aunt (H. D. and Kay Williams, Glenda Cooper, and Ladonna Cooper), my in-laws (Andy and Becky Minister), my brother-in-law (Stephen Minister) and his family, Justin Allen for being an information node, relieving me of the responsibility, and, finally, to everyone who laughed at my jokes about death instead of staring at me with horror (an especially high mention to folks who crafted new jokes).

Introduction

Engaging Rape Culture, Reimagining Religious Studies

Rhiannon Graybill, Meredith Minister, and Beatrice Lawrence

#MeToo. These two simple words, often presented via social media hashtag, began as a way of naming experiences of sexual violence and rape culture; they have grown to encompass a powerful and potent social movement. As a hashtag on social media and as a broader advocacy campaign, #MeToo has emerged as a powerful force for social change, as well as a marker of the fraught conversation surrounding rape culture. In 2017, the #MeToo campaign went viral as survivors of sexual violence felt increasingly empowered to share their stories. Allegations of sexual violence against prominent media and political figures soon followed, leading to the downfalls of film producer Harvey Weinstein, comedian Louis C.K., actor Kevin Spacey, television personalities Charlie Rose and Matt Lauer, and many others. On social media, in newspapers and magazines and blogs, and in conversations small and large, women and men have begun to share their experiences of sexual violence, sexual harassment, and everyday encounters of rape culture. Many others have joined in, adding simply "#MeToo."

While many of the most spectacular #MeToo revelations have involved celebrities in Hollywood or the media, sexual violence and rape culture are hardly limited to those milieus. #MeToo is also a movement by and for people who describe experiences of sexual misconduct that span from the troubling to the horrifying. #MeToo thus names the pervasiveness of rape and rape culture (as well as the ways in which the consequences of sexual violence are linked to social capital, or the lack of it).[1] Aggressors, in other words, face more infrequent consequences when their accusers have less social capital in the forms of race, sexuality, class, language, or ability. The #MeToo movement has joined an already powerful movement against sexual violence on college and university campuses. Student activists have worked to draw attention to the sexual violence occurring on campus, and to demand change from their institutions. Frequently cited is the statistic that 1 in 5 college women will be sexually assaulted, along with a smaller percentage of men.[2] The issue has begun to attract heightened national attention, including Jon Krakauer's book *Missoula: Rape and the Justice System in a College Town* (2015), the Oscar-nominated documentary *The Hunting Ground* (2015), and the "It's On Us" campaign (2014 to present), originally sponsored by the White House and headed up by then vice president Joe Biden.

As teachers and scholars of religious studies, we find ourselves in a critical moment. We live and work in communities touched by sexual violence. The same is true of our students. Responding to this moment, *Rape Culture and Religious Studies: Critical and Pedagogical Engagements* brings the conversation about sexual violence, especially sexual violence on college and university campuses, to Religious Studies. As a discipline, Religious Studies has a lengthy history of engaging with social issues. Gender, race, sexuality, ability, and class are all familiar categories of analysis in the discipline; we talk about these questions in the classroom and take them up in our research. And yet the conversation about campus sexual violence has remained largely separate from conversations within Religious Studies, including conversations about pedagogy. This is striking given the prevalence of sexual violence in religious texts, traditions, and communities and on the very campuses where religious studies experts work and teach. What would happen, if instead of covering our ears or burying our heads in the sand (or in committee work), we listened to the #MeToos echoing around us, in our classrooms, our texts, our syllabi, and our institutions?

Rape Culture and Religious Studies: Critical and Pedagogical Engagements undertakes this work of listening for #MeToos, as well as engaging, critically and compassionately, with them. The present volume offers both a response and an addition to these ongoing conversations. It is a response to this conversation because many of the contributions argue that we need deeper and more critical analyses of sexual violence in order to intervene effectively. It is an addition to this conversation because each essay suggests that the problem of sexual violence has important connections to religion and religious traditions, that understanding sexual violence in religious texts and traditions can shed light on the problem of sexual violence writ large, and that we need better ways to teach about religious texts and traditions that overtly promote or include sexual violence.

In the remainder of this introduction, we offer a brief overview of the #MeToo movement, the idea of "rape culture," and the significance of both as they relate to religious studies. We conclude with some specific comments about the essays contained within this volume. Our hope is that this volume will intervene in the problem of sexual violence at the level of cultural analysis and, ultimately, change.

A BRIEF HISTORY OF #METOO

Though #MeToo gained international fame in 2017, its origins lie much earlier. Most people heard about the campaign in relation to the hashtag and its encouraged use by celebrity activists such as Alyssa Milano and Ashley Judd. But the movement in fact began in 2006, and Tarana Burke, its founder, points to a moment a decade prior to that as the unofficial start of the movement. Burke was a youth camp director counseling a camper who had been abused. After meeting with the girl, Burke realized that the simple phrase "me too" had the potential to make connections that empower survivors, particularly in minority communities.[3] Two decades after Burke's realization, this phrase has become a way for survivors to share their stories.

#MeToo remains a powerful and popular statement. However, it is not without complications. The #MeToo movement has been accused of eliding important differences between different forms of sexual violence, of denying due process or fair treatment to the accused, and of empowering white women while continuing to ignore or even silence women of color. Reflecting on #MeToo, actress and sexual violence survivor Gabrielle Union told the *New York Times*, "I think the floodgates have opened for white women. I don't think it's a coincidence whose pain has been taken seriously. Whose pain we have showed historically and continued to show."[4] In her remarks, Union touched upon a critique that has been increasingly leveled against #MeToo: that the movement, though ostensibly concerned with all survivors of sexual violence, is in practice a campaign of, by, and for white women. Similar critiques have been raised with respect to sexuality (i.e., that #MeToo excludes gay, lesbian, and queer survivors), gender identity (#MeToo is only concerned with cisgender survivors), and disability (#MeToo excludes disabled survivors).[5]

Some of these critiques have been voiced by Tarana Burke herself. In particular, Burke raises questions over how a hashtag born in black communities was popularized largely by highly privileged white women responding to sexual violence, sexual harassment, and widespread sexism in Hollywood.[6] This concern that the #MeToo movement is being shifted away from marginalized people comes across clearly in an interview between Burke and Elizabeth Adetiba. When asked by Adetiba to explain her fear that the hashtag would move the conversation in a different direction, Burke responds, "I mean moving away from marginalized people. And to some degree, it's still happening. The conversation is largely about Harvey Weinstein or other individual bogeymen. No matter how much I keep talking about power and privilege, they keep bringing it back to individuals."[7] As Burke describes, #MeToo often functions as a highly individual, and individualizing, response to sexual violence. The risk is that this individualizing will subvert and even erase the *systemic* analysis of sexual violence that Burke and others insist is crucial to bringing about real change. Such systemic analysis of the problem of sexual violence threatens to be overwhelmed as individual takedowns (of Harvey Weinstein, of Louis C.K., of Charlie Rose) become the normalized response to allegations of sexual violence.

Burke is not alone in her concerns. Both popular and scholarly communities have debated, challenged, and worked to reimagine the world of, and beyond, #MeToo. In the introduction to *Where Freedom Starts: Sex, Power, Violence, #MeToo*, Jessie Kindig explains some of the limitations of the current conversations around sexual violence:

> The weapons we have to protect our bodies and our rights are not good enough, for they sit within a legal framework which doesn't recognize the undisciplined nature of desire and sex nor the systemic violence of capitalism, white supremacy, patriarchy. Stories of sexual assault, when they are told, often rely on binary language: consent/rape, victim/perpetrator, trauma/pleasure, man/woman, sex/power, yes/no. The language of politics and legal justice can itself reflect these binaries: individual/collective, oppressed/free, resistant/complicit. All, in different ways, can be almost as misleading and entrapping as silence. Bodies and desire, sex and politics, freedom and violence, are much more complicated, rich, and fraught.[8]

Sexual violence, in other words, must be resituated within broader contexts of power, contexts that challenge easy binaries that have come to dominate the conversation since the popularization of the hashtag.

Although #MeToo has increased public awareness around issues of sexual violence, making the current situation feel new, it is a problem with a long history. Feminist scholarship has long worked to describe and analyze sexual violence and to propose cultural, political, and legal interventions. Already in 1892, Ida B. Wells argued that white men accused black men of rape as a way of threatening violence in the form of lynching, thus promoting black subservience and stymieing black economic progress.[9] Wells's analysis of rape reveals how it has been used as a tool not only of male supremacy but also of white supremacy. For these reasons and the reasons Burke identifies, a race-aware analysis of sexual violence and rape culture is necessary.

This race-aware analysis was not, however, taken up in the feminist theories of rape that emerged in the 1970s. Ann Cahill identifies two strands of 1970s feminist philosophy on rape, represented by Susan Brownmiller and Catharine MacKinnon. Brownmiller, according to Cahill, represents the position that rape is primarily about violence as opposed to sex, while MacKinnon argues that the compulsory nature of heterosexuality made rape continuous with heterosexual sex, the presence or absence.[10] Cahill's 2001 study *Rethinking Rape* finds both theories lacking because they "fail to account sufficiently for the intricate interplay of social and political power, sexual hierarchization, and embodiment."[11]

The 1993 volume *Transforming a Rape Culture*, edited by Emilie Buchwald, Pamela Fletcher, and Martha Roth, offers one example of the types of intervention offered by feminist scholars. Like Burke's claim that sexual violence is about much more than individual perpetrators, the contributors to *Transforming a Rape Culture* challenge the idea that rape is an individual problem by contextualizing the problem of rape within broader assumptions about gender and expectations for gender roles. Peggy Miller and Nancy Biele state, "The individualism of the 1980s exacted its toll; there is now a whole industry, comprising diagnosis, therapy, medications, books, films, and tapes, that aim to move the reality of rape from its social context to an individual problem."[12] Against this tendency, Miller and Biele argue that responding to sexual violence requires changing social assumptions about gender. The situation that they diagnose in the 1980s remains a problem today; rape and sexual violence are routinely treated as individual, rather than social, matters. Recent movements such as #MeToo and "It's on Us" would do well to take the historical contributions of feminist scholarship into account. Responses to sexual violence are not new.

Activism has long occurred through activities such as "Take Back the Night," originally a loose collection of rallies and events, now a foundation that attempts to make it safer for women to move between spaces, especially when it's dark. In a 1979 speech written for a "Take Back the Night" march, Andrea Dworkin argues, "A Take Back the Night March goes right to our emotional core. We women are especially supposed to be afraid of the night. The night promises harm to women. For a woman to walk on the street at night is not only to risk abuse, but also—according to the values of male domination—to ask for it."[13] In response to the ways in which fear of the night is used to constrain women's movement, Dworkin suggests that women's movement is a precondition for women's freedom. Women who cannot move cannot be free. Dworkin's speech also addresses the racialized connotations of fear of the night: "In this context, the association of night, black men, and rape becomes an article of faith. Night, the time of sex, becomes also the time of race-racial fear and racial hatred . . . we will have to take back the night so that it cannot be used to destroy us by race or by sex."[14] Dworkin's speech builds on the legacy of Ida B. Wells while foreshadowing Burke's appeal to intersectionality. The long history of sexual violence is intertwined with racism and racially charged violence.

While #MeToo has created new possibilities for standing up to even the most egregious individual perpetrators, Burke and others consistently remind us that it is a movement about power. While individuals abuse power, the movement must begin to offer new ways of organizing personal and professional relationships to limit the possibilities of these abuses before they occur. Moreover, Burke reminds us that the movement fails if it becomes a movement for white women alone. In this, we must consider who benefits from the movement and how these responses (and lack of responses) perpetuate systems of power that ultimately support rape culture.

WHAT DOES RAPE CULTURE HAVE TO DO WITH RELIGION?

What does rape culture have to do with religion? A great deal, we suggest. Texts, practices, and the academic study of religion are all touched by rape culture in significant ways. First, sexual violence, from rape to more diffuse manifestations of rape culture, is present in a wide range of religious literature. The Hebrew Bible/Old Testament contains what Susanne Scholz calls "a wealth of rape texts." Scholz summarizes:

> In Genesis 19, Lot's daughters are threatened with rape when their father offers them to the mob outside the house. In Genesis 34, Dinah is raped by Shechem, and in 2 Samuel 13, Amnon rapes Tamar, his half-sister. In Ezekiel 23, God condemns Aholah and Aholibah to sexual violations by their former lovers. Rape laws appear in the book of Deuteronomy, and the stories of enslaved women who are forced into sexual intercourse are detailed in Genesis and the books of Samuel.[15]

These are only the most famous examples; there are also stories of rape threats (such as the threat of male rape in Samson and Delilah, Judg. 16), poems promising divine rape (e.g., Nah. 3:4–7), gang rapes and mass kidnappings (Judg. 19–21), and rape culture more broadly. While it is difficult to reconstruct the particulars of rape in ancient Israel,[16] sexual violence was clearly as much a part of lived experience then as now.

Rape and sexual violence are also found in the New Testament and its world. The rape of slaves was part of Roman society, and informs the New Testament texts, such as Paul's letter to Philemon.[17] Nowhere is this more evident than Revelation, which includes the violent rape and murder of the whore of Babylon (Rev. 17–18), rape threats to John's rival Jezebel (Gen. 2), and other instantiations of rape culture. The violence is present to such a degree that John W. Marshall can rightly assert "Sexualized violence against women is one of John's primary modes of depicting God's judgment."[18] The Jewish and Christian traditions that draw on these texts did not leave the biblical acceptance of rape behind. Rather, these traditions continue to perpetuate sexualized violence in theologies and practices. One example is unachievable Christian expectations around sexual purity and how the unachievable standards set forth by purity culture become an excuse for violence. In this way, Christian purity culture normalizes sexual violence.[19]

Biblical texts and Jewish and Christian traditions are not alone in offering religious justifications for sexual violence. Religious traditions reflect the norms of their socio-historical contexts, which is why biblical texts and postbiblical traditions often appear to condone sexual violence. Many societies constructed their traditions in ways that accepted sexual violence. Scholars of the Qur'an have studied the interpretive pluralities around 4:34, for example, which has been used to legitimate men's domestic use of physical violence as a mechanism for controlling women.[20] Other Qur'anic verses suggest that men should not treat women unkindly, which demonstrates that interpretive communities determine the meaning and application of sacred texts.[21] There are also tradition-reports that indicate the Prophet Muhammad punished a rapist based solely on the testimony of a rape victim; however, many premodern Muslim scholars imposed stricter evidentiary rules in rape cases. Although these competing traditions reflect tension in textual and historical Islamic approaches to rape, violence continues to be legitimated in contemporary legal structures. Hina Azam argues, "Legal institutions in many majority-Muslim states function to promote violence against women in systematic ways, ranging from establishing and enforcing male authority and power over females, to phrasing laws in ways that appear neutral but in fact are structurally discriminatory toward women, to providing legal cover for males who perpetuate violence against females."[22] These justifications for sexual violence reveal the persistence of the problem of sexual violence across religious traditions.

Buddhism, too, is not immune. Here, the Shambhala community, a large international Buddhist organization, provides a timely example. In 2018, the Shambhala community released a statement recognizing the harms caused by sexual violence that have taken place within their own community. Community leadership acknowledged,

> In our complex history there have been instances of sexual harm and inappropriate relations between members and between teachers and students. We are still emerging from a time in which such cases were not always addressed with care and skill. In particular, inappropriate or even abhorrent sexual behavior by some men in the community has caused some women to feel unsafe. Members have at times not felt heard or have been treated as though they are a problem when they tried to bring complaints forward. We are heartbroken that such pain and injustice still occurs.[23]

While this statement attempts to move the community forward past instances and accusations of sexual harm, it does not offer the possibility that the structures of the community itself, particularly the organization of the relations between students and teachers and the possibilities for submitting a complaint against another member of the community, lend themselves to instances of sexual violence. Effective responses to sexual violence must be willing to consider how established communal norms, such as the legal norms Azam describes in relation to legal systems in majority-Muslim states, perpetuate sexual violence.

There are, of course, many other examples. As scholars and teachers of religion, we are repeatedly confronted with the question of how to respond to sexual violence, both in the material we study and in presenting this and other sexually violent material to students. Often, encountering sexual violence in religious texts, contexts, or traditions is traumatizing for students in ways that can catch professors or experienced readers off guard. This is a point taken up in conversation with ancient Greek and Roman literature by Madeleine Kahn in her wryly named *Why are We reading Ovid's Handbook on Rape?*. Kahn takes up the question expressed in her title, which comes from a frustrated student (Ovid's *Metamorphoses* is filled with tales of rape, mostly of young women by lascivious gods.)[24] As Kahn describes, reading the *Metamorphoses* produces strong reactions from students, in part because it powerfully intersects with some of their most intimately painful experiences. Student reactions challenge not only Ovid and the *Metamorphoses* but also Kahn's authority as an instructor for her choice of a text that so clearly colludes with patriarchal culture. The reactions of Kahn's students to this ancient text begin to reveal the connections between recent conversations around sexual violence and ancient texts.

RAPE CULTURE IN THE RELIGIOUS STUDIES CLASSROOM

The sexual violence found in religious texts, traditions, and communities poses significant challenges in the classroom. At least in part, this is because sexual violence is not simply a theoretical or textual problem. In classrooms, the legitimation of sexual violence in sacred texts and traditions meets the lived experiences of students. In this meeting, the problem of sexual violence becomes a pressing pedagogical concern. Teaching about violent texts and traditions, including those discussed above, does not occur in a vacuum. A simple review of the literature on sexual violence and risk suggests that there is at least one survivor of a recent sexual assault sitting in nearly every classroom; likely, several more.[25] The sheer prevalence of sexual assault makes it a trauma that cannot (and should not) be reduced to an individual problem and must, therefore, be taken up intentionally and thoughtfully in classroom contexts. At the same time, professors and teachers must be ready to address it in other casual contexts with students.

Teaching about sexual violence, however, also poses a problem because professors are often teaching material beyond their immediate expertise. The lack of expertise can, understandably, cause faculty to be hesitant to openly discuss controversial or sensitive topics. This volume introduces some of the key conversations around sexual violence on college campuses to faculty members in the hopes that they will find ways these conversations intersect with the content of their teaching.

The question that began this project was simple: How should scholars of religion respond to the prevalence of rape and other forms of sexual violence in sacred texts and religious traditions? We were interested in thinking critically about sexual violence as a problem in religion, and in connecting this problem to the academic study of religion. All of the essays in this volume address this question, though in a variety of ways. This question, moreover, opens onto several other fields of inquiry.

First, as we have already suggested, rape and other forms of sexual violence are a part of the everyday experience of students. Inside the classroom and beyond it, rape culture is lived reality. We are scholars of religion, but we are also teachers and members of campus communities. Rape is a reality not simply in the materials that we teach, but also in our students' lives. What does it mean, practically and ethically, to reckon with both of these truths simultaneously? Instead of evading or downplaying the issues, how might we use the classroom, and scholarly materials we teach, to engage them?

While rape culture and sexual violence are widespread, there are also important differences, both in the texts and traditions we study and in the lived experiences of our students outside the classroom. This raises the question of to what degree, if at all, a "one size fits all" approach to rape culture and religion is possible. The question of universals is a familiar one in religious studies. What do different religious traditions have to do with each other? How do we understand variants within a tradition? What about the gaps between texts, practices, and ideologies? As religious studies experts, we are familiar with thinking and teaching about these issues. In this volume, we ask our contributors to bring this conversation to bear on the question of sexual violence, which both appears in a wide range of religious texts and traditions and assumes a specific form in each one.

These conversations about sexual violence touch, as well, on the question of "best practices" in teaching about sexual violence in the context of religious studies. In particular, what are the "best practices" in engaging and living with sacred texts that describe or even glorify sexual violence? This pair of questions speaks to the key pedagogical issues of the volume. The goal of *Rape Culture and Religious Studies: Critical and Pedagogical Engagements* is not just to critique, but to equip readers with real-life pedagogical reflections and tactics. Our contributors explore practical strategies for teaching about these issues, while also reflecting on the complications that such teaching often engenders. Sexual violence is not simply a phenomenon that we impassively observe in texts and communities. It affects real people—including the people that we teach, who may also be members of the religious communities over which rape culture exerts its grip. This is an issue to keep in mind as we teach. In addition, sexual violence raises important and difficult questions about our roles as scholars, observers, or participant-observers. Theorizing this question, and possible responses to it, is another goal of this volume.

Finally, as scholars, teachers, and learners, we aspire to learn from each other in a critical, engaged, and intersectional framework. The notion of intersectionality is an important one in feminist theory; it was coined by legal scholar Kimberlé Crenshaw to describe the multiple forms of oppression experienced by black women.[26] Since Crenshaw's article appeared in 1989, the term has gained wide currency in feminist theory and practice. Our contributors engage intersectional questions of race, class, sexuality, and gender in relation to sexual violence.

Rape Culture and Religious Studies is our response to the problems and provocations introduced above. While much has been written about sexual violence and the university context, very little comes from the disciplinary space of religious studies, particularly with attention to undergraduate experience. This is a notable lack and one that has serious negative effects on scholars across religious studies, especially as we are called upon to participate in campus conversations, activism, and critique. While few authors have taken up the particular intersection of this volume, some have considered the intersection of rape culture and religion, including Gina Messina-Dysert in *Rape Culture and Spiritual Violence,* Amy Kalmanofsky and the contributors in *Sexual Violence and Sacred Texts,* Caroline Blyth, Emily Colgan, and Katie Edwards and the contributors in the three-volume edited series *Rape Culture, Gender Violence, and Religion,* with essays on Biblical Perspectives (volume 1), Christian Perspectives (volume 2), and Interdisciplinary Perspectives (volume 3), and Meredith Minister in *Rape Culture on Campus.*[27]

Building on this emerging conversation, *Rape Culture and Religious Studies* explores what it means to teach sacred texts within academic and seminary contexts that normalize sexual violence. Susanne Scholz's chapter, for example, locates teaching about biblical rape within the context of the contemporary debate about Title IX on college campuses, while Gwynn Kessler's chapter explores the line between pedagogy and activism in a course titled "Rape, Slavery, and Genocide in Bible and Culture." Furthermore, much of the existing literature operates within a framework of how sacred texts either collude with or challenge rape culture while several chapters in our book consider how sacred texts collude with and challenge rape culture simultaneously and the complications raised by these interpretations.

In addition, *Rape Culture and Religious Studies* speaks from and about a variety of faith traditions. The volume includes chapters not only on texts with long-standing authority in religious communities but also on recently developed texts that have become sacred within specific communities (T. Nicole Goulet's chapter on the comic book *Priya's Shakti*), on texts that have become sacred in light of their popular reception histories (Meredith Minister's chapter on rethinking affirmative consent using Octavia Butler's speculative fiction), and on the representations of textual bodies that continue to shape contemporary understandings of sexual violence (Jeremy Posadas's chapter on consent in the narrative of the virgin Mary). These chapters expand the definition of sacred texts, an expansion that creates space to explore the plurality of sacred texts and the relationship between sacred texts and contemporary contexts.

THINKING WITH AND BEYOND "RAPE CULTURE"

A framing notion for this volume and the essays within is that of "rape culture." Rape culture is at once a key feminist term and a contested one. An original form of the term first appeared in the 1970s as "rape supporting culture," in Susan Brownmiller's *Against Our Will: Men, Women, and Rape*.[28] In the 1975 documentary *Rape Culture*, filmmakers Margaret Lazarus and Renner Wunderlick are among the first in public discourse about rape to demonstrate that rape is not only an individual experience; it is an element of culture comprising "classic films, advertising, music and 'adult entertainment.'"[29] In other words, they seek to highlight how sexual assault is built into culture, especially popular culture, as a norm rather than a violation. In subsequent publications on the topic, scholars continued to pursue the questions and convictions of feminist writers that to address rape, we must address social constructs that allow it to happen. In 1984, Dianne F. Herman published a piece called, simply, "The Rape Culture" examining the ways sexual violence is encoded into prevailing models of heterosexuality including constructs of masculinity and femininity, resulting in the normalizing and propagation of sexual assault.[30] In *Transforming a Rape Culture* (1993), Buchwald, Fletcher, and Roth synthesize these earlier works, defining rape culture as "a complex of beliefs that encourages male sexual aggression and supports violence against women. It is a society where violence is seen as sexy and sexuality as violent."[31] It is a ubiquitous social force supported by jokes, advertisements, the fashion industry, media and entertainment, and the legal system. In a 2009 blog post titled "Rape Culture 101," feminist author Melissa McEwan suggests that people requesting a definition of rape culture are often looking for a description or "something substantive enough to reach out and touch, in all its ugly, heaving, menacing grotesquery."[32] Building on previous definitions, Meredith Minister has described rape culture in terms of the demand for purity and then the requirement to police that purity by violently clarifying the boundaries of who or what is pure and who or what is impure. She states, "I define rape culture as a socially-accepted pattern that legitimates violence to police socially non-conforming activities, including expressions of sexuality and gender."[33] These descriptions and attempts at a definition suggest that the naming and undoing of rape culture is difficult work, requiring a commitment to deep engagement with painful messages.

The term "rape culture" is not without controversy. Recent work, both feminist and non-feminist, has challenged the idea of "rape culture" and/or the usefulness of the term. One of the major charges against "rape culture" is that the phrase normalizes sexual violence. Thus feminist scholar Jennifer Doyle writes in *Campus Sex, Campus Security*, "'Rape culture,' used too liberally, reinforces the structure of a normative sexual culture."[34] She further argues that the fear of rape is used to keep established power structures in place, including such institutions as marriage and the family and the drive toward reproduction. As her analysis makes clear, this critique is often linked to a larger critique of heterosexuality and heteropatriarchy. Doyle describes a "continuum" between rape and other "coercive structures" of social organization. Jack Halberstam goes further and diagnoses the problem as heterosexuality itself, suggesting that rape culture is simply its outgrowth.[35]

This critique of rape culture as ignoring the continuum of coercion is related to a second critique, that the breadth of the term actually stymies efforts to address the problem it describes. Yasmin Nair, for example, has challenged the breadth of the term and the flattening effect of describing a wide range of offenses with a single name.[36] Nair proposes that the term "rape culture" forecloses specificity. The strength of the term—the claim that acts of sexual violence are not individual acts or moments, but rather part of a larger cultural construction—is also its potential weakness: there is no space for differentiating forms and degrees of harm. Nair is not alone in making this critique, which has also been advanced by Laura Kipnis in *Unwanted Advances: Sexual Paranoia Comes to Campus*.[37]

Though "rape culture" is not a universally accepted term, and though salient critiques have raised important points about ways in which rape culture must be consistently re-evaluated, we contend that is a valuable, valid, and necessary perspective in the work we seek to do, which is ultimately about change. These debates over "rape culture" have informed, and continue to inform, our own conversations about sexual violence. In spite of the critiques, we still find "rape culture" a useful shorthand for describing a complex constellation of acts, ideologies, and cultural figurations of sexual violence. This is one reason we use it here. Second, by using "rape culture," we signal our own commitments to participating in a feminist culture critiquing sexual violence. While imperfect, "rape culture" remains a powerful discursive formulation.

SCOPE OF THE VOLUME AND OVERVIEW OF CONTRIBUTIONS

Rape Culture and Religious Studies is a volume focused on the United States. Furthermore, all of our contributors are scholars working in institutions of higher education, chiefly colleges and universities. While many of the essays engage global contexts—T. Nicole Goulet writes about sexual violence in India, for example—they remain grounded in U.S. university contexts. This focalizing of the volume is intentional. Because laws and policies addressing sexual violence and sexual assault are location specific, we have found it useful to limit *Rape Culture and Religious Studies* to the U.S. context. In the United States, the most important law regulating sexual violence on college campuses is Title IX, which guarantees equal access to education, regardless of sex. Failure to comply with Title IX can lead to the loss of federal funding, a potential death threat for many institutions of higher education. While Title IX was originally applied mainly in the case of college sports, since 2001 it has been applied to sexual violence as well. Additional guidance released in 2011 by the Obama administration was rescinded by the Department of Education headed by Betsy DeVos in 2017.[38] The degree to which the law has influenced U.S. conversations about sexual violence is inarguable, and it is one reason that we maintain a U.S. emphasis here.[39]

In this context of endemic sexual violence in and around college and university campuses, *Rape Culture and Religious Studies* offers a practical and theoretical intervention. We have sought to curate an accessible, critically-informed volume on sexual violence, rape, and rape culture as they intersect with the discipline of religious studies, with a particular focus on the space of the classroom. Our contributors offer historical backgrounds, cross-cultural comparisons, and literary engagements. They are equally comfortable addressing pedagogy and the issue of sexual violence as it plays out in the classroom. We have intentionally solicited scholars who bring diverse backgrounds, perspectives, and sensibilities to the material. At the same time, the volume is intentionally framed as a feminist work. Both as a collection and as individual essays, the pieces we present here are critical, intersectional, and theoretically informed; they bring together feminist scholarship, practices, and pedagogy. This reflects our assertion that religion is an important field for the study of rape culture, for its naming and its transformation. The contributors to this work also come from diverse disciplines within religious studies, which reflects our assertion that religion is an important field for the study of rape culture. The work of naming and transforming rape culture needs to take place in multiple communities, and as such, the analysis of elements of multiple traditions is a vital task.

In "Reading Biblical Rape Texts beyond a Cop-Out Hermeneutics in the Trump Era" (chapter 1) Susanne Scholz examines the impact Title IX and contemporary awareness of rape and rape culture have on biblical studies, which has traditionally been dominated by historical-critical perspectives, aligned with historically male scholarship. The result of such methodological hegemony has been a discrediting of feminist approaches to the text; Scholz argues that not only do biblical scholars have an obligation to identify and examine rape texts in the Bible, but that methodologically the field needs to open more to feminist and sociological perspectives.

Turning to an Indian context, T. Nicole Goulet approaches responses to the 2012 rape and murder of Jyoti Pandey in "Constructions of Hindu Mythology after the Rape of Jyoti Singh Pandey: Coupling Activism with Pedagogy" (chapter 2). Goulet bring the attack into conversation with Hindu mythology via the graphic novel *Priya's Shakti*. This novel is part of the response to Pandey's attack, and functions in the realm of traditional Hindu explorations of the deities who, in this case, learn of the rape of a young woman and respond. The combination of the novel with modern media (art, workshops, and videos), gives new life to the Hindu *purana* and brings the issue of rape into conversation with both contemporary Hindus and their traditions.

Gwynn Kessler takes readers into the biblical studies classroom in her chapter, "Teaching Rape, Slavery, and Genocide in Bible and Culture" (chapter 3). She describes her approach to teaching students about the presence of rape, genocide, and slavery in the Bible, linking these texts to historical and contemporary realities, through an introductory exercise involving "texts of terror." Using specific texts from Deuteronomy as a focal point, she combines inductive pedagogy with feminist theory, critical race theory, and posthumanist philosophy, inviting students to see both the text and the world in new ways.

"On #MosqueMeToo: Lessons for Nuancing and Better Implementing the Goals of #MeToo" (chapter 4) by Kirsten Boles describes how so-called "Muslim #MeToos" highlight issues of inclusivity and accessibility within the larger #MeToo movement, as well as how they call attention to the specific ways that accusations of sexual violence are often racialized. In relation to the #MeToo movement, Boles asks, how do we ensure that the same age-old colonial and exclusionary paradigms are not recreated when doing the critical pedagogical work that the #MeToo movement advocates? And how can educators and scholars leverage the important cultural labor "Muslim #MeToos" are doing to help nuance, expand, and ameliorate conversations about sexual violence and consent?

Minenhle Nomalungelo Khumalo's essay, "Judges 19 and Non-Con: Sado-Kantian Aesthetics of Violence in the Tale of an Unnamed Woman" (chapter 5), examines the graphically violent story of the concubine of Gibeah in Judges 19. Linking this story of gang rape and dismemberment to contemporary non-consensual pornography (focusing in particular on video game pornography *Kunoichi: Broken Princess*), Khumalo shows how the text of Judges 19 avoids depicting the victim's experience, but instead creates a "rape fantasy," wherein the woman is narratively at the disposal of men's interests. Rape, then, is a both a narrative and a mythical tool for the text, de-emphasizing the suffering of the woman at the center of the tale.

A female figure central to Christian theology is the focus of Jeremy Posadas's chapter, "To Confess the Fundamental Marian Dogma: Postulating the Doctrine of Mary's Reproductive Justice" (chapter 6). He asks the pointed question: What is the relationship of the traditional narrative of Mary's impregnation to rape culture? By emphasizing Mary's own responses to her annunciation, and by bringing Mary into intersubjective conversation with God, Posadas works to imbue the story of Christ's conception with a critique against rape culture.

In "Rape Culture in the Rabbinic Construction of Gender" (chapter 7), Beatrice Lawrence examines texts from midrash and Talmud in the seventh chapter to identify and examine patterns of gender construction that propagate rape culture. This involves not only texts *about* rape, but also texts describing the theological anthropology of the rabbis which presents gendered expectations of aggression, passivity, and hypersexualization.

The final two chapters of this volume deal with critical, theoretical critiques of approaches to the epidemic of sexual assault, especially on college campuses: the emphasis on affirmative consent, and the nature of common critical and pedagogical tactics in teaching about rape culture. In "Sex and Alien Encounter: Rethinking Consent as a Rape Prevention Strategy" (chapter 8), Meredith Minister explores the nature of consent in two parts: first, in an analysis of the history and assumptions of consent; and second, in conversation with the speculative fiction of Octavia Butler. Through analyzing two of the fictional worlds created by Butler, Minister demonstrates the shortcomings of contemporary treatments of consent. Finally, in "Good Intentions are Not Enough" (chapter 9), Rhiannon Graybill focuses attention on four topics relevant to analysis of rape culture: the nature of "harm" and the insights of carceral feminism, critical race theory, postcolonial approaches to the question of "saving women," and the issue of pleasure. Graybill targets her analysis in particular at the field of religious studies, identifying critiques that can and should be a part of the work of naming and transforming rape culture in scholarly discourse and in the classroom.

There are no easy answers to the problem of sexual violence. This is as true in the classroom as it is in the world at large. Nor does religion, whether as an object of academic study, a collection of texts and practices, or a lived experience, offer straightforward answers. And yet thinking critically about the intersections of religion, sexual violence, and pedagogy is both necessary and important. Students will encounter sexual violence in the subject matter, and in their lives, regardless of how hard we try to protect them. At the same time, the academic study of religion, and the religious studies classroom, create a unique and valuable space for thinking through, and challenging, sexual violence. The essays in this volume offer a resource in this vital task.

NOTES

1. Collier Meyerson, "Sexual Assault When You're on the Margins: Can We All Say #MeToo?" *The Nation* October 19, 2017, https://www.thenation.com/article/sexual-assault-when-youre-on-the-margins-can-we-all-say-metoo/; Bernice Young, "The Unreckoned: Seventeen Women tell why #MeToo Still Hasn't Come for Them," *The Cut*, September 5, 2018, https://www.thecut.com/2018/09/unreckoned-left-behind-by-metoo.html.

2. This statistic, which appeared in the 2011 OCR Dear Colleague letter on Title IX and in popular accounts of sexual violence such as Jon Krakauer's *Missoula* and the documentary *The Hunting Ground* has a somewhat complicated history but was validated in a Post-Kaiser Poll. See Nick Anderson and Scott Clement, "1 in 5 women say they were violated," *Washington Post*, June 12, 2015, https://www.washingtonpost.com/sf/local/2015/06/12/1-in-5-women-say-they-were-violated/?tid=a_inl_manual. Also see Christopher Krebs and Christine Lindquist, "Setting the Record Straight on '1-in-5,'" *Time*, December 15, 2014, http://time.com/3633903/campus-rape-1-in-5-sexual-assault-setting-record-straight/; Christopher Krebs et al., "Campus Climate Survey Validation Study: Final Technical Report," Bureau of Justice Statistics, U.S. Department of Justice, January 2016, http://www.bjs.gov/content/pub/pdf/ccsvsftr.pdf); Callie Marie Rennison and Lynn A. Addington, "Violence Against College Women," *Trauma, Violence, and Abuse* 15, no. 3 (2014): 159–69; "Rape and Sexual Assault Victimization Among College-Age Females, 1995–2013," Bureau of Justice Statistics, U.S. Department of Justice, December 2014, http://www.bjs.gov/content/pub/pdf/rsavcaf9513.pdf. For a readable discussion of the various statistics and their limitations geared at a more popular audience, see Vanessa Grigoriadis, *Blurred Lines: Rethinking Sex, Power, and Consent on Campus* (New York: Houghton Mifflin Harcourt, 2017), pages 112–17. At this point, it is also important to mention that women 18–24 not enrolled in college are at an even higher risk for sexual assault. See Sofi Sinozich, and Lynn Langton, *Rape and sexual assault victimization among college-age females, 1995–2013*. Washington, DC: U.S. Department of Justice, Office of Justice Programs, Bureau of Justice Statistics, 2014; http://jpp.whs.mil/Public/docs/03_Topic-Areas/07-CM_Trends_Analysis/20150918/05_BJS_SpecialReport_SexAsslt_CollegeAge_Females.pdf.

3. Elizabeth Adetiba, "Tarana Burke says #MeToo Should Centered Marginalized Communities" in *Where Freedom Starts: Sex Power Violence #MeToo*. A Verso Report, ed. Verso, 2018, 25. Also see Me Too Movement, "About," accessed August 6, 2018, https://metoomvmt.org/.

4. Hayley Krischer, "We're Going to Need More Gabrielle Union," *New York Times*, December 5, 2017, https://www.nytimes.com/2017/12/05/style/gabrielle-union-memoir.html. While Union has criticized certain aspects of #MeToo, especially in practice, she has also been a voice for survivors. She contributed an essay to the anthology *Not That Bad: Dispatches from Rape Culture* (Gabrielle Union, "Wiping the Stain Clean," in Roxane Gay, ed., *Not that Bad: Dispatches from Rape Culture* (New York: Harper Perennial, 2018), pp. 203–6). *Not That Bad* contains a number of recent reflections on race, positionality, and lived experiences of rape culture.

5. For a resource on identifying voices that have been excluded from the #MeToo movement, see Rebecca Reingold, "#MeToo: Who is Being Left Out?" *Georgetown Law*, December

20, 2017, http://oneill.law.georgetown.edu/metoo-who-is-being-left-out/. On trans-inclusivity, see Gabriel Arkles, "Making Space for Trans People in the #MeToo Movement," *The American Civil Liberties Union*, April 13, 2018, https://www.aclu.org/blog/womens-rights/violence-against-women/making-space-trans-people-metoo-movement. Angela Onwuachi-Willig raises concerns about racial awareness in the movement, in "What About #UsToo?: The Invisibility of Race in the #MeToo Movement," *The Yale Law Journal*, June 18, 2018, https://www.yalelawjournal.org/forum/what-about-ustoo. On questions about disability awareness, see Emily Flores, "The #MeToo Movement Hasn't Benn Inclusive of the Disability Community," *Teen Vogue*, April 24, 2018, https://www.teenvogue.com/story/the-metoo-movement-hasnt-been-inclusive-of-the-disability-community.

6. A number of famous women of color have also shared #MeToo stories, including Salma Hayek, Lupita Nyong'o, Viola Davis and America Ferrera. "Time's Up," a movement against "sexual assault, harassment and inequality in the workplace" that began in Hollywood in 2018, includes significant participation and leadership by women of color, including a significant number of signatories on the original letter published January 1, 2018 in the *New York Times*. See Times Up. "Times Up Now," accessed September 10, 2018, https://www.timesupnow.com/.

7. Adetiba, "Tarana Burke says #MeToo Should Centered Marginalized Communities," 27.

8. Adetiba, "Tarana Burke says #MeToo Should Centered Marginalized Communities," 20–21.

9. Ida B. Wells, *Southern Horrors: Lynch Law in All Its Phases* (The Floating Press, 2013), 1892.

10. Ann J. Cahill, *Rethinking Rape* (Ithaca and London: Cornell University Press, 2001), 2–3.

11. Cahill, *Rethinking Rape*, 3.

12. Peggy Miller and Nancy Biele, "Twenty Years Later: The Unfinished Revolution," in *Transforming a Rape Culture*, ed. Emilie Buchwald, Pamela Fletcher, and Martha Roth (Minneapolis: Milkweed, 1993), 52.

13. Andrea Dworkin, "The Night and Danger," in *Letters from the War Zone: Writings 1976–1989* (New York: Lawrence Hill Books, 1989), 13.

14. Dworkin, "The Night and Danger," 15–16.

15. Susanne Scholz, *Sacred Witness: Rape in the Hebrew Bible* (Minneapolis: Fortress, 2010), 2.

16. See discussion in Scholz, *Sacred Witness*, 5–7. Kawashima offers a useful overview of the question of sexual consent in ancient Israel, although we disagree with his conclusion that the lack of a notion of consent means that sex without consent is not rape. See Robert S. Kawashima, "Could a Woman Say 'No' in Biblical Israel? On the Genealogy of Legal Status in Biblical Law and Literature," *AJS Review* 35, no. 1 (2011): 1–22.

17. Joseph A. Marchal, "The Usefulness of an Onesimus: The Sexual Use of Slaves and Paul's Letter to Philemon," *Journal of Biblical Literature* 130, no. 4 (2011): 749–70.

18. John W. Marshall, "Gender and Empire: Sexualized Violence in John's Anti-Imperial Apocalypse," in *A Feminist Companion to the Apocalypse of John*, ed. Amy-Jill Levine with Maria Mayo Robbins, Feminist Companion to the Bible (Bloomsbury Publishing, 2010), 19; Tina Pippin, *Death and Desire: The Rhetoric of Gender in the Apocalypse of John* (Louisville, Ky: Westminster/John Knox Press, 1992).

19. Meredith Minister, *Rape Culture on Campus* (Lanham, MD: Lexington Press, 2018).

20. Karen Bauer. '"Traditional" Exegesis of Q 4:34,' Comparative Islamic Studies, 2.2 (2006), pp. 129–42.

21. For example, 4:20 or 4:35.

22. Hina Azam, *Sexual Violation in Islamic Law: Substance, Evidence, and Procedure* (Cambridge: Cambridge University Press, 2015), 1.

23. Shambala.org, Facebook post, February 12, 2018, https://www.facebook.com/Shambhala.org/posts/1999897840264640. See also Sarah Marsh, "Buddhist Group Admits Sexual Abuse by Teachers" *The Guardian*, March 5, 2018, https://www.theguardian.com/world/2018/mar/05/buddhist-group-admits-sexual-abuse-by-teachers.

24. Madeleine Kahn, *Why Are We Reading Ovid's Handbook on Rape?: Teaching and Learning at a Women's College* (Boulder: Paradigm Publishers, 2006).

25. For statistics on the prevalence of sexual violence among college women, see note 2. These statistics suggest that given a college class of 20, it is safe to assume the presence of multiple survivors in every classroom. In addition, it is important to acknowledge that classrooms also include perpetrators. For an analysis of this, see Beatrice Lawrence, "When Perpetrators Are Our Students," *Teaching Theology and Religion* 20, no. 1 (2017): 80–84.

26. Kimberlé Crenshaw (1989). "Demarginalizing the intersection of race and sex: a Black feminist critique of antidiscrimination doctrine, feminist theory and antiracist politics." *University of Chicago Legal Forum, special issue: Feminism in the Law: Theory, Practice and Criticism*. University of Chicago Law School: 139–68.

27. Gina Messina-Dysert, *Rape Culture and Spiritual Violence: Religion, Testimony, and Visions of Healing* (Abingdon and New York: Routledge, 2015), Amy Kalmanofsky (ed.), *Sexual Violence and Sacred Texts* (Indianapolis: Dog Ear Publishing, 2017), Caroline Blyth, Emily Colgan, and Katie B. Edwards (eds.), *Rape Culture, Gender Violence, and Religion: Biblical Perspectives* (New York: Palgrave, 2018), Caroline Blyth, Emily Colgan, and Katie B. Edwards (eds.), *Rape Culture, Gender Violence, and Religion: Christian Perspectives* (New York: Palgrave, 2018), Caroline Blyth, Emily Colgan, and Katie B. Edwards (eds.), *Rape Culture, Gender Violence, and Religion: Interdisciplinary Perspectives* (New York: Palgrave, 2018), and Meredith Minister, *Rape Culture on Campus* (Lanham, MD: Lexington, 2018).

28. Susan Brownmiller, *Against Our Will: Men, Women, and Rape* (New York: Open Road Media, 1975).

29. Margaret Lazarus and Renner Wunderlick, "Rape Culture," Santa Barbara: CA: Cambridge Documentary Films, 1975.

30. Herman, "The Rape Culture," in *Women: A Feminist Perspective*, ed. by Jo Freeman (Palo Alto: Mayfield Publishing, 1984), 20-38.

31. Emilie Buchwald, Pamela R. Fletcher, Martha Roth, eds., *Transforming a Rape Culture* (Minneapolis: Milkweed Editions, 1993).

32. Melissa McEwan, "Rape Culture 101," *Shakesville* (blog), October 9, 2009, http://www.shakesville.com/2009/10/rape-culture-101.html.

33. Meredith Minister, *Rape Culture on Campus* (Lanham, MA: Lexington, 2018), 1.

34. Jennifer Doyle, *Campus Sex, Campus Security* (Semiotext(e)/Intervention Series 19, South Pasadena, CA: Semiotext(e), 2015).

35. Jack Halberstam, "Wieners, Whiners, Weinsteins and Worse," Bully Bloggers (blog), October 24, 2017, https://bullybloggers.wordpress.com/2017/10/23/wieners-whiners-weinsteins-and-worse-by-jack-halberstam/.

36. Michael Kinnucan, "An Interview with Yasmin Nair, Part Two: The Ideal Neoliberal Subject is the Subject of Trauma," *Hypocrite Reader* 43, August 2014, http://hypocritereader.com/43/yasmin-nair-two.

37. Laura Kipnis, *Unwanted Advances: Sexual Paranoia Comes to Campus* (New York: HarperCollins, 2017).

38. This is a fast moving and fraught political issue in the United States. The information we present in this volume is current as of spring 2019.

39. *Rape Culture and Religious Studies* is complemented by work in other national contexts. The Shiloh Project (http://shiloh-project.group.shef.ac.uk/) is an international collaboration between scholars at Sheffield University and the University of Leeds in the United Kingdom and the University of Aukland in New Zealand.

BIBLIOGRAPHY

Adetiba, Elizabeth. "Tarana Burke says #MeToo Should Centered Marginalized Communities." In *Where Freedom Starts: Sex Power Violence #MeToo*, edited by Verso, 24–31. London and New York: Verso, 2018.

Arkles, Gabriel. "Making Space for Trans People in the #MeToo Movement." *The American Civil Liberties Union Blog*, April 13, 2018. https://www.aclu.org/blog/womens-rights/violence-against-women/making-space-trans-people-metoo-movement.

Azam, Hina. *Sexual Violation in Islamic Law: Substance, Evidence, and Procedure*. Cambridge: Cambridge University Press, 2015.

Bauer, Karen. "'Traditional' Exegesis of Q 4:34." *Comparative Islamic Studies* 2, no. 2 (2006): 129–142.

Blyth, Caroline, Emily Colgan, and Katie B. Edwards, editors. *Rape Culture, Gender Violence, and Religion: Biblical Perspectives*. New York: Palgrave, 2018.

Blyth, Caroline, Emily Colgan, and Katie B. Edwards, editors. *Rape Culture, Gender Violence, and Religion: Christian Perspectives*. New York: Palgrave, 2018.

Blyth, Caroline, Emily Colgan, and Katie B. Edwards, editors. *Rape Culture, Gender Violence, and Religion: Interdisciplinary Perspectives*. New York: Palgrave, 2018.

Brownmiller, Susan. *Against Our Will: Men, Women, and Rape*. New York: Open Road Media, 1975.

Buchwald, Emilie, Pamela Fletcher, and Martha Roth, editors. *Transforming a Rape Culture*. 2nd edition. Minneapolis, MN: Milkweed Editions, 1995.

Bureau of Justice, "Rape and Sexual Assault Victimization Among College-Age Females, 1995–2013." Bureau of Justice Statistics. U.S. Department of Justice, December 2014. http://www.bjs.gov/content/pub/pdf/rsavcaf9513.pdf.

Cahill, Ann J. *Rethinking Rape*. Ithaca and London: Cornell University Press, 2001.

Crenshaw, Kimberlé. "Demarginalizing the intersection of race and sex: a Black feminist critique of antidiscrimination doctrine, feminist theory and antiracist politics." *University of Chicago Legal Forum, special issue: Feminism in the Law: Theory, Practice and Criticism* 140 (1989): 139–68.

Dick, Kirby. *The Hunting Ground*. Directed by Kirby Dick. Los Angeles: Chain Camera Pictures, 2015.

Doyle, Jennifer. *Campus Sex, Campus Security*. Semiotext(e) / Intervention Series 19, South Pasadena, CA: Semiotext(e), 2015.

Dworkin, Andrea. "The Night and Danger." In *Letters from the War Zone: Writings 1976–1989*. New York: Lawrence Hill Books, 1989.

Flores, Emily. "The #MeToo Movement Hasn't Benn Inclusive of the Disability Community." *Teen Vogue*, April 24, 2018. https://www.teenvogue.com/story/the-metoo-movement-hasnt-been-inclusive-of-the-disability-community.

Gay, Roxane, editor. *Not that Bad: Dispatches from Rape Culture*. New York: Harper Perennial, 2018.

Grigoriadis, Vanessa. *Blurred Lines: Rethinking Sex, Power, and Consent on Campus*. New York: Houghton Mifflin Harcourt, 2017.

Halberstam, Jack. "Wieners, Whiners, Weinsteins and Worse." *Bully Bloggers* (blog), October 24, 2017. https://bullybloggers.wordpress.com/2017/10/23/wieners-whiners-weinsteins-and-worse-by-jack-halberstam/.

Herman, D. "The Rape Culture." In *Women: A Feminist Perspective*, edited by Jo Freeman, 20–38. Palo Alto: Mayfield Publishing, 1984.

Kahn, Madeleine. *Why Are We Reading Ovid's Handbook on Rape?: Teaching and Learning at a Women's College*. Boulder: Paradigm Publishers, 2006.

Kalmanofsky, Amy, editor. *Sexual Violence and Sacred Texts*. Indianapolis: Dog Ear Publishing, 2017.

Kawashima, Robert S. "Could a Woman Say 'No' in Biblical Israel? On the Genealogy of Legal Status in Biblical Law and Literature." *AJS Review* 35, no. 1 (2011): 1–22.

Kinnucan, Michael. "An Interview with Yasmin Nair, Part Two: The Ideal Neoliberal Subject is the Subject of Trauma." *Hypocrite Reader* 43, August 2014. http://hypocritereader.com/43/yasmin-nair-two.

Kipnis, Laura. *Unwanted Advances: Sexual Paranoia Comes to Campus*. New York: HarperCollins, 2017.

Krakauer, Jon. *Missoula: Rape and the Justice System in a College Town*. New York: Anchor Books, 2016.

Krebs, Christopher, et al. "Campus Climate Survey Validation Study Final Technical Report." Bureau of Justice Statistics Research and Development Series, January 20, 2016. http://big.assets.huffingtonpost.com/BJSstudy.pdf.

Krebs, Christopher and Christine Lindquist, "Setting the Record Straight on '1-in-5.'" *Time*, December 15, 2014. http://time.com/3633903/campus-rape-1-in-5-sexual-assault-setting-record-straight/.

Krischer, Hayley. "We're Going to Need More Gabrielle Union." *New York Times*, December 5, 2017. https://www.nytimes.com/2017/12/05/style/gabrielle-union-memoir.html.

Lawrence, Beatrice. "When Perpetrators Are Our Students." *Teaching Theology and Religion* 20, no. 1 (2017): 80–84.

Lazarus, Margaret and Renner Wunderlick. "Rape Culture." Santa Barbara, CA: Cambridge Documentary Films, 1975.

Marchal, Joseph A. "The Usefulness of an Onesimus: The Sexual Use of Slaves and Paul's Letter to Philemon." *Journal of Biblical Literature* 130, no. 4 (2011): 749–70.

Marsh, Sarah. "Buddhist Group Admits Sexual Abuse by Teachers" *The Guardian*, March 5, 2018. https://www.theguardian.com/world/2018/mar/05/buddhist-group-admits-sexual-abuse-by-teachers.

Marshall, John W. "Gender and Empire: Sexualized Violence in John's Anti-Imperial Apocalypse." In *A Feminist Companion to the Apocalypse of John*, edited by Amy-Jill Levine with Maria Mayo Robbins, 17–32. Bloomsbury Publishing, 2010.

Me Too Movement. "About." Accessed August 6, 2018. https://metoomvmt.org/.

McEwan, Melissa. "Rape Culture 101." *Shakesville* (blog), October 9, 2009. http://www.shakesville.com/2009/10/rape-culture-101.html.

Messina-Dysert, Gina. *Rape Culture and Spiritual Violence: Religion, Testimony, and Visions of Healing*. Abingdon and New York: Routledge, 2015.

Meyerson, Collier. "Sexual Assault When You're on the Margins: Can We All Say #MeToo?" *The Nation*, October 19, 2017. https://www.thenation.com/article/sexual-assault-when-youre-on-the-margins-can-we-all-say-metoo/.

Minister, Meredith. *Rape Culture on Campus*. Lanham, MD: Lexington Press, 2018.

Morgan, Joan. "The Pro-Rape Culture." *The Village Voice*, May 9, 1989: 39–40.

Nick Anderson and Scott Clement. "1 in 5 women say they were violated" *Washington Post*, June 12, 2015. https://www.washingtonpost.com/sf/local/2015/06/12/1-in-5-women-say-they-were-violated/?tid=a_inl_manual.

Onwuachi-Willig, Angela. "What About #UsToo?: The Invisibility of Race in the #MeToo Movement." *The Yale Law Journal*, June 18, 2018. https://www.yalelawjournal.org/forum/what-about-ustoo.

Pippin, Tina. *Death and Desire: The Rhetoric of Gender in the Apocalypse of John*. Louisville, Ky: Westminster/John Knox Press, 1992.

Reingold, Rebecca. "#MeToo: Who is Being Left Out?" *Georgetown Law*, December 20, 2017. http://oneill.law.georgetown.edu/metoo-who-is-being-left-out/.

Rennison, Callie Marie and Lynn A. Addington. "Violence Against College Women" *Trauma, Violence, and Abuse* 15, no. 3 (2014): 159–69.

Scholz, Susanne. *Sacred Witness: Rape in the Hebrew Bible*. Minneapolis: Fortress, 2010.

Shambala.org, Facebook post, February 12, 2018, https://www.facebook.com/Shambhala.org/posts/1999897840264640.

Sinozich, Sofi and Lynn Langton. *Rape and sexual assault victimization among college-age females, 1995–2013*. Washington, DC: US Department of Justice, Office of Justice Programs, Bureau of Justice Statistics, 2014; http://jpp.whs.mil/Public/docs/03_Topic-Areas/07-CM_Trends_Analysis/20150918/05_BJS_SpecialReport_SexAsslt_CollegeAge_Females.pdf.

Times Up. "Times Up Now." Accessed September 10, 2018. https://www.timesupnow.com/.

Wells, Ida B. *Southern Horrors: Lynch Law in All Its Phases*. The Floating Press, 2013, 1892.

Young, Bernice. "The Unreckoned: Seventeen Women tell why #MeToo Still Hasn't Come for Them." *The Cut*, September 5, 2018. https://www.thecut.com/2018/09/unreckoned-left-behind-by-metoo.html.

Chapter One

Reading Biblical Rape Texts beyond a Cop-Out Hermeneutics in the Trump Era

Susanne Scholz

With the election of the 45th President of the United States of America in November 2016 much has changed, including the public discourse on sexual harassment, sexual violence, and rape. Six months after President Trump's inauguration, the U.S. Department of Education, under the leadership of the new U.S. Secretary of Education, Betsy DeVos, withdrew the Dear Colleague Letter on Sexual Violence dated April 4, 2011, and the Questions and Answers on Title IX Sexual Violence dated April 29, 2014.[1] In a new Dear Colleague letter of September 22, 2017, the Acting Assistant Secretary for Civil Rights of the U.S. Department of Education, Candice Jackson, explains the withdrawal of the "well-intentioned" 2011 and 2014 "guidance documents," stating that "the guidance has not succeeded in providing clarity for educational institutions or in leading institutions to guarantee educational opportunities on the equal basis that Title IX requires."[2] The public is informed that:

> the Department has decided to withdraw the above-referenced guidance documents in order to develop an approach to student sexual misconduct that responds to the concerns of stakeholders and that aligns with the purpose of Title IX to achieve fair access to educational benefits. The Department intends to implement such a policy through a rulemaking process that responds to public comment. The Department will not rely on the withdrawn documents in its enforcement of Title IX.[3]

In light of the highly partisan approach characterizing contemporary politics in the United States and in light of the extraordinary change of political power in the 2016 presidential, progressive analysts predicted the dramatic enforcement change of the Title IX application as previously interpreted by the Obama administration.[4] The brief moment in which the Department of Education recognized the problem of rampant sexual violence on U.S. colleges and universities was unique. That the Trump administration has quickly removed any effort to deal with the epidemic is the logical conclusion of the long-term practice of hegemonic androcentrism in its intersectional manifestations.

The polarized treatment of sexual violence should, however, not surprise anybody who knows anything about the history of reading biblical rape texts. After all, for most of the interpretation history, biblical rape texts are not usually known as literature about sexual violence. Instead, many interpreters advance biblical rape texts as passages about marriage, love, or consensual heteronormative sex, perhaps gone awry but always acceptable within the socio-ethical parameters of the reconstructed ancient time period. Moreover, biblical rape texts are not usually known, as Christian and Jewish lectionaries do not include many of them. Accordingly, many scholarly interpreters do not usually specify biblical rape texts because, to them, they are about marriage and thus all is well.

So what shall feminist Bible readers do about this long-standing denial while we also realize that during the last half century feminist theorists have exposed and offered alternative views on the matter? Feminists have advised society to side with raped victim survivors and to be suspicious of the alleged rapists. Since the Trump administration rejects the Title IX interpretation of the Obama administration, predictably the alleged rapists are back in the center of attention. Trump's Education Secretary, Betsy DeVos, worries about them being falsely accused and she promptly met with men's rights groups and male students accused of sexual assault.[5] We also hear of mothers whose sons are accused of rape; they defend them with vigor and confidence of their innocence.[6] The question is what these developments have to do with interpreting biblical rape texts. The answer is: everything. They indicate that past and present culture is filled with assumptions and notions about sexual violence that shape how people read the Bible. This essay explores what their readings tell us about their ideas about sexual violence. The first section explains the nature of a cop-out hermeneutics and how even some feminist scholars interpret biblical rape texts with this kind of hermeneutics. The second section discusses how to move beyond the cop-out hermeneutics. The conclusion reiterates the importance to articulate biblical meanings beyond the kyriarchal[7] and phallogocentric status quo of the Trump era.

WHAT IS A COP-OUT HERMENEUTICS?

A cop-out hermeneutics is a way of reading biblical rape texts that does not take seriously rape-victim survivors. In contrast, feminist scholars have taught us to take victim-survivors seriously and to read the world through their eyes. This insight is also the basis of the unique approach to Title IX, initiated under the Obama Presidency, until the Trump administration dismantled it in September 2017. For the first time in U.S. history, colleges and universities were mandated to reduce, if not to eliminate, sexual harassment, which was defined to include sexual assault. Thus, a cop-out hermeneutics of the Bible avoids addressing sexual violence in biblical texts. It either ignores the topic altogether or it finds other ways to sidestep the topic. Most often, it relies on scientific-positivist explanations that eliminate sexual violence from the ancient worlds of the Bible. It accommodates and perhaps even aims to please the fathers and lords of the field and probably also of religious organizations. Feminist exegete Elisabeth Schüssler Fiorenza has written abundantly on the shortcomings of this approach, called scientific positivism. One quote from one of Schüssler Fiorenza's many books shall suffice to illustrate her critique of this paradigm:

> Although the scientific-positivist paradigm demands objectivity, disinterestedness, and value-neutrality in order to control what constitutes the legitimate, scientifically established, true meaning of a text, it is patently *kyriocentric* and *Eurocentric*.[8]
> At stake is the exegetical relationship to the structures of power. Moreover, the adherence to positivism is a particularly *white* feminist hermeneutical preference because many minority-positioned exegetes—feminist, womanist, and otherwise—talk openly about the disciplinary pressures that make them avoid, downplay, or even reject socially located readings of the Bible.[9]

Is the adherence of many (white feminist) Bible exegetes to the scientific-positivist epistemology related to not only the need to please "the fathers" but also to keep their academic positions, such as precarious tenure-track or adjunct teaching positions? Why are many white feminist and nonfeminist scholars so reticent to venture into epistemologically and hermeneutically more adventurous territories when the topic is sexual violence? Please note that I am observing a tendency here, not an absolute condition.

The effects of this tendency are considerable. I want to mention only one example to illustrate the limitations of the scientific-positivist epistemology in biblical interpretations on rape. It comes from Hilary B. Lipka's comprehensive study, *Sexual Transgression in the Hebrew Bible*.[10] Lipka articulates the chosen hermeneutical position in the following three sentences, which makes her study such a good illustration: "I argued that we can only talk about a concept of rape in a biblical text if two elements are present. First, there must be evidence of some belief on the author's part that the sexual act is forced upon an individual against his or her will. Second, there must be evidence of a conception that this forced act violates the victim on a personal level."[11]

Lipka establishes two requirements in her hermeneutical analysis of sexual violence in biblical literature. The first requirement relates to the preference of authorial meaning. This highly modern preference assumes that it is possible, desirable, and relatively obvious to know what the original authors thought about sexual violence. The second requirement prioritizes the individualism of the victim-survivor, yet another modern assumption, as it has developed since the emergence of the Western modern worldview in the sixteenth century. It stresses the priority of the individual over the collective. Thus, perhaps unsurprisingly, Lipka treats biblical rape texts with a historical-literary approach that tries to decipher what the text meant to the Israelite writers. Importantly, however, Lipka does not explain why she makes the two requirements so central to her analysis or even how she came up with them in the first place.

In other words, Lipka privileges intentional meaning to a socially located hermeneutic. But why? Confusion and silence about the rationale prevail. While Lipka acknowledges the existence of rape in biblical literature, she does not consistently use the vocabulary of rape. The inconsistency is already obvious in the book's title that classifies sexual violence as "sexual transgression."[12] Why sexual transgression and not rape? Lipka argues that her study is broader than rape, as it also includes texts about incest, adultery, and other sexual activities. The terminological choice of "sexual transgression" minimizes and obfuscates rape, as the phrase "sexual transgression" contributes to the silencing effect we encounter even today when it comes to rape and sexual violence in the Bible and elsewhere. "Transgression" implies "wrongdoing" without clarifying who is doing the wrong. The terminology leaves open the possibility that the victim-survivor and the perpetrator are both "transgressing."

Furthermore, Lipka's claim to present the views of the original authors relies on a notion of historiography that presupposes objectivity, universality, and value neutrality. She believes the phrase "sexual transgression" avoids anachronism, and she repeatedly states that she wishes to avoid "imposing our own cultural meanings upon ancient texts."[13] Yet this scientific-positivist goal is, of course, unattainable because an escape from particularity, locatedness, and partiality is impossible.[14] It also affirms the prevailing structures of domination because it does not side explicitly with the victim-survivor and it does not question the existing power structures. Predictably, then, Lipka's study leaves unaddressed questions of power, intersectionality, and issues of social location.

Certainly, Lipka's work is not unique, as this epistemological maneuver appears in many other publications.[15] The widespread reluctance of disrupting the enduring dominance of the scientific-positivist paradigm characterizes many studies. Their focus stays with the male characters, even when female characters suffer grave violence. Sometimes the notion of the lesser of two evils excuses it, especially when the survival of an Israelite tribe is at stake. Interpreters acquiesce to sexual violence by talking about ancient marriage customs, even when they classify these customs as problematic to today's readers. Yet few of them articulate substantive positions of solidarity with raped victim-survivors although sometimes they end up questioning God.[16]

In sum, many interpreters claim to read biblical rape texts from an apparently neutral space. They offer exegetical details, theological judgment, and ethical consideration beyond a partisan approach while accommodating the sociopolitical status quo of a phallogocentric, kyriarchal society that tolerates misogyny and sexual violence. Representing one of the most treacherous features of the exegetical cop-out hermeneutics, this hermeneutical tolerance for silence to and complicity with rape-prone customs, features, and conventions indicates the high level of tolerance for sexual violence in past and present culture.

HOW TO MOVE BEYOND A COP-OUT HERMENEUTICS

If all biblical interpretation is located socially, culturally, politically, economically, and religiously, as argued convincingly by Bible scholars who are usually located on the ethnic, racial, and geopolitical margins of the biblical studies enterprise,[17] then we ought to read biblical texts from the perspectives of victim-survivors and deconstruct kyriarchal conventions, habits, and argumentation structures as they have been produced in the extensive biblical interpretation histories. Feminist biblical scholars cannot give up and we have to continuously develop counternarratives because exegetical resistance to the classification of biblical rape stories as tales about marriage, love, or even consensual sex is urgent. We need to move beyond a cop-out hermeneutics and produce biblical readings that align with the legal efforts to take seriously the Title IX debate so that biblical rape texts will no longer be read in ways that support the silence, obfuscation, and marginalization of violence, including sexual violence, so pervasive in the world even today. Three important pedagogical and theoretical moves are central in this feminist effort. First, we have to commit to teaching about biblical and scholarly rape discourse whenever and wherever we can. Second, we have to challenge the persistent gender essentialism in biblical studies and elsewhere. Third, we have to integrate feminist theories and practices into the field of biblical studies. These three moves will ensure that feminist biblical interpreters contribute to social-political and cultural-religious practices that take "seriously its public responsibility, because the bible shaped and still shapes not only the church but also the cultural-political self-understanding of the American imagination."[18]

First, feminist interpreters will have to teach about biblical rape texts whenever and wherever we have the opportunity. Our commitment is important because very few people outside of biblical studies have heard of *feminist* Bible readings, no less of feminist approaches to biblical rape texts. The situation is surely regrettable, but it is also easily explained. The intellectual, theological, and cultural resistance to alternative Bible readings goes deep. Often it is not limited to feminist exegesis but also affects postcolonial, antiracist, queer, or ecological biblical readings. Emerging from the civil-rights and anti-colonial socio-political struggles of the 1960s and 1970s, these approaches have found a hearing only in the most progressive Christian and Jewish communities. In contrast, kyriocentric historical and religiously conservative approaches still dominate mainstream religious (both Jewish and Christian) approaches to biblical texts, as well as conservative, evangelical, and fundamentalist groups, and even extend to secularized settings.

It needs to be acknowledged that, in Western societies, Bible readers are a shrinking group of people because of the pervasive notion that the Bible belongs to a long-gone world and offers antiquarian information about the past. The feminist conviction that the interpretation of biblical rape texts is significant for the understanding and transformation of society seems bizarre to many people, whether they are secular, mainstream religious, or fundamentalist conservative. Substantial ignorance, manufactured for different intellectual and religious reasons, prevails and most people see little need for the feminist study of the Bible. As a result, entire commentary series are still published without any substantive or even marginal engagement with feminist biblical scholarship. The same is true for many preachers and teachers of the Bible who talk as if nothing ever changes in the field of biblical studies.

Yet when feminist Bible exegetes include biblical rape texts and their interpretation histories as part and parcel of a regularly taught Bible curriculum, students learn to connect exegetical, historical, socio-political, cultural, and theological rape-prone assumptions to their own readerly expectations for biblical meanings. Thanks to the recent activism on campus rape and Title IX, this kind of teaching has become considerably easier than in previous decades. Nowadays, students grasp the significance of their own hermeneutical preferences for a reading of the Bible as a political artifact on rape. They recognize the socio-political, cultural, and religious structures of domination that make them assume rape-prone interpretations before they ever read this or that biblical rape text. Ignorance about the content and value of the Bible morphs into a theological-exegetical maturing process, as students begin to recognize the Bible as an integral part of past and present rape cultures.[19]

Second, another crucial step in moving beyond a cop-out hermeneutics and producing biblical readings that counteract the silencing efforts of the Trump administration has to do with the persistent gender essentialism in biblical studies and elsewhere. Essentialism is the idea that the core identity of a person or a thing consists of an essence that is rooted in biological characteristics. Because proponents of essentialism regard gender as a physical characteristic independent of societal norms and conventions, they assume that women are different from men in their essence. Exegetes who take for granted essentialist notions about gender usually ignore feminist-theoretical research. They also disregard the emergence of queer and masculinity studies that have further explored the historical, cultural, socio-political, economic, and religious reasons for the prevalence of essentialism in gender discourse.

Interestingly, feminist exegetes of the 1970s and early 1980s often *seemed* like proponents of gender essentialism. They uplifted female characters, vocabulary, and themes as they countered hegemonic androcentrism that for centuries ignored women as worthy research subjects. However, feminist exegetes also demonstrated that traditional notions of scholarly universality, objectivity, and value neutrality are quite particular, subjective, and biased in favor of men. Feminist works established that androcentric readers are almost exclusively interested in male characters and their texts. Consequently, early second-wave feminist exegetes often articulated seemingly essentialist interpretations but with the goal of subverting and exposing androcentric biases and assumptions. Yet as they stayed within an apparently essentializing gender binary, many of them opened the door for alternative, feminist readings of the Bible.[20]

In addition, early feminist biblical researchers were usually in conversation with the feminist movement of the late 1960s and 1970s, even when they did not make this connection explicit. As feminists asserted women's centrality over against androcentric conventions, laws, and practices in society, they emphasized the category of woman as a politically, culturally, and socially significant research area. Usually, they did not intend to advance essentializing views but to develop the study of women as a mandatory research topic for the transformation of the world. Accordingly, some early feminist Bible scholars articulated already then that the study of biblical women was not necessarily a feminist move. For instance, Schüssler Fiorenza explained in 1983 that the collection "of so-called data and facts on 'Women in the Bible' . . . take[s] the androcentric dynamics and reality constructions of patriarchal texts at face value."[21] She observed that a focus on "women" often legitimizes "societal and ecclesiastical patriarchy and . . . women's divinely ordained place,'"[22] serving doctrinal claims that turn the Bible into "an absolute oracle revealing timeless truth and definite answers to the questions and problems of all times."[23]

Said differently, essentialist views about gender are not indigenous to feminist biblical studies. Instead, feminist exegetes have employed the concept of intersectionality to emphasize the interrelatedness of various structures of domination, including gender, shaping the production of biblical meanings.[24] Yet this constructivist conceptualization of feminist biblical research is not always the basis for investigations of gender and sexuality in biblical studies. In fact, resistance to intersectional feminist biblical scholarship comes from many quarters.

One of the biggest obstacles exists in the institutional power of academic gatekeepers who have cemented their exegetical superiority and authority by ignoring innovative exegetical developments, including feminist exegesis. The academic hallways are filled with stories from feminist Bible scholars who did not gain entry into academia due to their feminist convictions. Even when feminist exegetes succeed in being fully credentialed with the highest academic degrees, producing long publication lists, and holding respectable academic positions, they still face overt and subtle practices of exclusion, discrimination, and marginalization. The hegemonic architecture of academic and religious institutions is not friendly to feminists in any field but the ease with which feminist Bible scholars are sidelined is remarkable. Often, therefore, potential feminist interpreters advance their careers by following the path of least resistance. Accepting essentialist notions of gender, they avoid explicit feminist topics. Unsurprisingly, safe essentialist publications on biblical women are common even today. Disregarding critical gender theories, they reinforce the common misperception that feminist exegesis focuses on biblical women, as if such a focus challenged the hegemonic forces of kyriarchal power in biblical studies and elsewhere in society.

The problem of essentialism is also reinforced in the Christian Right's interpretations of the Bible that essentialize gender in countless popularizing books. The Christian Right consists of Christian evangelical and fundamentalist groups that advance a relatively wide spectrum of conservative theological and political convictions. Commonly they read the Bible with essentializing notions of gender and a strict view of the Bible as the inerrant word of God. There are many examples for popularly written and successfully distributed Christian Right books that assume essentializing notions of gender.[25] They articulate women's experiences as monolithic and unified, and as rooted in women's biological functions and roles. Accordingly, they attribute ontological autonomy to the category of woman, as if the concept is independent of time and space. Since they apply the same idea to the category of man, Christian Right's interpretations stabilize the heteronormative gender binary in the Bible and beyond. The essentializing framework within which the construct of woman is upheld also prevents the possibility for acknowledging differences among women. Very few of the Christian Right's books explore intersectional issues of class, race, ethnicity, or geopolitics in their retellings of biblical women's stories. As a result, almost all of them privatize, sentimentalize, and spiritualize biblical meanings. They universalize women's experiences into the single grouping of "women," not recognizing that women are a diverse group facing different issues in society.

Of course, Christian Right books are not the only ones essentializing gender in the Bible. Many scholarly books in biblical studies fail to contribute to gender justice in its various intersectional manifestations. Esther Fuchs characterizes this tendency of essentializing discourse on biblical women as a neoliberal hermeneutical preference that lacks feminist-theoretical engagement.[26] Yet, ultimately, the charges against essentializing readings of women in the Bible are even more serious. These interpretations do not only lack feminist-theoretical engagement, but they also fail to conceptualize the feminist study of the Bible as a constructive-contextual democratic practice. They are complicit with the ethos of empire requiring submission and passivity to violence, and so they function in maintaining exploitation, injustice, and violence. As such, they not only reinforce essentialist views about gender but also stand in opposition to Schüssler Fiorenza's proposal that biblical scholars, theologians, preachers, teachers, and communities of faith be educated to participate critically and responsibly in public discourses in which the Bible is used for nondemocratic purposes.[27]

Third and finally, feminist interpreters aiming to move beyond a cop-out hermeneutics have to engage feminist theories and practices as they are articulated and lived in the world. Unfortunately, feminist Bible exegetes are often reticent to engage feminist theories and to orient their scholarship accordingly. In fact, Fuchs observes that very few feminist biblical scholars work with feminist theoretical notions when they develop the definition, purpose, and trajectory of their work. Since feminist theorists maintain that all feminist work is "the site of production, contestation, and dialogue between and among various feminist discourses," that all feminist work avoids "normative, authoritative, or prescriptive language in describing its own projects," and that all feminist work stands in an epistemological evolution or genealogy that engages "previous or adjacent feminist work" as "its point of departure," feminist biblical studies ought to be self-critical and skeptical of "emerging orthodoxies, individual authoritative voices, or consensus."[28] It ought to be "inclusive of different 'feminisms'" and define these differences politically and in theoretical terms. It also ought to be intersectional and nurture "a politics of alliance and solidarity."[29] These are only a few of Fuchs's ideas about the development of feminist biblical interpretations in conversation with feminist theories.

As Fuchs elaborates on feminist theoretical ideas, she recognizes the aspirational aspects of feminist readings of the Bible. If we defined it accordingly, she explains, we would see it "as a mapping of a trajectory, a movement toward a kind of knowledge that may not be achievable."[30] Feminist exegesis might then turn into a form of "nomadic scholarship" that transcends "traditional disciplines in its quest for ever more radical questions."[31] As such, the posture of feminist biblical scholars should be one of dialog "between feminism and other discourses of oppression."[32] The tentative, nomadic, or diasporic qualities of feminist biblical scholarship find expression in womanist, postcolonial feminist, or queer exegesis, all of which emphasize the intersectionality of various structures of oppression, including misogyny, sexism, and heteronormativity.[33] Although such work does not always engage feminist theories, it illustrates the need for theoretical engagement with academic discourses beyond the traditional confines of biblical studies.

The significance of feminist theories is also related to another important issue. It has to do with feminist methodologies. Pamela J. Milne explains that feminist theorists have produced extensive works on the topic that would be beneficial to feminist biblical scholarship.[34] Yet so far, these works are rarely engaged in feminist exegesis. Milne believes that the lack of clarity on this theoretical-hermeneutical matter contributes to the irrelevance of biblical studies in the academic world. This is a harsh judgment. However, Milne's astute observation that feminist exegetes do not usually articulate the feminist purposes of their research, the assumptions of their readings, or the kinds of data collected and highlighted in their studies is important.

In short, the lacuna of feminist theoretical conversations within the field of feminist biblical studies indicates considerable theoretical deficiency. It also contributes to the difficulties of moving beyond the cop-out hermeneutics when the topic is sexual violence and rape in the Bible. One should thus take note whether feminist exegetes subscribe to Cartesian positivism or whether they participate in the ongoing struggles for socio-political, economic, geopolitical, and religious justice. One should also ponder what topics contribute to an end of gendered domination in its intersectional manifestations and which topics reinforce the status quo. Since every interpreter makes choices, one has to ask what choices are made and for what reasons. One needs to decipher which exegetical methods are employed, what purposes are served, and how the choices relate to the political goals of gender justice. It is also important to consider why some feminist interpreters relegate such considerations beyond the task of biblical exegesis. What power dynamics do they advance and why?

These and many other theoretical considerations bring feminist clarity to the value of one's research project and how it contributes to dismantling the cop-out hermeneutics. The considerations also promise to move feminist exegesis beyond the status quo of sexual violence and rape-prone assumptions and habits of thought and practice. It is high time for feminist Bible interpreters to address these complex meta-level issues within feminist-theoretical frameworks so that feminist biblical exegesis contributes to feminist practice in the world. What will be the feminist exegetical questions in light of contemporary culture, politics, and religion, and how will feminist theories, epistemologies, methodologies, and hermeneutics shape feminist biblical readings beyond the cop-out hermeneutics that avoids, redefines, or obfuscates in various ways biblical rape texts? It is an exciting time to be part of the ongoing feminist effort to examine biblical texts and their interpretation histories from exegetical positions that take seriously the experiences and perspectives of rape victim-survivors, despite the most recent relegation of Title IX legislation to the waste bins of the Trump administration.

PREPARING A FEMINIST EXEGETICAL PATH FOR TOMORROW: CONCLUDING CONSIDERATIONS

All in all, it has not been easy to convince readers to let go of the cop-out hermeneutics in the reading of biblical rape texts. Deeply ingrained are assumptions and habits about what constitutes accurate, faithful, and legitimate ways of interpretation. On the one hand, many readers aim for personal truth when they read the Bible; they are on a quest for privatized, personalized, and sentimentalized (PPS) biblical meaning. This quest is deeply felt and students may shed tears when they are asked to relinquish their PPS hermeneutics. On the other hand, readers look for historical "accuracy" in their Bible readings. They ask if the events described in a biblical text really happened or who its authors were, when they wrote it, and what their circumstances were that made them compose the various texts. Literary critics of the 1950s dismantled the idea of intentionality,[35] but they may as well have said it on the moon. Ordinary or scholarly Bible readers believe in authorial intention with a vengeance that makes it almost impossible for them to listen to any other hermeneutical position. Quickly they reject any meta-level explanations that locate the historical quest for biblical meanings into readerly contexts of the modern-western era. They insist on defining biblical meanings on the basis of historical accuracy. Their insistence indicates that many readers still regard biblical rape texts as documents delivering historical information about ancient marriage practices or heteronormative love even when those readers acknowledge their ethical difficulties with the ancient points of views. Under such circumstances it is an uphill battle to convince readers that they could also interpret these texts from feminist perspectives that expose and do not assume kyriarchal and phallogocentric perspectives. The cop-out hermeneutics will not disappear any time soon.

But its persistence does not mean we should not keep working against it. The #MeToo movement of 2017 demonstrates that one never knows when voices of refusal to comply with the unjust status quo gain strength in numbers so that sexual harassers and assaulters are fired *en masse*.³⁶ The women's march on January 21, 2017, taking place one day after the inauguration of Donald Trump as the 45th President of the United States, galvanized feminist energies into the global public.³⁷ The president himself has been accused of sexual harassment after he admitted on the so-called Hollywood tape to groping women and their genitalia.³⁸ Since 2017, feminist resistance in solidarity with the sprawling anti-Trump resistance movement has gained strength. Feminist exegetical resistance to the cop-out hermeneutics ought to follow suit. It is about time.

NOTES

1. See "Department of Education Issues New Interim Guidance on Campus Sexual Misconduct" (September 22, 2017); https://www.ed.gov/news/press-releases/department-education-issues-new-interim-guidance-campus-sexual-misconduct. For more detailed comments on the contemporary Title IX debates for the reading of biblical rape texts, see my book *The Bible as Political Artifact: On the Feminist Study of the Hebrew Bible* (Minneapolis, MN: Fortress Press, 2017), 259–77. This article is a version of this previously published book chapter but it is updated in recognition of the changed times for people living in the Trump era.

2. The letter is available online at https://www2.ed.gov/about/offices/list/ocr/letters/colleague-title-ix-201709.pdf (accessed on December 22, 2017).

3. See the letter available online at https://www2.ed.gov/about/offices/list/ocr/letters/colleague-title-ix-201709.pdf.

4. See, e.g., Lindsay Gibbs, "The Trump administration is systematically dismantling Title IX: On the 45th anniversary of the landmark legislation, there are reasons to worry about its future," *ThinkProgress*, June 23, 2017, https://thinkprogress.org/how-the-trump-administration-is-systematically-attacking-title-ix-21bde2f73fc6/; Christina Cauterucci, "What Will Happen to Title IX Under Trump?," *Slate*, February 2, 2017, http://www.slate.com/articles/double_x/doublex/2017/02/trump_could_undo_obama_s_title_ix_protections_for_rape_victims_and_trans.html.

5. Tess Owen, "DeVos to meet with men who say they were falsely accused of campus rape," *VICE News*, July 12, 2017, https://news.vice.com/en_us/article/qvzn3m/devos-to-meet-with-men-who-say-they-were-falsely-accused-of-campus-rape.

6. Anemona Hartocollis and Christina Capecchi, "'Willing to Do Everything': Mothers Defend Sons Accused of Sexual Assault," *New York Times*, October 22, 2017, https://www.nytimes.com/2017/10/22/us/campus-sex-assault-mothers.html?_r=0.

7. The renowned feminist biblical scholar, Elisabeth Schüssler Fiorenza, coined the neologism "kyriarchy"; it originates from the Greek *kryios* for "lord" and *archein* for "to rule/dominate," and expresses structures of domination that combine both gender and class oppression.

8. Elisabeth Schüssler Fiorenza, *Democratizing Biblical Studies: Toward an Emancipatory Educational Space* (Louisville, KY: Westminster John Knox, 2009), 68.

9. See, e.g., Gay L. Byron and Vanessa Lovelace eds., *Womanist Interpretations of the Bible: Expanding the Discourse* (Atlanta: SBL Press, 2016).

10. Hilary B. Lipka, *Sexual Transgression in the Hebrew Bible* (Sheffield: Sheffield Phoenix Press, 2006).

11. Lipka, 220.

12. For Lipka's detailed explanation on the meaning of "sexual transgression," see Lipka, 22.

13. Lipka, 247.

14. For an elaboration on this point, see Jeffrey T. Nealon, *Post-postmodernisms or, The Cultural Logic of Just-In-Time Capitalism* (Stanford: Stanford University Press, 2012).

15. For other examples, see, e.g., M. I. Rey, "Reexamination of the Foreign Female Captive: Deuteronomy 21:10–14 as a Case of Genocidal Rape," *JFSR* 32, no. 1 (2016): 37–53; Alexander I. Abasili, "Was It Rape? The David and Bathsheba Pericope Re-examined," *VT* 61, no. 1 (2011): 1–15.

16. For many other examples from the mainstream commentary literature on Judges 21, see my essay "How to Read the Bible in the Belly of the Beast: About the Politics of Biblical Hermeneutics within the U.S.A.," in *La Violencia and the People's Life: Politics, Culture, and the Interpretation of the Hebrew Bible*, ed. Susanne Scholz and Pablo Andiñach (Semeia Studies; Atlanta, GA: Society of Biblical Literature, 2016), 137–62.

17. The list is long but for one the first publications forcefully making this point, see Fernando F. Segovia and Mary Ann Tolbert (eds.), *Reading from This Place, vol. 1: Social Location and Biblical Interpretation from This Place; vol. 2: Social Location and Biblical Interpretation in Global Perspective* (Minneapolis, MN: Fortress Press, 1995).

18. Elisabeth Schüssler Fiorenza, *The Power of the Word: Scripture and the Rhetoric of Empire* (Minneapolis, MN: Fortress, 2007), 55.

19. For detailed commentary on the challenges of teaching biblical rape texts in U.S.-American and Western academic institutions of higher education, see my essays "Redesigning the Biblical Studies Curriculum: Toward a 'Radical-Democratic' Teaching Model" and "Occupy Academic Bible Teaching: The Architecture of Educational Power and the Biblical Studies Curriculum," chaps. in *The Bible as Political Artifact*. See also my essay "How to Read the Bible in the Belly of the Beast: About the Politics of Biblical Hermeneutics Within the U.S.A.," in *La Violencia and the People's Life: Politics, Culture, and the Interpretation of the Hebrew Bible*, ed. Susanne Scholz and Pablo Andiñach (Semeia Studies; Atlanta, GA: Society of Biblical Literature, 2016), 137–62.

20. For a more detailed discussion on these and related issues, see especially chapter 7 in my *Introducing the Women's Hebrew Bible: Feminism, Gender Justice, and the Study of the Old Testament* (2nd rev. and exp. edn; London: Bloomsbury T&T Clark, 2017).

21. Elisabeth Schüssler Fiorenza, *In Memory of Her: A Feminist Theological Reconstruction of Christian Origins* (New York: Crossroad, 1983), xxiii–xxiv, 30.

22. Schüssler Fiorenza, *In Memory of Her*, 7.

23. Schüssler Fiorenza, *In Memory of Her*, 5.

24. Cheryl Anderson, *Ancient Laws and Contemporary Controversies: The Need for Inclusive Interpretation* (Oxford: Oxford University Press, 2009).

25. Scholz, *Introducing the Women's Hebrew Bible*, 149–69.

26. Esther Fuchs, *Feminist Theory and the Bible: Interrogating the Sources* (Feminist Studies and Sacred Texts; Lanham, MD: Lexington Books, 2016), 55–70.

27. Elisabeth Schüssler Fiorenza, *Democratizing Biblical Studies* (Louisville: Westminster John Knox, 2009), 20. For a discussion with examples, see my essay "The Forbidden Fruit for the New Eve: The Christian Right's Adaptation to the (Post)modern World," chap. in *The Bible as Political Artifact: On the Feminist Study of the Hebrew Bible* (Minneapolis, MN: Fortress Press, 2017).

28. Fuchs, *Feminist Theory and the Bible*, 1.

29. Fuchs, *Feminist Theory and the Bible*, 1–2.

30. Fuchs, *Feminist Theory and the Bible*, 9–10.

31. Fuchs, *Feminist Theory and the Bible*, 10.

32. Fuchs, *Feminist Theory and the Bible*.

33. See, e.g., Gay L. Byron and Vanessa Lovelace (eds.), *Womanist Interpretations of the Bible: Expanding the Discourse* (Atlanta, GA: SBL Press, 2016); Mitzi J. Smith (ed.), *I Found God in Me: A Womanist Biblical Hermeneutics Reader* (Eugene OR: Wipf and Stock, 2015); Deryn Guest and Robert E. Goss, Mona West, Thomas Bohache (eds.), *The Queer Bible Commentary* (London: SCM Press, 2006); Musa W. Dube, *Postcolonial Feminist Interpretation of the Bible* (St. Louis, MO: Chalice Press, 2000).

34. Pamela J. Milne and Susanne Scholz, "On Method and Methodology in Feminist Biblical Studies: A Conversation," in *Feminist Interpretation of the Hebrew Bible in Retrospect, vol. 3: Methods*, ed. Susanne Scholz (Sheffield: Sheffield Phoenix Press, 2016), 19–34.

35. W. K. Wimsatt, Jr. and Monroe Beardsley, "The Intentional Fallacy," *The Sewanee Review* 54, no. 3 (July–September 1946): 468–88. Revised and republished in William K. Wimsatt, *The Verbal Icon: Studies in the Meaning of Poetry* (University of Kentucky Press, 1954), 3–18. See also Roland Barthes, "The Death of the Author," *Aspen* 5–6 (1967).

36. See, e.g., Sophie Gilbert, "The Movement of #MeToo: How a hashtag got is power," *The Atlantic*, October 16, 2017, https://www.theatlantic.com/entertainment/archive/2017/10/the-movement-of-metoo/542979/; Jean McGregor, "Will the #MeToo movement speed up the number of women in leadership or slow it down?" *The Washington Post*, December 26, 2017, https://www.washingtonpost.com/news/on-leadership/wp/2017/12/26/will-the-metoo-movement-speed-up-the-number-of-women-in-leadership-or-slow-it-down/?utm_term=.ffa3b98a3bf3.

37. See "2017 Women's March," entry in the online Wikipedia and available at https://en.wikipedia.org/wiki/2017_Women%27s_March (accessed December 29, 2017).

38. See, e.g., Dan Merica, "Women detail sexual allegations again," *CNN*, December 12, 2017, http://www.cnn.com/2017/12/11/politics/donald-trump-women-allegations/index.html; Maggie Haberman and Jonathan Martin, "Trump Once Said the 'Access Hollywood' Tape Was Real: Now He's Not Sure," *New York Times*, November 28, 2017, https://www.nytimes.com/2017/11/28/us/politics/trump-access-hillwood-tape.html.

BIBLIOGRAPHY

Abasili, Alexander I. "Was It Rape? The David and Bathsheba Pericope Re-examined." *VT* 61, no. 1 (2011): 1–15.

Anderson, Cheryl. *Ancient Laws and Contemporary Controversies: The Need for Inclusive Interpretation*. Oxford: Oxford University Press, 2009.

Barthes, Roland. "The Death of the Author." *Aspen* 5–6 (1967).

Byron, Gay L. and Vanessa Lovelace, editors. *Womanist Interpretations of the Bible: Expanding the Discourse*. Atlanta: SBL Press, 2016.

Cauterucci, Christina. "What Will Happen to Title IX Under Trump?" *Slate*, February 2, 2017. http://www.slate.com/articles/double_x/doublex/2017/02/trump_could_undo_obama_s_title_ix_protections_for_rape_victims_and_trans.html.

Dube, Musa W. *Postcolonial Feminist Interpretation of the Bible*. St. Louis, MO: Chalice Press, 2000.

Fuchs, Esther. *Feminist Theory and the Bible: Interrogating the Sources*. Feminist Studies and Sacred Texts; Lanham, MD: Lexington Books, 2016.

Gibbs, Lindsay. "The Trump administration is systematically dismantling Title IX: On the 45th anniversary of the landmark legislation, there are reasons to worry about its future." *ThinkProgress*, June 23, 2017. https://thinkprogress.org/how-the-trump-administration-is-systematically-attacking-title-ix-21bde2f73fc6/.

Gilbert, Sophie. "The Movement of #MeToo: How a hashtag got is power." *The Atlantic*, October 16, 2017. https://www.theatlantic.com/entertainment/archive/2017/10/the-movement-of-metoo/542979/.

Guest, Deryn, Robert E. Goss, Mona West, Thomas Bohache, eds. *The Queer Bible Commentary*. London: SCM Press, 2006.

Haberman, Maggie and Jonathan Martin. "Trump Once Said the 'Access Hollywood' Tape Was Real: Now He's Not Sure." *New York Times*, November 28, 2017. https://www.nytimes.com/2017/11/28/us/politics/trump-access-hollywood-tape.html.

Hartocollis, Anemona and Christina Capecchi. "'Willing to Do Everything': Mothers Defend Sons Accused of Sexual Assault." *New York Times*, October 22, 2017. https://www.nytimes.com/2017/10/22/us/campus-sex-assault-mothers.html?_r=0.

Lipka, Hilary B. *Sexual Transgression in the Hebrew Bible*. Sheffield: Sheffield Phoenix Press, 2006.

McGregor, Jean. "Will the #MeToo movement speed up the number of women in leadership or slow it down?" *The Washington Post*, December 26, 2017. https://www.washingtonpost.

com/news/on-leadership/wp/2017/12/26/will-the-metoo-movement-speed-up-the-number-of-women-in-leadership-or-slow-it-down/?utm_term=.ffa3b98a3bf3.

Merica, Dan. "Women detail sexual allegations again." *CNN*, December 12, 2017. http://www.cnn.com/2017/12/11/politics/donald-trump-women-allegations/index.html.

Milne, Pamela J. and Susanne Scholz. "On Method and Methodology in Feminist Biblical Studies: A Conversation." In *Feminist Interpretation of the Hebrew Bible in Retrospect, vol. 3: Methods*, edited by Susanne Scholz, 19–34. Sheffield: Sheffield Phoenix Press, 2016.

Nealon, Jeffrey T. *Post-postmodernisms or, The Cultural Logic of Just-In-Time Capitalism*. Stanford: Stanford University Press, 2012.

Owen, Tess. "DeVos to meet with men who say they were falsely accused of campus rape." *VICE News*, July 12, 2017. https://news.vice.com/en_us/article/qvzn3m/devos-to-meet-with-men-who-say-they-were-falsely-accused-of-campus-rape.

Rey, M. I. "Reexamination of the Foreign Female Captive: Deuteronomy 21:10–14 as a Case of Genocidal Rape." *JFSR* 32, no. 1 (2016): 37–53.

Scholz, Susanne. "How to Read the Bible in the Belly of the Beast: About the Politics of Biblical Hermeneutics within the U.S.A." In *La Violencia and the People's Life: Politics, Culture, and the Interpretation of the Hebrew Bible*, edited by Susanne Scholz and Pablo Andiñach, 137–62, Semeia Studies; Atlanta, GA: Society of Biblical Literature, 2016, 137–62.

———. *The Bible as Political Artifact: On the Feminist Study of the Hebrew Bible*. Minneapolis, MN: Fortress Press, 2017.

———. *Introducing the Women's Hebrew Bible: Feminism, Gender Justice, and the Study of the Old Testament*, 2nd edition revised and expanded. London: Bloomsbury T&T Clark, 2017.

———. *The Bible as Political Artifact: On the Feminist Study of the Hebrew Bible*. Minneapolis, MN: Fortress Press, 2017.

Schüssler Fiorenza, Elisabeth. *Democratizing Biblical Studies*. Louisville: Westminster John Knox, 2009.

———. *Democratizing Biblical Studies: Toward an Emancipatory Educational Space*. Louisville, KY: Westminster John Knox, 2009.

———. *In Memory of Her: A Feminist Theological Reconstruction of Christian Origins*. New York: Crossroad, 1983.

———. *The Power of the Word: Scripture and the Rhetoric of Empire*. Minneapolis, MN: Fortress, 2007.

Segovia, Fernando F. and Mary Ann Tolbert, editors. *Reading from This Place, vol. 1: Social Location and Biblical Interpretation from This Place*. Minneapolis: Fortress Press, 1995.

———. *Reading from This Place, vol. 2: Social Location and Biblical Interpretation in Global Perspective*. Minneapolis: Fortress Press, 1995.

Smith, Mitzi J., editor. *I Found God in Me: A Womanist Biblical Hermeneutics Reader*. Eugene OR: Wipf and Stock, 2015.

United States Department of Education Office for Civil Rights. "Dear Colleague Letter." April 4, 2011. http://www2.ed.gov/about/offices/list/ocr/letters/colleague-201104.html.

———. "Department of Education Issues New Interim Guidance on Campus Sexual Misconduct." September 22, 2017. https://www.ed.gov/news/press-releases/department-education-issues-new-interim-guidance-campus-sexual-misconduct.

Wimsatt, W.K., Jr., and Monroe Beardsley. "The Intentional Fallacy." *The Sewanee Review* 54, no. 3 (July–September 1946): 468–88.

Wimsatt, William K. *The Verbal Icon: Studies in the Meaning of Poetry*. University of Kentucky Press, 1954.

Chapter Two

Constructions of Hindu Mythology after the Rape of Jyoti Singh Pandey

Coupling Activism with Pedagogy

T. Nicole Goulet

On the evening of December 16, 2012, 23-year-old medical student Jyoti Singh Pandey was gang-raped and mutilated by five men and one juvenile on a moving bus in Delhi, India. After going out to a movie with her friend Avanindra Pratap Pandey (of no relation), the two had difficulties getting transport home, and so boarded a charter bus after the juvenile encouraged them to come aboard. Once on the bus, both were attacked. People outside the bus could not see through the tinted windows, nor apparently hear their calls for help while the bus was moving. On December 29th Pandey (who became referred to in the press as Nirbhaya, or "fearless") died of her injuries, but not before providing a full account of the incident, including the names of her attackers. The attackers were subsequently brought to trial, with four of the adult perpetrators convicted of rape and murder, sentenced to death by hanging, and the juvenile also convicted of rape and murder, and sentenced to the three-year maximum prison sentence allowable for those under eighteen years of age. The juvenile has since served his time. One of the adult males did not contest the charges, but died either of suicide or murder before trial. Through a series of appeals, India's Supreme Court upheld the remaining three males' convictions and sentences. The men, as of the writing of this essay, have yet to be executed.[1]

On December 19, following Pandey's assault, small groups of protesters converged at the residence of Sheila Dikshit, then chief minister of Delhi. At least one report claimed that these protesters consisted mostly of female students and feminist organizations that were troubled by Dikshit's failure to take any responsibility for the Pandey case, as well as by the government's general failure to adequately address violence against women.[2] Protests escalated on December 22nd and 23rd, with increased numbers and diverse groups now attending, and clashes with police followed. The geographical focus of the protests was originally India Gate in Delhi, however by the second day of escalation, protests were being held across the country.[3] India Gate is a World War I memorial commemorating soldiers of the Indian Army. Due to its location near both the Parliament of India and the Supreme Court of India, and because there is no vehicle traffic allowed near the site, it is an ideal location for public gatherings, and is particularly popular for protests over legal and political issues. According to Debolina Dutta and Oishik Sircar, the protests were understood by some Indian people as the "Arab Spring for India," a moment in which widespread protest and activism could potentially lead to political and legal reforms; reforms, in the case of India, that would protect women against gender based violence (GBV).[4] Dutta and Sircar also argue that Pandey became "India's national property" in this process, used by activists, nationalists, and lawmakers alike to push their diverse, though sometimes overlapping, agendas.[5] Further evidence of how Pandey represented diverse national agendas can be found in *India's Daughter*, a documentary which tracked the attitudes and perspectives of both those directly involved in the incident as well as those on peripheries.[6] *India's Daughter*, which included footage of one of the perpetrators and his lawyer admitting they viewed Pandey at fault for her assault, proved so controversial the Indian government (led by the Bharatiya Janata Party, or BJP) had the documentary banned from release in India. Various government and party authorities cited reasons for that suppression which included the likelihood that it would incite riots and that the film defamed India.[7]

Subsequent reforms were limited and generally dissatisfying for the majority of feminists, who viewed the minor changes as maintaining the status quo. Many protestors had placed their hope in the three-member Justice Verma Committee, which was set up by the Indian government to create a report and provide recommendations for changes in the legal system as it pertained to GBV. While the Committee made some reforms such as legislating against new crimes including stalking and acid attacks as well as stiffening extant penalties, the government of the Indian National Congress continued to refuse to acknowledge some forms of GBV such as marital rape, or to recognize rape as a gender-specific crime.[8] This resistance was in part due to the persistence of the brahminical ideals espoused in certain types of Hinduism. As Jean Chapman argues in her article, "Violence against Women in Democratic India: Let's Talk Misogyny," brahminical Hinduism normalizes both overt and subtle types of misogyny. As a result of this normalization, Chapman argues: "Rape is not random. It is structured."[9] Rape culture, in this line of argument, is institutionally supported and accepted within Hinduism, to the point that it becomes an inevitable outcome of orthodox, brahminical ideals. Certainly, despite the findings and recommendations of the Justice Verma Committee, rape in certain contexts continued to be protected by both secular courts and religiously based patriarchal systems, sustaining patriarchal controls over what counts as rape.

In the aftermath of the trial, the protests, and the report, attempts to understand what happened to Pandey and why produced a diversity of explanations. Some commentators, such as Hindu nationalists Asaram Bapu and Kailash Vijayvargiya, used cultural or religious arguments to blame Pandey for her predicament. Both evaluated Pandey's behavior in terms of the theological concept, *Lakshman rekha*, or the moral limits or lines people should not cross, as they were derived from the *Ramayana*. In the *Ramayana*, the *Lakshman rekha* was utilized as a warning to Sita about how she conducted herself in front of Rama's brother Lakshmana. In this context, it is used to explain why such a bad thing happened to such a serious, dedicated, hardworking young woman. If Pandey had not stayed out late with a male companion, if she had voiced God's name when they started to assault her, or if she hadn't been so western in her pursuit of an education, she never would have been attacked and killed in the first place.[10] Another line of argument, taken by mainline news outlets in North America, including CNN and *New York Times*, blamed the marginalization of impoverished male migrant workers for the incident. The assailants, who fit neatly into this category, were depicted along with other fellow migrants as backward villagers who raped women because such behavior was acceptable within villages.[11] If the country could work toward economic and cultural reforms, they could avert future instances of violence like the one Pandey experienced.[12]

Other explanations, such as those examined in this chapter, analyzed the crime in the context of a systemic sexism closely tied to religion and assumptions about women's roles, and sought to address the problem of rape culture within an explicitly Hindu framework. A particularly interesting example, and the subject of this chapter, is the Priya comic series co-created by Ram Devineni and Dan Goldman, which can be understood as an element of a much larger movement to address GBV. Their comic series attempts to not just explain what happened but transform the way violence against women is conceived. What I am calling the "Priya movement" began in 2014 with the publication of a comic book entitled *Priya's Shakti*, and promotional posters and digital pictures that allow supporters to assert, "I'm with Priya." The initial enthusiasm for the comic, which soon became a series, led to linked educational workshop initiatives, international media coverage, and support from The United Nations Entity for Gender Equality and the Empowerment of Women (UN Women).[13]

The conception of *Priya's Shakti* was a direct result of the Jyoti Singh Pandey case, and it was a deliberate attempt to participate in efforts to stop

GBV.[14] The comic book tells the story of Priya, a young girl living in a rural community. Her father tells her she can no longer attend school (despite her dreams of becoming a teacher) and must instead stay home and help her mother with chores. Once she is a young woman, she is regularly harassed by men as she shops in the market, until one day she is beaten and raped by local village men as she fetches water. Priya's family subsequently rejects her as she is no longer pure. The goddess Parvati, a popular figure amongst the poor and impoverished and the wife of Shiva, laments the treatment of female devotees such as Priya. She decides to incarnate as Priya in order to look for justice in the world—yet she finds none. Instead, Parvati (in the body of Priya) becomes the object of another sexual attack which prompts her to reveal herself to the perpetrator, scaring him off. Shiva awakens out of his meditation to feel the experiences of Parvati. He is enraged, and vows to destroy a degenerate humanity. Parvati, who has since left Priya's body, pleads with him to show mercy—his actions would also destroy the innocent, and in particular the women she wants to protect—and eventually he acquiesces. In the end, Parvati visits Priya who has isolated herself in a forest, and bestows upon her a mantra: speak without shame. Priya is given a tiger as a steed which is identified as *shakti* (female power) and rides from village to village to preach her message: first, that women are equal to men so they should be treated with respect; second, that all children, regardless of gender, should be educated; third, intervene when you see a woman in crisis; and fourth, reveal injustice so that it can be stopped (speak without shame).

Devineni, Goldman, and co-author Paromita Vohra published another comic entitled, *Priya's Mirror*, the "chapter 2" to *Priya's Shakti* retroactively labeled, "chapter 1." Premiering at the New York Film Festival on September 30, 2016, this second comic reprises the character Priya and continues drawing awareness to GBV around the world by focusing on the real-life experiences of women who were victims of acid attacks. This second comic follows up the "speak without shame" mandate of the first with an additional message: through courage, we can change and the world can change. A third chapter to this series is currently in production, titled *Priya and the Lost Girls*. While the date of release has not been determined, this issue addresses the trafficking of girls across India.[15] With each comic, we can see how the comics adapt to issues of gender as they arise in society.

Unlike the debates in traditional media that attempted to explain why Pandey was raped, assaulted, and killed by focusing on the legal system, the Priya movement seeks to educate, inform, and change people's behaviors through sociocultural and religious reform. By drawing awareness to the prevalence of GBV in India, violence against women can be addressed and discussed rather than normalized or ignored. Because of the socially and culturally diverse origins of actors in this movement, polarizing binaries such as urban/rural, western/eastern, modern/backward, upper caste/lower caste are not given much credence, let alone reinforced. This could, arguably, be viewed as problematic by feminist organizations who recognize class and caste as factors in how a rape is perceived and whether or not it will go unreported,[16] but because one of the aims of the Priya movement is to reach and teach the widest audience possible, including outside the Indian context, it makes sense that the specificities of the structure of Indian society are not overemphasized. Thus, it does not matter who you are—male or female, upper caste or lower caste, rich or poor—everyone should learn to speak out against GBV without shame. Yet the "Indian roots" of this project are recognizable, and, as I will argue, may even be likened to a contemporary Purana (sacred writings about the gods and goddesses). By framing the comic as a Purana we can see how the idea of global accessibility remains critical to the project even while specifically Hindu concepts and practices ground it in South Asian experience and culture. What makes the *Priya's Shakti* project so very attractive from a pedagogical perspective is, as we shall see, the way it problematizes the often taken-for-granted relations of the local to the global, of the traditional to the modern, and elite or orthodox representations of Hinduism to popular or even subaltern ideas of what the gods are, and what they are for. If students in religious studies classrooms are paying close attention to this material, a lot of theoretical heavy-lifting can be accomplished just by talking thoughtfully about how this event and its aftermath was integrated into religious discourse in India and beyond.

PRIYA'S SHAKTI AS A PURANA

The success of *Priya's Shakti*, with its blending of contemporary issues with Hindu mythology, could be partially explained by considering the comic as a modern Purana. *Priya's Shakti* offers a new story about the Hindu pantheon which is formulated to speak to feminist concerns of female empowerment, human equality, and non-violence. The reframing of the Goddess promotes the anti-GBV message without overstepping boundaries (such as the *Lakshman rekha*) that are so easily imagined between the secular and the religious.

The Puranas originate between the fourth and sixteenth centuries CE and contain stories of hundreds of gods and goddesses. Highly diverse and spanning hundreds of years in their creation, the Puranas are an example of smriti literature. Smriti can be translated as "that which is remembered," and refers to a body of texts authored by humans and revised over time. Shruti literature, or "that which is heard," by contrast, refers to texts that are considered revealed and without author. Both bodies of texts are important to the Hindu tradition(s), and are used and emphasized differently, depending on the sect and practitioner. For example, the Puranas, as smriti literature, have long been considered by scholars as "the Veda of the common people," used as a means to access Vedic messages, or shruti literature, in the form of legends and myths.[17] This literature includes origin stories about gods and goddesses, as well as stories about kings and other significant individuals. They may suggest moral lessons, but they also may not. That is, there is not a clear organizational structure shared by all Puranas, nor is the content necessarily consistent between them.

This may be due to the possibility that, according to some scholars, in contrast to other religious texts found in Hinduism, the Puranas were never meant to be in book form. These texts are compilations of various and diverse oral narratives, rife with local variations that have accumulated over centuries and which never underwent a process of codification or standardization—the diversity and breadth of the Puranas are testament to this.[18] Though the majority of the Puranas are in Sanskrit, their language is colloquial and informal to the point that they are referred to by scholars of Sanskrit poetry as the "pulp fiction of ancient India."[19] The use of such a moniker suggests a certain normative attitude about the Puranas' value and function. Certainly, those who viewed themselves as authoritative purveyors of authentic Hinduism, such as the Sanskrit scholars, often viewed the Puranas as secondary to shruti texts. But there is also the recognition that they are entertaining and bring enjoyment to mass audiences, in contrast to the Vedas, which were generally reserved for the upper castes to read as part of serious study, to fulfill one's ashrama as a student. Whereas the Vedas are perceived as the sophisticated philosophical and intellectual foundation of the Hindu tradition(s), Puranas are the popular and devotional material that enables average devotees to participate in that tradition.

There are easy parallels to be made here between attitudes toward the Puranas and comic books. Both are popular forms, which have been frequently marginalized and disregarded by cultural elites. And while both are important forms of communication and reflect the culture within which they were created, and contribute to its formation, neither have been taken all that seriously by those who decide what should be studied in the first place. It is only in recent years, for example, that we see the genre of comic books (renamed "graphic novels" to make them more elite-friendly) getting recognized as legitimate cultural forms in the academy.[20] Likewise, the Puranas, though always connected to the study and understanding of certain forms of Hinduism, have rarely been studied except in so far as they are a particular manifestation of what is deemed by many scholars and large numbers of practitioners to be authentic brahminical Hinduism.[21]

Comics, like the Puranas, are intended for a popular audience and are not taken particularly seriously by literary and intellectual elites. *Priya's Shakti* as a comic in particular, has the religious content to justify the argument that it is a Purana. But it is not just the religious content that makes the claim interesting, as it is the way in which the *Priya's Shakti* is used. Specifically, it functions not simply as a repository of religious stories but as a mode of worship in which mantras are introduced and new relations with the divine are established. Just as ancient religious texts are embedded with mantras that aid practitioners in spiritual realization, the "mantras" in *Priya's Shakti* may also influence the behaviors and attitudes of people by way of reception and repetition. The Puranas are not only an argument for the practice of *bhakti*, but a means to achieve it, so too with *Priya's Shakti*. *Bhakti* refers to loving devotion of a deity, devotion which entails the practice of puja or worship toward a chosen deity or deities. The emergence of *bhakti* as a religious practice, which coincided with the increasing popularity of the Puranas, occurred in the twelfth century and was in sharp contrast to previous emphasis on the proper Vedic ritual of Upanishadic meditation to achieve enlightenment. In *bhakti*, as it was promoted in the Puranas, new gods and goddesses were incorporated into the existing pantheon, Vedic gods were revived and reconsidered, and the practice of *bhakti* itself extended to those who were previously excluded from ritual worship.[22] Hillary Rodrigues argues the Puranas facilitate the democratization of religious practice in Hinduism (a process that occurred in other Indian religions as well, such as Jainism) and provide a means by which women and lower castes can legitimate their capacity to worship in ways that departed from the strict rules and orthodoxy associated with the Vedic period. Essentially, the Puranas are religious texts that provide spiritual knowledge and techniques to populations formerly excluded by elites from the practice of orthodox Hinduism. One can see why, then, brahminical elites would scoff at the lack of standardization, the use of vernaculars and "low" Sanskrit (if there is such a category) found in the Puranas. One can also see why they were so popular, as they opened the door to new possibilities for the religious practitioners who were excluded from the "official" Hindu tradition. In the case of *Priya's Shakti*, orthodoxy is overturned through Priya's devotion to Parvati, as demarcated by their personal relationship and interactions. It is *bhakti* that results in Priya's ability to overcome her rape, and her performance of *bhakti* toward Parvati that emboldens her to live a life independent of her traditional Hindu family.

As a contemporary Purana, *Priya's Shakti* also challenges the status quo, but does not do so outside of the bounds already set by the ancient smriti texts. It doesn't challenge the established Hindu pantheon to add new gods or goddesses, but maintains existing popular deities, albeit imagining them in new ways. Nor does it counter widely held assumptions about the sacred, but instead uses the sacred to reconsider contemporary social practice. Readers are informed about *bhakti* throughout, as it's a central feature that propels the story forward. We see how practitioners call upon their deities and the rewards that they receive for their loyalty. Relationships between humans and deities are forged and affirmed to the benefit of humanity as a whole.

Critically, it is Priya's piety—her practice of *bhakti* toward Parvati—that precipitates Parvati's manifestation and engagement with humanity. It is only when Priya calls out in distress, "Help me Goddess Parvati, I have nowhere to turn," that Parvati pays attention.[23] Until then, Parvati is either unaware of Priya's plight or doesn't care, as she is too immersed in her relationship with Shiva. But when Parvati's attention is finally drawn to her worshipper, the goddess becomes aware of Priya's life experiences, both past and present, and comes to understand the dire situation that Priya is in. The act of *bhakti* creates a relationship that is not one of precise and formal ritual overseen by a priest and reminiscent of the Vedas, but is rather an intimate and spontaneous result of Priya's supplication in a moment of distress and anguish. As a devotee, Priya is not rejected as she would be in brahminical traditions as a result of her caste, class or gender, or her impurity, but accepted on the basis of her commitment and devotion to the goddess.

When Parvati bestows Priya with her power and provides her with the *vahana* (mount/vehicle) of a tiger, it is an indication that Priya's devotion has resulted in Parvati's ongoing protection. At this time, Parvati also claims Priya as her chosen one, who is given a mantra to share with others: "speak without shame and stand with me, bring about the change we want to see."[24] Priya subsequently rides the tiger from village to village while repeating the mantra. The tiger's eyes are depicted with the same colored green as Parvati's, indicating Priya and Parvati's continued connection to one another, even when Parvati is no longer physically present. And Priya's eyes take on the same color after receiving her mount. Thus, Parvati's power and the tiger become interchangeable, or one in the same; likewise is the interchangeable or shared power of Priya and Parvati.

The ongoing relationship between Priya and Parvati is also evident when Parvati appears briefly in the second comic, *Priya's Mirror*. While Parvati's role is not as pivotal as in the first comic, she does direct Priya to encourage a group of women burned by acid to escape a demon named Ahankar. The tiger remains Priya's mount and remains a continued marker of Priya's connection to Parvati. *Bhakti* is also explicitly referred to in the second comic when a fictional woman named Kusum prays to the god Shiva for her love interest's protection. Again, the act is spontaneous, made by a devotee during a time of distress. But it is also highly repetitive, as Kusum calls over and over again: "Oh Shiva, Shiva, please don't let him die because of me."[25] There is no formalized ritual, but instead a simple and repeated call, which is enough to capture the attention of a deity. My point here is that the comic series may be understood not simply as a morality tale couched in religious terms but as a reminder to people of the ways and reasons Hindus might participate in *bhakti* in contemporary times. It is in this sense, not only because of the popular content, tone, and mode of delivery, but because of its ritual component, that *Priya's Shakti* is so very reminiscent of the Puranas.

It is also important to point out that the very medium of *Priya's Shakti* itself—a story coupled with visuals in comic form—provides visual aids to help practitioners in their efforts to gain access the gods and goddesses, and that the use of such visual cues is not particularly modern. The use of murtis (statues/depictions of deities) has long been an element of Hinduism and is especially significant to the practice of *bhakti*. For example, Wendy Doniger argues the popularity of the Puranas coincided with the rise in temple worship, which in turn allowed for people who could not read Sanskrit texts to have access to Sanskrit myths and rituals by way of carved images on temples. Iconography allows worshippers to transcend illiteracy and develop a religious imaginary even if they cannot read the texts.[26] This type of association between temple images and the democratization of worship with *bhakti* is critical when considering that *Priya's Shakti* targets women denied education who are therefore often illiterate or semi-literate. Priya, after all, is depicted as a girl who loves to go to school and longs to be a teacher. Her dream is thwarted when her father pulls her from school to focus on helping her mother with maintaining the household.

Priya's chance to pursue an education is further diminished by the rape. While obviously these events happened through no fault of her own, Priya was the one who bore the responsibility of the transgression. This is because her value to her orthodox family is dependent on her sexual purity and not her intelligence, independence, or even future earning potential. There are resemblances to the Pandey case here, for both of the victims are blamed for circumstance. If she were more traditional and religious, the argument goes, the rape would not have happened. Notably, the issue of lack of education for girls is less the case in the second comic, *Priya's Mirror*, which is concerned more with educated women, such as a character named Anjali, who after placing first in a series of tests for law school, is attacked with acid by a male acquaintance. Interestingly, the Hindu pantheon also figures less prominently in this comic, and instead depicts the powers of humans, in this case mostly women, who fight against the human-turned-demon Ahankar. However, the general principle, that the visual medium of the comic is as crucial to our understanding of it as its literal message, holds true when we consider the larger project of which it is a part. In *Priya's Mirror* too, Priya is depicted on her tiger mount armed with a mirrored shield fighting Ahankar—an image highly suggestive of Durga fighting Ravana, a key Puranic story. Durga is a powerful warrior goddess who is the only one who can defeat Ravana, a king and demigod, after all the other gods have failed. It is Durga's *shakti* (female divine energy) that contributes to her success, and her refusal to depend on a male consort only enhances her image as a powerful and autonomous force. Priya's transformation into someone independent, brave, and strong is a reflection of Durga's power and the idea that mortal women may channel it.

As I have argued, there is considerable overlap between *Priya's Shakti* and the Puranas in both function and content, but there is also considerable divergence, particularly when identifying the ways that certain deities are represented. Aside from her connection to Shiva, for example, the Parvati in *Priya's Shakti* features no specific characteristics associated with the goddess as she is traditionally understood within the Hindu tradition. In the opening scenes of the comic book, Parvati is at first glance very much the deity one might expect. She stays steadfastly by Shiva's side on Mount Kailash, where she and Shiva are described as in "complete devotion to each other."[27] When he leaves her to go and meditate, she says a prayer for him, wishing that he does not disturb the balance of the universe. In this way, she maintains her quintessential role as householder to Shiva's renouncer, ensuring that he does not renounce so much that in so doing he destroys the universe with his power. Yet she also functions independently of Shiva and is depicted as having more knowledge and compassion about the universe and humanity than Shiva. Traditionally, Parvati's power resides in her connection to Shiva, for she is his consort and manifestation of *shakti*. As such, the Puranas depict her not so much as having her own followers, but instead as having a relationship with those who follow her husband Shiva. In *Priya's Shakti*, Parvati is depicted as acknowledging that she has her own devotees with whom she interacts independently, rather than functioning primarily as an intermediary to Shiva's followers. This innovation in the comic shows how Parvati as a distinct power, separate from her husband, is a compassionate deity who believes in the overarching goodness of humanity. There are certainly extant myths that emphasize her compassion for Shiva's impoverished followers, but in these instances she tends to make requests of Shiva to take care of them accordingly rather than intervene directly.[28] In contrast to Shiva who is depicted in fairly traditional ways in the comic—he goes off to meditate for long periods of time, acts spontaneously and violently, and generally seems out of touch with humanity—Parvati, represented as the personification of feminist values, is radically new. Her compassion for humanity requires her to protect the women who have been harmed. And she arms humans with the power (in this case *shakti*) to join in her fight, going so far as to manifest as Priya and experience her rape, showing how all—even the gods—are ultimately impacted by the violence directed toward women, and therefore all must join the fight against GBV.

Priya's Shakti has been able to tap into more traditional understandings of Hinduism while simultaneously adapting to a contemporary message with some success. Strikingly, cultural watchdogs like Rajan Zed and the Hindu American Foundation have said nothing about this feminist incarnation of Parvati. Zed is a Nevada-based self-proclaimed Hindu cleric who works on interfaith initiatives, but is also highly critical of contemporary representations of Hinduism around the world, including representations of deities for public, non-Hindu consumption.[29] Considering Zed's project to present a unified orthodox Hinduism to the Western world, it is surprising that he has said nothing, at least to my knowledge, about the comic series. Given his concerns about representations of goddesses outlined on his own webpage, one can only surmise that it will be a matter of time before he formulates some sort of statement about *Priya's Shakti*. As his webpage states: "Zed indicated that reimagining Hindu scriptures, symbols, concepts and deities for commercial or other agenda [sic] was not okay as it hurt the devotees."[30] Likewise, the Hindu American Foundation, which purportedly has links to the Hindu nationalist groups Vishva Hindu Parishad and Hindu Swayamsevak Sangh, has offered no critiques or concern about the comic. Perhaps *Priya's Shakti*'s success is not only because of the relevancy of the message, but because Parvati is represented in a way that does not explicitly challenge the basic role of a Hindu deity: she protects the faithful, intercedes where possible on their behalf, and rewards complete devotion. What is challenged, however, are traditional wifely roles and submissiveness, which Parvati no longer embodies; feminism is smuggled into the debate under the cover of a Puranic style.

PRIYA'S SHAKTI AS PEDAGOGICAL ACTIVISM

Priya's Shakti functions as a forum to educate people about GBV and to empower those women who have already been victimized. As noted already, the final scenes of *Priya's Shakti* depict an empowered Priya upon her tiger mount bestowed with her new mantra: speak without shame. In addition to the mantra she is provided with directives on education, respect, and responsibility of others. These are directives that are not just to be presented to Priya, but are meant to be shared with humanity and actively applied to the world.

There is nothing exclusively or characteristically "Hindu" about Priya's mantra or the mandates, meaning that in this case, they do not mimic or repeat the content of mantras evident in Hindu texts. That is because the message to educate is rooted in the idea that all women, no matter where they live, what religion they practice, whether they even practice a religion at all, can be subject to GBV; therefore, the entire world needs an education on how to treat women. The availability and accessibility of the comic are evidence of attempts at global reach. *Priya's Mirror* is available in five languages: English, Spanish, Italian, Portuguese, and Hindi. All of the comics are also available in any digital format and are free to download.[31] There are no sign-up requirements, nor any collection of personal data. The primary goal is to simply make the message available to as many people as possible.

In addition to the comic book, the creators of the series, Ram Devinini and Dan Goldman, established a free "augmented reality" (AR) app, two years before the launch of Pokémon Go, with the sponsorship of a company named Blippar. They claim their use of this technology is "the first of its kind with international outreach and social engagement."[32] The AR allows women to share their own experiences of victimization with the larger readership in their own words. Their stories are subsequently inserted into specific pages of the comic. Readers and supporters of the Priya series can have access to these personal accounts once they have downloaded the app. While the voices used are of the women who experienced GBV, they are drawn as comics and their identities are masked.[33] Care is taken to protect the women's identities and their names are not revealed. Devinini's production company Rattapallax, which is also responsible for producing the series, has posted some of these mini documentaries on YouTube. Each woman is drawn to look directly at the viewer, situated in front a plain background of solid color which changes intermittently from colors like orange to red to beige. As the women tell of their experiences, word bubbles come from their mouths in keeping with comic book style of the project.

The women do not simply relay their experiences of abuse, but also the impact that rape has on their lives. One woman tells of how she was gang raped in her village when she was a teen. When she told her parents, they immediately supported her and went to the police. But their experience with the police only brought disappointment; because her perpetrators were politically connected, the police did little but offer the woman and her family money. The impact of the injustice was devastating: her father committed suicide and her family was exiled from their community, but she remained determined to help others who had similar experiences.[34] In another story of gang rape, a woman tells a similar story of how she had family support but none from the police. The anger of seeing her perpetrators on the street while she has no recourse to justice has led her to call for greater education among boys on how to treat women.[35]

Both examples depart somewhat from Priya's story, yet hit similar notes that help to emphasize the timeliness and importance of the series. Priya's family rejects her for the rape, while the women in these examples have family support. In these stories it is the lack of police support, especially the refusal to press charges against their perpetrators, that is most striking, and which was also the central issue of the Pandey case. Yet in the story of Priya, there is no mention or example of the police whatsoever. That is because, I would argue, in the same way which *Priya's Shakti* does not overtly criticize or diverge from traditional representations of the Hindu Pantheon, it does not engage critically with a well-entrenched political institution like the legal Indian system. Instead, both the comic series and the women in the AR docuseries emphasize the ways that citizens can inform and educate to cease GBV.

The combination of the comic with the Youtube clips are also useful as a pedagogical tool on a smaller scale, such as in a classroom setting. As a guest lecturer in a class on spiritual autobiography, I used these products collectively to critically challenge assumptions about the shape and content of memoir. The use of comic and video in this case, can be used to show how people are engaging in creative new ways to impart certain messages and personalized stories, even if based in the broader fictitious story of Priya. The anonymity of the contributors of the videos, coupled with the general story of Priya, allow for a free-form discussion of GBV and rape in particular, in ways that do not endanger those who have experienced violence first hand. Discussing these alternative forms of memoir, which contrast traditional text, allowed students to discuss the broader issue of GBV as tied to India and Hinduism, while also recognizing the personal stories and agency of the individual women who participated in the project. By sharing these initiatives, students were also able to see how pedagogical activism takes root in (Hindu) Indian contemporary society.

Currently, for example, *Priya's Shakti*'s primary supporter, and for whom they raise funds, is the NGO Apne Aap Women Worldwide. This India-based organization seeks to educate girls and young women by bringing *Priya's Shakti* to schools, as well as to provide help to at-risk females.[36] Mostly, their goals are to end the sexual exploitation of youth via their outreach, which includes a base not only in India but an international office in the United States. While their primary focus is on Indian girls and women, it is evident that they situate themselves amidst a greater international framework. Founded by former sex workers, the organization has a number of initiatives over and above their connections to *Priya's Shakti*, which include self-empowerment groups in brothels and red-light districts, influencing policies to protect women, and creating environments that emphasize community based solutions related to the plight of women.[37]

Other examples include street art that was commissioned by local Indian artists, painted in Mumbai and Delhi in 2015 as part of the *Priya's Shakti* initiative. These painted murals which depict Priya on her tiger advertised and celebrated the series by using the image of Priya that is most reminiscent of Durga—one of the few independent goddesses in the Hindu pantheon, rather than emphasizing Parvati.[38] As mentioned previously, Durga's *shakti* is the only divine power that can conquer the demon king Ravana. Nor is Priya is ever referred to in such promotionals as a goddess but instead an "iconic superhero" who fights against violence toward women. This again speaks to the idea that the series never pushes the boundaries of what is acceptable to orthodox Hindu elites too far. Rather than representing Priya as an incarnation of Parvati, she is entirely human, accessing the sacred power through her devotion and dedication. The importance of these murals is not simply a sort of branding, but also that when one uses the app against them they become animated. Participants (as they are no longer simply readers) are invited to insert themselves into the murals, just as they were with the comics, or to place their phone over an image to hear the stories shared by others, watch movies, and see additional plot developments. As people gather around the murals, they are learning about the experiences of other women, and how to prevent future violence from happening to them.

With the release of *Priya's Mirror*, a new mural was commissioned in 2016. This one is situated in Bengaluru and has a different image of Priya. Instead of comfortably sitting upon her tiger looking relatively relaxed, as in the first series of murals, this time Priya rides the back of the tiger leaping ferociously into action against Ahankar, the demon-human. She is holding a mirror that reflects Ahankar's reflection—a reflection that will make him realize that he must change his ways.[39] The function of the mural is the same as the earlier ones—it is both a method of promotion, but also an AR space in which stories of women's experiences, this time concerning acid attacks, can be shared.

The comic and murals demand responses and participation from audiences that go beyond the Hindu context. At the same time, the Hindu context is evident through the imagery and storytelling involved. In taking these innovations to the classroom, students in the academic study of religion can see the ways in which Hinduism can be fluid and diverse (specifically when likening *Priya's Shakti* to a Purana), but can also help students understand how certain groups respond to societal issues using their religion. For example, when I taught the course Hindu Goddesses, we looked at various texts and summaries of key Hindu goddesses as well as discussed whether the Goddess is/could be a feminist. On many levels it seems impossible to think of a Hindu goddess as a feminist, given that the Hindu tradition itself, like the rest of the major world religions, are created and informed by patriarchal socio-cultural ideals. But *Priya's Shakti* provides a counter-narrative to this assumption, showing students that a "reworking" of traditional understandings of the Hindu pantheon does not necessarily mean that new representations of goddesses run counter to more traditional religious commitments.

CONCLUSION

Devinini and Goldman's hypermodern process of participant-immersion integrates a very cosmopolitan educational mission and fund-raising project with a grassroots effort, which suggests at least two target audiences. First, there are the Indian Hindus as well as Indian organizations such as Apne Aap, for whom GBV have modelled a highly localized approach. In using the

Hindu pantheon, the creators of the series are recreating a familiar though contemporary model of religious belief so as to speak to systemic problems relating to class, caste, and gender as experienced specifically in India. Second, there is the transnational Western and diasporic audience that includes academics and potential donors. This international audience contributes to the spreading of the *Priya Shakti* message through sponsorship and attending events, as well as the broader application of women's rights to international contexts. Specifically, the latter audience focuses on the idea that GBV is prevalent around the world no matter where we live, and that we must all do something to change this.

The fact that *Priya's Shakti* has gained the attention of both audiences shows us how the initiatives tied to *Priya's Shakti* are far-reaching. What started out as a response to the rape and murder of Jyoti Singh Pandey has subsequently resulted in a long-term initiative that has no evidence of slowing down. This success is partially due to the ways that the comic reformulates Hindu mythology to address contemporary concerns of GBV, while challenging certain aspects of orthodox Hinduism. In its thoughtful "reboot" of the goddess Parvati, *Priya's Shakti* functions as a contemporary Purana reminiscent of the *bhakti* tradition at the same time as it presents Parvati as a powerful feminist figure. Through the use of comic books coupled with technological innovation, the creators are able to impart a message against GBV that is both highly specific to Hindu India and yet universalizing enough to have wide spread international appeal as well.

NOTES

1. C. Mackenzie Brown and Nupur D. Agrawal, "The Rape that Woke Up India: Hindu Imagination and the Rape of Jyoti Singh Pandey," *Journal of Religion and Violence* 2, no. 2 (Digital Commons @ Trinity): 2.

2. Karen Zitzewitz, "A Timeline of Events in the Delhi Gang-Rape Case," *The Feminist Wire*, February 2, 2013, http://www.thefeministwire.com/2013/02/a-timeline-of-events-in-the-delhi-gang-rape-case/.

3. Alan Taylor, "Violent Protests in India over Rape Case," *The Atlantic*, December 26, 2012, https://www.theatlantic.com/photo/2012/12/violent-protests-in-india-over-rape-case/100429/.

4. Debolina Dutta and Oishik Sircar, "India's Winter of Discontent: Some Feminist Dilemmas in the Wake of a Rape," *Feminist Studies* 39, no. 1 (2013): 294.

5. Dutta and Sircar, 299.

6. *India's Daughter*, directed by Leslee Udwin, *BBC*, 2015. Netflix.

7. Anoosh Chakelian, "Silencing India's Daughter: Why has the Indian government banned the Delhi rape film?," *NewStatesman*, March 5, 2015, https://www.newstatesman.com/world-affairs/2015/03/silencing-india-s-daughter-why-has-indian-government-banned-delhi-rape-film.

8. Dutta and Sircar, 301.

9. Jean Chapman, "Violence Against Women in Democratic India: Let's Talk Misogyny," *Social Scientist*, 42, no. 9 (Sept.–Oct. 2014): 52.

10. Brown and Agrawal, 5–6.

11. Poulami Roychowdhury, "The Delhi Gang Rape": The Making of International Causes," *Feminist Studies* 39, no. 1 (2013): 283.
12. Roychowdhury, 286.
13. "Gender Equality Champion," Priya's Shakti, accessed December 14, 2017, http://www.priyashakti.com/#outreach.
14. "About," Priya's Shakti, accessed December 14, 2017, https://www.priyashakti.com/about.
15. "Priya's Shakti," Kinjin, accessed September 20, 2017, https://kinjin.co/priyashakti/.
16. Sarbani Guha Ghosal and Sarbani Guha Ghosa, "Socio-political Dimensions of Rape," *The Indian Journal of Political Sciences* 70, no. 1 (Jan.–Mar. 2009): 117–18.
17. Ludo Rocher, *A History of Indian Literature: The Puranas* (Wiesbaden: Otto Harrassowitz, 1986), 16.
18. Klaus Klostermaier, *A Survey of Hinduism*, 2nd ed. (New York: SUNY, 1994), 95.
19. Wendy Doniger, *The Hindus, An Alternative History* (New York: Penguin Press, 2009), 379.
20. Simon Armstrong, "Why Academics are taking Comic Books Seriously," *BBC News*, October 18, 2013, http://www.bbc.com/news/uk-england-24458521.
21. B.N. Krishnamurti Sharma, *A History of the Dvaita School of Vedanta and Its Literature* (India: Motilal Banarsidass, 2008), 128–31.
22. Hillary Rodrigues, *Introducing Hinduism* (New York: Routledge, 2006), 189.
23. "Priya's Shakti," 4.
24. "Priya's Shakti," 24–25.
25. "Priya's Mirror," 17.
26. Doniger, 381.
27. "Priya's Shakti," 3.
28. David Kinsley, *Hindu Goddesses, Visions of the Divine Feminine in the Hindu Religious Tradition* (Berkeley: University of California Press, 1988), 47.
29. One example is Zed's denouncements of an art exhibit by Argentinians Marianela Perelli and Pool Paolini entitled, "Barbie—The Plastic Religion," in which Mattel's Barbie was refashioned into religious figures including the Hindu goddess Kali. See Narayan Lakshman, "Anger over Barbie Doll Cast as Hindu Goddess," *The Hindu* (Sept. 26, 2014), http://www.thehindu.com/news/international/world/anger-overbarbie-dollcast-ashindu-goddess/article6448740.ece.
30. "Upset Hindus urge removal of goddess Parvati from FGO mobile game where she is a "servant," Rajan Zed, accessed October 20, 2017, http://www.rajanzed.org/upset-hindus-urge-removal-of-goddess-parvati-from-fgo-mobile-game-where-she-is-a-servant/.
31. "Rape & Acid Attack Survivors Appear in New Augmented Reality Comic Book at New York Film Festival at Lincoln Center," Press Release, Priya's Shakti, Mumbai, September 26, 2016, accessed September 30, 2017, http://www.priyashakti.com/.
32. "Augmented Reality Comic Books & Art," About, Priya's Shakti, accessed November 2, 2017, http://www.priyashakti.com/about.
33. "Augmented Reality Comic Books & Art."
34. "Priya's Shakti: The power story of a survivor of gang rape in India," March 9, 2015, Rattalpallax, video, 5:48, https://www.youtube.com/watch?v=WMl95Jc-X1Y.
35. "Priya's Shakti: The story of a survivor of gang rape in India still pursing justice," March 14, 2015, Rattalpallax, video, 2:56, https://www.youtube.com/watch?v=ABKtA7llGdM.
36. "NGO Partner Apne Aap Women Worldwide," Priya's Shakti, accessed November 20, 2017, http://www.priyashakti.com/apne_aap/.
37. "About Us," Apne Aap Women Worldwide, accessed November 3, 2017, http://apneaap.org/about-us/.
38. "Priya's Shakti Augmented Reality Street Art," Priya's Shakti, accessed September 1, 2017, http://www.priyashakti.com/street_art/.
39. "Priya's Shakti Augmented Reality Street Art."

BIBLIOGRAPHY

Apne Aap Women Worldwide. "About Us." Accessed November 3, 2017. http://apneaap.org/about-us/.

Armstrong, Simon. "Why Academics are taking Comic Books Seriously." *BBC News*, October 18, 2013. http://www.bbc.com/news/uk-england-24458521.

Brown, C. Mackenzie, and Nupur D. Agrawal. "The Rape that Woke Up India: Hindu Imagination and the Rape of Jyoti Singh Pandey." *Journal of Religion and Violence* 2, no. 2: 234–80. https://digitalcommons.trinity.edu/cgi/viewcontent.cgi?article=1002&context=relig_faculty.

Chakelian, Anoosh. "Silencing India's Daughter: Why has the Indian government banned the Delhi rape film?" *NewStatesman*, March 5, 2015. https://www.newstatesman.com/world-affairs/2015/03/silencing-india-s-daughter-why-has-indian-government-banned-delhi-rape-film.

Chapman, Jean. "Violence Against Women in Democratic India: Let's Talk Misogyny." *Social Scientist* 42, no. 9 (Sept.–Oct. 2014): 49–61.

Doniger, Wendy. *The Hindus, An Alternative History*. New York: Penguin Press, 2009.

Dutta, Debolina, and Oishik Sircar. "India's Winter of Discontent: Some Feminist Dilemmas in the Wake of a Rape." *Feminist Studies* 39, no. 1 (2013): 293–306.

Ghosal, Sarbani Guha, and Sarbani Guha Ghosa. "Socio-political Dimensions of Rape." *The Indian Journal of Political Sciences* 70, no. 1 (Jan.–Mar. 2009): 107–20.

Kinjin. "Priya's Shakti." Accessed September 20, 2017. https://kinjin.co/priyashakti/.

Kinsley, David. *Hindu Goddesses, Visions of the Divine Feminine in the Hindu Religious Tradition*. Berkeley: University of California Press, 1988.

Klostermaier, Klaus K. *A Survey of Hinduism*. 2nd edition. New York: SUNY, 1994.

Lakshman, Narayan. "Anger over Barbie Doll Cast as Hindu Goddess." *The Hindu*, September 26, 2014. http://www.thehindu.com/news/international/world/anger-over-barbie-dollcast-ashindu-goddess/article6448740.ece.

Priya's Shakti. "About." Accessed December 14, 2017. https://www.priyashakti.com/about.

———. "Augmented Reality Comic Books & Art." About. Accessed November 2, 2017. http://www.priyashakti.com/about.

———. "Comic Books." Accessed September 12, 2016. https://www.priyashakti.com.

———. "Comic Books for Social Change Workshops." Accessed December 14, 2017. http://www.priyashakti.com/workshops/.

———. Facebook. https://www.facebook.com/priyas.shakti/.

———. "Gender Equality Champion." Accessed December 14, 2017. http://www.priyashakti.com/#outreach.

———. "NGO Partner Apne Aap Women Worldwide." Accessed November 20, 2017. http://www.priyashakti.com/apne_aap/.

———. "Priya's Shakti Augmented Reality Street Art." Accessed September 1, 2017. http://www.priyashakti.com/street_art/.

———. "Rape & Acid Attack Survivors Appear in New Augmented Reality Comic Book at New York Film Festival at Lincoln Center," Press Release, Mumbai, September 26, 2016. Accessed September 30, 2017. http://www.priyashakti.com/.

———. Twitter, https://twitter.com/priyas_shakti?lang=en.

Rattalpallax. "Priya's Shakti: The power story of a survivor of gang rape in India." Published March 9, 2015. Video, 5:48. https://www.youtube.com/watch?v=WMl95Jc-X1Y.

———. "Priya's Shakti: The story of a survivor of gang rape in India still pursing justice." Published March 14, 2015. Video, 2:56. https://www.youtube.com/watch?v=ABKtA7llGdM.

Rocher, Ludo. *A History of Indian Literature: The Puranas*. Wiesbaden: Otto Harrassowitz, 1986.

Rodrigues, Hillary. *Introducing Hinduism*. New York: Routledge, 2006.

Roychowdhury, Poulami. "'The Delhi Gang Rape': The Making of International Causes." *Feminist Studies* 39, no. 1 (2013): 282–92.

Sharma, B.N. Krishnamurti. *A History of the Dvaita School of Vedanta and Its Literature*. India: Motilal Banarsidass, 2008.
Taylor, Alan. "Violent Protests in India over Rape Case." *The Atlantic*, December 26, 2012. https://www.theatlantic.com/photo/2012/12/violent-protests-in-india-over-rape-case/100429/.
Udwin, Leslee, dir. India's Daughter. *BBC*, 2015. Netflix.
Zed, Rajan. "Upset Hindus urge removal of goddess Parvati from FGO mobile game where she is a "servant." Accessed October 20, 2017. http://www.rajanzed.org/upset-hindus-urge-removal-of-goddess-parvati-from-fgo-mobile-game-where-she-is-a-servant/.
Zitzewitz, Karen. "A Timeline of Events in the Delhi Gang-Rape Case." *The Feminist Wire*, February 2, 2013. http://www.thefeministwire.com/2013/02/a-timeline-of-events-in-the-delhi-gang-rape-case/.

Chapter Three

Teaching Rape, Slavery, and Genocide in Bible and Culture

Gwynn Kessler

What—and where—is the line between pedagogy and activism? Such a question strikes me as simultaneously naive and taboo, necessary and beside the point at the same time. Better, probably, to consider the *relationship between* pedagogy and activism, where and how each informs the other, and to reckon honestly with the complex relationships, possible tensions, and muddied waters between them rather than query hard and fast lines.

In the spring of 2016, I offered a course called "Rape, Slavery, and Genocide in Bible and Culture." A number of cultural currents were sweeping across, or at least gaining ground, in the United States in the few years leading up to the class (and of course many years prior). Such currents may be exemplified by, just to name some of the more well-known, the beginning of the Black Lives Matter movement (2013) in response to the increasing awareness of the frequency of racially motivated police brutality and killings, the publication of Ta-Nehisi Coates's article "The Case for Reparations" (2014), the letters by the Office for Civil Rights at the Department of Education published in 2011 and 2014 about Title IX procedures, and the release of *The Hunting Ground* (2015), a documentary about sexual assault on college campuses. On the global front, wars were being fought during these years, many still ongoing, in Afghanistan, Iraq, Syria, Somalia, Libya, Pakistan, and Gaza, with direct or tacit U.S. involvement. On a more personal level, I had been placed on the Sexual Misconduct Task Force at Swarthmore College that was formed in 2013 and served as one of two faculty members on that committee from then until 2015; at the time of this writing, the report we authored and the recommendations we made remain largely unheeded, as students are currently, once again, speaking out against the administration's lack of consistent, transparent, and effective ways to acknowledge, confront and combat sexual violence on campus.

My course "Rape, Slavery, and Genocide in Bible and Culture" was designed as an upper-level seminar, and it comprised seven students, of diverse religious and non-religious backgrounds and affiliations, as well as differing ethnicities, races, socio-economic backgrounds, and gender identities. The course readings and discussion were primarily focused on the Hebrew Bible, but some readings about New Testament texts were incorporated.[1] Our class meetings were discussion based, and students shared reactions and reflections about the assigned readings; we also examined primary biblical texts in class, applying the secondary readings to the texts and then interpreting the texts in multiple ways as the class session progressed. Two of the students went on to write senior theses that emerged from readings and discussions in the class, and at least two were active in campus discussions, organizing, and journalism around Title IX issues on campus.

There were, as is often the case, many reasons as well as numerous goals embedded in such a "timely" course offering. Part of this essay is devoted to rendering such motivations and goals transparent in order to reflect upon them retrospectively, with some more depth and perhaps the clarity of hindsight. I also consider how such goals might be better seen as bringing into sharper relief, as opposed to standing in stark contrast to, the goals that I set for other, not quite as explicitly topical, timely, or "relevant" classes that I regularly offer about the Bible and religion more generally. But the bulk of this essay focuses on examining three texts from the biblical book of Deuteronomy that we read together on the first day of class in order to begin to examine "what the Bible says" about rape, slavery, and genocide and how these texts illuminate their interconnectedness.

At the outset, it was—and remains—important to be clear that the class did not aim to locate the cause of, or the blame for, certain of our current culture's struggles with sexual violence, racism, and genocide in the Bible itself. Much of the Bible's influence on U.S. culture, while I do think such influence exists, is simply too hard to pin down in any facile, straightforward, manner. However, the course did aim to provide a place where current occurrences of sexual violence, framed as an outgrowth of misogyny and structural sexism, and racial violence, understood as an outgrowth of white supremacy and persistent systemic racism, could be critically examined and discussed. Thus the course did not expect that we bracket contemporary debates in our discussions about biblical texts. Rather it sought to integrate—though not conflate—textual materials from another time and place with contemporary cultural realities that both we and our students confront. Ultimately, I hoped the class would "work" on multiple levels; I wanted us to "think with" the Bible about contemporary violence, to begin the work of historicizing it, and use contemporary discourses about violence to "think the Bible." For, as

Regina Schwartz has warned, "if we do not think about the Bible, it will think (for) us."[2]

The specific objectives for the course that I listed on the syllabus included introducing students to the academic study of the Bible as well as to the general topic of violence and religion and, more specifically, violence and the Bible. I also specified some of the components of what I consider to be part of the academic study of the Bible: introducing students to the background and historical context of biblical texts and developing critical reading skills for primary (biblical) and secondary (scholarly) sources. Other course objectives listed included exposure to the complexity of the Bible and its legacy for today, exploration of possible connections between biblical texts and contemporary culture, and finally, the development of skills for discussing challenging topics in sensitive, sophisticated, and nuanced ways.[3]

What strikes me about these course objectives upon looking back is, on the one hand, their timidity, their partialness bordering on incompleteness, and even their blandness. In certain ways such course objectives stand in tension with the boldness of the course title. I had dismissed, at the planning stage of the class, naming the course "The Bible and Violence" or "Violence and Religion"; there is, I decided, a power, as well as a necessity, in naming specific types of violence. Furthermore, in simultaneously singling out specific types of violence yet stringing them together—rape, slavery, genocide—the course title conjures what I saw as a foundational objective of the course, though it is not explicitly listed: to consider the connections between violence on a more personal, individual scale and violence on a collective, species, and massive scale. Also missing from the stated course objectives is the interrogation of the hierarchical binary between human(s) and animal(s), which formed the basis of some of the last assigned readings in the section about genocide at the end of the course. Indeed, rethinking, by which I mean challenging and ultimately exposing a number of hierarchical binaries—between human and animal, male and female, enslaved and free, Israelite and non-Israelite, us and them—as potential acts of violence in and of themselves, remained absent from my specified course objectives. And, of course, nowhere is it mentioned that what I wanted to do, through or along with the academic study of the (Hebrew) Bible, was help students articulate, or if need be locate, and reckon with, their anger, their outrage, at the injustices pervasive in our culture, and to begin to account for our complicity in such structures. Better to play it safe, to at least conform and comport what is, after all, an academic endeavor to the still powerful illusion that there exist dispassionate, "objective," objectives to courses, that knowledge—either its acquisition or its transmission—is itself objective.

On the other hand, a second look at the stated course objectives, while partial or even incomplete, might reveal that they are neither timid nor bland. Studying the Bible academically, which entails, among numerous other things, questioning assumptions about biblical authorship, inerrancy, consistency, universality, timelessness, even Truth, and especially historical accuracy and objectivity, is perhaps in and of itself both a challenging and lofty goal. In a college classroom, studying the Bible entails confronting a text that many have only experienced in religious settings, and others, even if they have no prior knowledge of the Bible, assume to be of religious import, in a critical, secular setting. Studying the Bible academically, unmoored from prior religious teaching and/or distanced from an aura of "the sacred/the holy," is therefore, I submit, neither a simple, nor timid endeavor. It involves questions of no less import and urgency than those of agency and authority; it demands an awareness of social location and situatedness,[4] those of the contemporary reader(s) as well as those of the ancient text(s).

Teaching the Bible academically means helping our students activate, and I think ultimately increase, their agency as critical readers, thinkers, and inhabitants of and participants in society. Such increased agency embeds within it not only questions of meaning(s)—what does any given biblical text *mean* (and we must add to whom)—but also questions of authority—*who decides*. Beginning to answer such questions requires that students engage the texts and confront them as directly as possible. Since I teach the Bible in English translation, directly engaging the text means re-inscribing the act of reading as an active, dynamic, and complex, process, or relationship, between text and reader, reader and text, as well as readers, texts, and cultures—past and present. Critical reading begins when one asks, "The text says this?!" or "This is in the Bible?!" or even, "This is the Bible?!" It continues when one asks how is this—this text, passage, book—to be understood and interpreted.

One of the strategies useful in the academic study of the Bible, shared with ethnography and religious studies more generally, is commonly described as rendering the strange familiar and the familiar strange. Academic, critical study of the Bible begins with a willingness to distance oneself from their assumptions, preconceptions, prior beliefs, and expectations. This works from different angles for different students. If one believes that the Bible is the word of God, or divinely inspired, or that it is central to their identities, one should re-situate themselves in relation to these beliefs; if a student believes that the Bible is made up stories, "make-believe," always and only harmful, and irrelevant for their lives and even identities, they too need to imagine otherwise. The academic study of the Bible—as education in general—is not about staying within our "comfort zones"—all the more so when the texts represent, and seem to justify, violence.

On the first day of class, after the familiar ritual of reading over the syllabus is completed, I distributed a handout with three excerpts from the biblical book of Deuteronomy. It is my invitation to the students to ask "This is (in) the Bible?!" The "strangeness" of the passages strikes, I hope, on multiple levels, from the de-centering of better known biblical stories to the focus on less known biblical laws, to the differing types of violence that appear in the passages, and further, to the shared elements that intersect among the passages. Of course, these texts were only a partial, far from complete, selection of what one may find on the topics of rape, slavery, and genocide in the Bible. (And of course, texts that extol the virtues of peace, shared responsibility and care for other beings and the land are not represented at all.) But as I hope to show, they offer one fruitful opening to learning and inquiry about the central topics of the course as well as studying the Bible academically.

Deuteronomy 7:1–11

> [1]When the Lord your God brings you to the land that you are about to enter and possess, and he dislodges many nations before you—the Hittites, Girgashites, Amorites, Canaanites, Perizzites, Hivites, and Jebusites, seven nations much larger than you—[2]and the Lord your God delivers them to you and you defeat them, you must doom them to destruction: grant them no terms and give them no-quarter. [3]You shall not intermarry with them: do not give your daughters to their sons or take their daughters for your sons. [4]For they will turn your children away from Me to worship other gods, and the Lord's anger will blaze forth against you and he will promptly wipe you out. [5]Instead, this is what you shall do to them: you shall tear down their altars, smash their pillars, cut down their sacred posts, and consign their images to the fire. [6]For you are a people consecrated to the Lord your God: of all the peoples on earth the Lord your God chose you to be his treasured people. [7]It is not because you are the most numerous of peoples that the Lord set his heart on you and chose you—indeed, you are the smallest of peoples; [8]but it was because the Lord favored you and kept the oath he made to your fathers that the Lord freed you with a mighty hand and rescued you from the house of enslavement (*bayt avadim*), from the power of Pharaoh king of Egypt. [9]Know, therefore, that only the Lord your God is God, the steadfast God who keeps his covenant faithfully to the thousandth generation of those who love him and keep his commandments, [10]but who instantly requites with destruction those who reject him—never slow with those who reject him, but requiting them instantly. [11]Therefore, observe faithfully the Instruction—the laws and the rules—with which I charge you today.

Deuteronomy 15:12–17

> [12]If a fellow Hebrew, man or woman, is sold to you, he shall serve you (*v'avadekha*) six years, and in the seventh year you shall set him free. [13]When you set him free, do not let him go empty-handed: [14]Furnish him out of the flock, threshing floor, and vat, with which the Lord your God has blessed you. [15]Remember that you were a slave (*eved*) in the land of Egypt and the Lord your God redeemed you; therefore I enjoin this commandment upon you today. [16]But should he say to you, "I do not want to leave you"—for he loves you and your household and things go well for him with you—[17]you shall take an

awl and put it through his ear into the door, and he shall become your slave (*eved*) in perpetuity. Do the same with your female slave (*l'amatkha*).

Deuteronomy 21:10–14

[10]When you go out to war against your enemies, and the Lord your God delivers them into your hands and you take some of them captive, [11]and you see among the captives a beautiful woman and you desire her and would take her to wife, [12]you shall bring her into your house, and she shall trim her hair, pare her nails, [13]and discard her captive's garb. She shall spend a month's time in your house lamenting her father and mother; after that you can come to her and possess her, and she shall be your wife. [14]Then, should you no longer want her, you must release her outright. You must not sell her for money: you shall not treat her as a slave (*lo titamer bah*)[5] because you have afflicted her (*initah*).[6]

These texts serve a number of pedagogical purposes. As mentioned above, they introduce students to one possibly "strange" aspect of biblical texts—their presentation as "law." These texts are immediately disarming, and perhaps confusing, to *some* readers, especially those who might expect a biblical text to be more obviously narrative in structure.[7] Who are the characters, the protagonists? What is the context? How are these laws to be understood as part of the unfolding story of Israel and God? In other words, how do we situate, read, engage, and understand biblical laws and their scope? And then there's the violence in the texts, sometimes seemingly erupting off the page with excessive force and at other times almost muted if not hidden, buried, or silenced in the text—but no less potent. What is the relationship between violence and "the sacred"? How does violence function in the Bible? Do these texts, does the Bible, justify, *authorize*, violence—genocide, slavery, rape? These are perhaps the questions that initially arise. But the academic study of the Bible demands, and thus promises, more.

The passages on the handout are presented in the order they appear in Deuteronomy, but this ordering also renders legible different types of violence—moving from the more explicit to the more implicit and even hidden.[8] Thus Deuteronomy 7 begins with divinely commanded genocidal violence; Israel is commanded to utterly destroy seven nations, to "tear down their altars," "smash their pillars," "cut down their sacred posts," and "burn their images." If Israel does not "doom to destruction" these seven nations, then God's rage will strike at Israel, destroying the Israelites instead. Deuteronomy 15 shifts from the earlier chapter's depiction of national war and ethnic destruction to a setting of domesticity; its violence is more muted and yet pervasive. The violence in this text resides in a social structure where people can be purchased and freed—not of their own accord—as well as in the bodily harm done to the slave, "the piercing of the ear into the door." Finally,

Deuteronomy 21 brings us to both the battlefield and the home; here genocide and domesticity in the previous excerpts meet.[9] A captured beautiful woman is brought into her captor's house, to be "married" and then to remain or be cast out—according to her captor's whim. Here the violence in the text, that the woman is taken against her will and raped[10] until her master[11] tires of her, is almost completely hidden. The woman is utterly silent, her consent not only rendered irrelevant but seemingly unimaginable to the biblical author(s).[12]

My primary goal in introducing these texts is not simply to elicit certain reactions from the students—"this is (in) the Bible?," "where and when do violence and religion intersect?"—but to broaden our understanding of violence and what counts as violence.[13] If the genocidal violence of Deuteronomy 7 appears self-evident, how does one come to recognize the other two passages (and many others) as also containing, even brimming with, violence? How do we learn to recognize structural oppression and its silencing as violence—in texts and in our culture?

By structural violence I mean the very presumption of the texts (Deut. 15; Deut. 21) that people can be bought, sold, and owned, or women can be captured and raped, kept, or discarded, as a matter of course. That the texts are presented as law and thus presented as authoritative, encourages readers to read them passively, accepting these laws, at least initially, with little or no question. Since readers are less likely to question such texts, they are also less likely to see them as the mechanisms of structural oppression, which I am framing as (a type of) violence.

Framing these texts as containing violence—both in that systems of oppression are embedded in and produced by the texts and that to some extent this violence is contained through the medium of legal discourse—invites further inquiry into these texts. In fact, framing the texts as violence beckons deeper engagement, questioning, and even some inevitable pushback against this very framing.

Students might point out that Deuteronomy 15:12–17, for example, sets a term limit on how long one can be enslaved, and further, it dictates that the enslaved person, when freed, cannot be sent forth empty-handed. A case for reparations indeed.[14] Further still, the enslaved person, in some instances and as if on their own accord, might declare, "I do not want to leave you." All of this is correct, and yet, these "benevolent" sounding provisions do not abrogate that the text assumes and (re)produces a system where people can be purchased, owned, and then freed (or discarded)—by someone else. How are we to read the enslaved person's declaration that they do not want to leave? The narrative adds, or the narrator supplies, the stated reasons: he loves his owner and his owner's house, and things are better for him if he remains—but how reliable is this report?[15] Even if reliable, to what extent is an enslaved person free to choose to remain enslaved, or is it only the recognition of and capitulation to a system of oppression that makes this the most viable "choice"? Finally, we should ask about this passage's limited scope of concern for the treatment of enslaved "kinsmen"; the passage only legislates the ownership of Israelites, or Hebrews, who are enslaved by other Israelites. How does biblical law legislate the ownership and treatment of non-Israelite enslaved peoples? Thus Deuteronomy 15:12–17 serves as an opening to other biblical texts that will be encountered over the course of the semester that discuss non-Israelite enslaved people in the Hebrew Bible (e.g., Exodus 21; Leviticus 25).

Having asked these questions, noting that these texts are only some of many and beginning to acknowledge that our own assumption that it is wrong to enslave people might be operating in our own readings, we have engaged with the text more deeply. And, having acknowledged some of our limitations regarding textual materials and our own situated positions, we are in a better position to examine what the underlying assumptions of a society that condones such a system might be—our disagreement placed at some distance. (Of course, this will require more than three biblical texts and more than one introductory class period.)

Furthermore, having engaged with Deuteronomy 15 more deeply, we are able to compare it with Deuteronomy 21 to deepen our engagement with that text as well. In contrast to the enslaved Hebrew, male or female, who speaks—whether or not reliably so—the non-Israelite captive woman is utterly silent. Deuteronomy 21 affords her no opportunity to speak. Indeed, what would she say, we might ask.[16] Given that Deuteronomy 21:10–14 is most commonly framed as legislation about the "marriage" of captive women, we might then begin to query some of the commonalities between this and other "marriage laws." If a woman could not consent to marriage, it being conceived of as a transaction between men,[17] are instances of what we would call rape far more pervasive in biblical Israel than imagined and imaginable? Again, these are questions to be explored far beyond one, two, or even three texts and one introductory class session.

More germane to my point, in this article and on the first day of class, is to consider the intertextual resonances and thematic connections between Deuteronomy 15 and 21, and ultimately Deuteronomy 7, which allow us to think slavery, rape, and genocide together. As part of this thinking, we should ask, what are the apparent connections between the captured, raped woman who is taken in "marriage" and the enslaved person who is purchased with money? What does it mean when Deut. 21:14 insists of the discarded woman, "you shall not treat her as a slave since you have afflicted her"? Are both people not suffering from structural oppression and violence? Are they not both treated more as property than persons? Shifting the question from whether or not (captured) women and enslaved peoples *are* property to how they are treated as such moves us away from that still debated question;[18] it simultaneously moves us closer to a performative conception of identities and allows us to see how the performance of violent acts by adult male Israelites (and biblical law itself) is foundational to the identity of adult male Israelites (and biblical law as well). Finally, do both (captured) women and enslaved peoples exemplify and suffer "social death"?[19]

"Social death" is a concept characterized by violence, separation from one's larger culture, and the alienation from and loss of intergenerational links—those between the socially dead's ancestors and their progeny, their past and future.[20] The concept as related to enslaved peoples has developed from the work of Orlando Patterson; it has been broadened and used in the field of Genocide and Holocaust Studies and further developed to include other marginalized peoples, genders, and ethnicities.[21] In what follows, I mobilize this broader usage in order to explore some possible links between enslaved Israelites and captured women in the biblical texts I have been discussing.[22]

The recognition of the social death of the captured woman and the enslaved Israelite in Deuteronomy 15 and 21, respectively, provides an additional broad thematic link, beyond that of the violence they share, between these chapters and Deuteronomy 7. For Deuteronomy 7, while prescribing genocide, demonstrates how genocide and social death coincide. Claudia Card, in her work which explores the connections between genocide and social death, writes, "Social death is not necessarily genocide. But genocide is social death" (2010: 237).[23] She further writes, "Putting social death at the center of genocide takes the focus off body counts" (2010: 238). It shifts our sole or at least primary focus from the killing of people(s) in genocide to include the destruction of their cultural markers and ways of life. Both types of destruction are prescribed in Deuteronomy 7.

Deuteronomy 7 clearly prescribes total destruction and death to the seven nations: "You must doom them to destruction: you shall make no covenant with them nor show mercy to them" (7:2).[24] Perhaps, however, acknowledging that there are always survivors,[25] and that total destruction requires more than dead bodies, it continues, "you shall tear down their altars, smash their images, cut down their Asherim, and burn their carved idols" (7:5). That which is prescribed in Deuteronomy 7 is both physical and social death. Our reading of the social death suffered by enslaved person and captured woman in Deuteronomy 15 and 21 enhances and deepens our reading of Deuteronomy 7, encouraging us, not to look away from the physical death prescribed, but to look further and see the destruction of specifically religio-cultural aspects of these nations: their altars and their gods.

In fact, we need not choose whether physical or social death is more central, but the text allows us, on one reading, to imagine that the religio-cultural aspects are key motivating factors for the destruction. The fear expressed in the text is that, through intermarrying, the foreign daughters will lead the sons astray from following God to the worship of other gods (7:4) and that as a consequence, God will destroy Israel (7:4). Israel then, risks suffering both social death, in that through the worship of other gods they will lose their culture and "religion"—their links to their past ways and its future—and physical death as well, in that God will destroy Israel, "with haste," according to the text.

In addition to the broad thematic link between Deuteronomy 7, 15, and 21 through the shared theme of social death, there are some more specific connections that also become apparent when the texts are read together. As just mentioned, Deut. 7:4 discusses the exchange of women, here daughters. Deuteronomy 7:3 states, "And you shall not make marriages with them; your daughter you shall not give to his son, nor his daughter shall you take to your son."

In other biblical texts that deal with genocide, including Deut. 20:13–15,[26] Numbers 31, Judges 21, and, as seen already in Deut. 21,[27] women are expected to be taken as part of war. Yet Deut. 7:4 (and Deut. 20:16–17) explicitly forbid taking the women of these seven nations. Still, that these texts proscribe the taking of these women while prescribing genocide demonstrates that under other circumstances, women are taken and married—without their (or their fathers') consent. Thus Deuteronomy 7 acknowledges, here through its negation, certain connections between genocide, gender, and sexual violence. If we read the text complacently, or passively, without slowing down, engaging with it, and asking questions of it, the assumption that the text makes that other women are taken as part of the spoils of war could pass unnoticed, the gendered violence of genocide subsumed by and subordinated to the more explicit or obvious violence of total destruction. But having examined Deut. 21:10–14, noting the fate of the captive woman, her silencing and the systemic oppression and violence that are encoded in that text, we have become, or are on our way to becoming, better readers of biblical texts.

Becoming better readers of the biblical text involves reading along with, and against, the narrator or the text. It entails acknowledging that the narrator/text has a perspective, and we do best to read both with—and against—this perspective. It includes asking who is silenced in, and by, the text. It encourages us to read from different, often competing, perspectives.[28] These are all aspects of the academic study of the Bible that are introduced, yet surely not fully digested, on the first day of class through our engagement with just three excerpts from Deuteronomy. But I want to circle back to the very beginning of Deuteronomy 7 to make one more connection between the excerpts on the handout for this first class session.

Deuteronomy 7:1 states, "When the Lord your God shall bring you into the land which you are entering to possess, and has cast out many nations before you, the Hittites, and the Girgashites, and the Amorites, and the Canaanites, and the Perizzites, and the Hivites, and the Jebusites, seven nations greater and mightier than you." We know what happens next, but it is worth pausing here, to see where the text situates us.

The text addresses "you" and "your God," and thus we are situated as reading along with, if not as, the Israelites. And then it continues to name the seven nations who will be displaced and killed so that Israel can possess the land. It is worth naming them, as the Bible itself takes care to do: the Hittites, Girgashites, Amorites, Canaanites, Perizzites, Hivites, and Jebusites.

When we read Deuteronomy 7:1 together in class, when one student reads it out loud, they often struggle with the names, as they do when we read various genealogies from Genesis later in the course. But reading these genealogies or lists of those doomed to destruction, pausing to struggle with the names, slows down our reading process; instead of encouraging readers to skim, or worse, skip, such biblical passages, we must pause to see the work that they do within the text, for the narrative, and for us to recognize, and memorialize, both that which is built up in and by genealogies and that is brought down in lists of utter destruction. Thus when we encounter and explore Genesis 10:15–17, as we will later in the course, we recognize the connections between Deuteronomy 7:1 and Gen. 10:15–17: "And Canaan fathered Sidon his firstborn, and Heth, And the Jebusite, and the Amorite, and the Girgashite, And the Hivite, and the Arkite, and the Sinite." Between Deuteronomy 7:1 and Genesis 10:15–17, we recognize the identity of these nations, who are to be "sacrificed"[29] so that Israel might live in their land; we learn that they are related to each other and that six out of the seven are Canaan and his descendants.[30] Who is Canaan? Canaan is the son of Ham and grandson of Noah, whom Noah curses, stating, "Cursed be Canaan; a slave of slaves shall he be to his brothers" (Gen. 9:25). A slave of slaves. Thus we would have to ask, what does Deuteronomy 7 have to do with enslavement? The importance of this question lies in its being asked, not answered—at least on the first day of class. On the first day of class, we are doing well simply to recognize that Deuteronomy 7 builds on the backs of enslaved non-Israelites. And we are doing well to acknowledge that, at least according to these three excerpts, there is reason enough to explore the inner-biblical resonances and connections between genocide, enslavement, and sexual violence that appear within the Bible itself as part of our thinking about the links among these types of violence in our own day.

But the last question I simply wish to introduce—on this first day of class—is what happens when we read the Bible as/with enslaved Israelites, as/with non-Israelite captured women, and as/with conquered Canaanites[31] —as well as with and from the perspective(s), for there are always multiple perspectives within groups too—of Israelites?

If I had it to do over again, I would add a fourth text to the first day's handout, in order to introduce and anticipate our later course readings and class discussions that will expand the rubric of genocide to include the killing of non-human animals. The fourth text could even be incorporated simply by excerpting more of Deuteronomy 7, "And God will love you, and bless you, and multiply you; he will also bless the fruit of your womb, and the fruit of your land, your grain, and your wine, and your oil, the produce of your cows, and the flocks of your sheep, in the land which he swore to your fathers to give you. You shall be blessed above all people; there shall not be barrenness among your people, or among your beasts" (Deut. 7:13–14). We could thus begin to see how Israelite animals are blessed along with Israelite people, that according to the Bible, the continuation of every species is dependent on God.[32] In other words, we could begin to query the different types of relationship(s) between human animals and non-human animals, as well as the different types of relationships between animals—human and non-human—and God, that the Bible offers in order to help us think more deeply and perhaps differently about the "companion species" with whom we share the world today.[33] We would then be more equipped to read the Bible with, and as, the animals that therefore we most definitely are.[34]

I cannot stress enough that these three biblical texts encountered on the first day of class offer only a partial, utterly incomplete sampling of "what the Bible says" about rape, slavery, and genocide.[35] And how could any introductory session (or even semester long course) on these topics, treated separately or, all the more so, grouped together, be otherwise? Numerous books, not to mention countless articles, have been written on each of these topics—from broad surveys on war, rape, and slavery to monographs focused on one specific text or group of related texts.[36] And I should also stress that many of the connections between Deut. 15 and 21 and among Deut. 7, 15, and 21, which I made in this essay, were at best broached in the most cursory of ways and others were left implicit or even somewhat dormant, to be returned to as the course progressed.

What I wanted to do on the first day of class, through the use of these three biblical texts, was simply—and not so simply—to introduce students to the Bible as a "strange" book, and to begin to make the critical, academic study of biblical texts a "familiar" exercise. I also sought to set the stage for the topics covered in this course (rape, slavery, and genocide), to begin to expand our definitions of violence and our scope of what constitutes violence to include systemic or structural oppression, and to begin to think about possible connections, by way of reading ancient texts, between racial, gendered, and global violence we are currently witnessing, if not experiencing first hand.

None of this was undertaken as a "purely" academic endeavor, but in the hopes of engaging our students as active, responsible, and yet in many ways complicit, agents in the world. As I mentioned at the beginning of this essay, various cultural currents—each in their own ways calling attention not only to specific types of violence pervading our culture but also to the violence of systemic oppression(s) upon which our culture relies—contributed to my thinking this specific course into being and into action. And, writing about this course offered me the opportunity to reflect upon the "action" of teaching, and how activism is expressed—and more importantly how knowledge is gained—through critical and pedagogical, personal and political, engagements with both the past and the present.

The process of writing about this specific course, "Rape, Slavery, and Genocide in Bible and Culture," also lent me greater clarity about my not-so-objective "objectives" to this course and others that I teach. It has brought into sharper focus my belief in the central, foundational importance of teaching toward the deconstruction of hierarchical binaries, by which I mean challenging and exposing the ways such binaries reflect and (re)produce violence in and of themselves.

The Bible, on one reading, canonizes and even appears to authorize, hierarchical binaries: male and female, Israelite and non-Israelite, enslaved and free, etc.[37] And yet, the Bible itself also complicates, perhaps even wreaks havoc, on these very binaries, making the Bible a splendidly teachable, exquisitely "anti-binary" text. Thus says the prophet Ezekiel to Israel: "Your birth and your origin is in the land of Canaan; your father was an Amorite, and your mother a Hittite" (Ezek. 16:3). The complexity of Ezekiel 16 cannot be addressed here, nor can its sexual violence and the gendered nature of it—for Israel is gendered female throughout this passage—be overlooked or condoned.[38] But for my purposes, it serves as but one, parting example, where the Bible subverts, overturns, or at bare minimum, complicates its own hierarchical binaries. Here Israel, by definition presumably *not* Canaan and *not* female, is imagined as both Canaanite and female—the daughter of the "slave of slaves'" descendants, the Hittite and the Amorite. What does this text mean? Who decides? We, as critical, engaged, readers, as well as purveyors and producers of our culture(s), do.

NOTES

1. For example, we read Avalos's chapter on "Slavery in the New Testament" as well as the introductory, Near Eastern, and Hebrew Bible chapters in his book, *Slavery, Abolitionism, and the Ethics of Biblical* Scholarship (Sheffield: Sheffield Phoenix Press, 2011). Other books we read at least significant portions of include: Susan Niditch, *War in the Hebrew Bible* (New York: Oxford University Press, 1993); Susanne Scholz, *Sacred Witness: Rape in the Hebrew Bible* (Minneapolis: Fortress Press, 2010); Haynes, *Noah's Curse: The Biblical Justification of American Slavery* (Oxford and New York: Oxford University Press, 2002); Trible, *Texts of Terror* (Philadelphia: Fortress, 1984); Exum, *Fragmented Women: Feminist (Sub)versions of Biblical Narratives* (Sheffield: Sheffield Academic Press, 1993); *The Bible and Posthumanism*, edited by Jennifer Koosed (Atlanta: Society of Biblical Literature, 2014) and *Divinanimality: Animal Theory, Creaturely Theology*, edited by Stephen D. Moore (New York: Fordham Uni-

versity Press, 2014). It should be noted that while the course focused on Hebrew Bible primary texts, many of the readings, by virtue of their interests in the role the Bible plays in the history of American enslavement and its after effects and sexual violence in contemporary U.S. culture, focus on Christian readings of these texts.

2. Regina M. Schwartz, *The Curse of Cain: The Violent Legacy of Biblical Monotheism* (Chicago: University of Chicago Press, 1997), 8.

3. The Society of Biblical Literature, the American Academy of Religion, and the Wabash Center for Teaching and Learning in Theology and Religion have a number of resources that discuss the methods and goals of teaching the Bible in college and university classroom settings. See *Teaching the Bible in the Liberal Arts Classroom*, edited by Jane S. Webster and Glenn S. Holland (Sheffield: Sheffield Phoenix Press, 2012) and *Teaching the Bible in the Liberal Arts Classroom Volume Two*, edited by Jane S. Webster and Glenn S. Holland (Sheffield: Sheffield Phoenix Press, 2015). Especially useful for me during the planning of the course were Janet Everhart, "Dildos and Dismemberment: Reading Difficult Biblical Texts in the Undergraduate Classroom," Amy Cottrill, "Reading Textual Violence as 'Real' Violence in the Liberal Arts Context," and Susanne Scholz "Occupy Academic Bible Teaching," all appearing in the first volume (2012).

4. Some classic articulations of the importance of situatedness and social location in feminist theory include, Dona Haraway, "Situated Knowledges: The Science Question in Feminism and the Privilege of Partial Perspective," *Feminist Studies* 14, no. 3 (1988): 575–99. And Sandra Harding "Feminist Standpoint Epistemology" in *Whose Science, Whose Knowledge?: Thinking from Women's Lives* (Ithaca: Cornell University Press, 1991).

5. Cf. Deut. 24:7.

6. On the word *initah* and whether it connotes rape or not, see, for example, Gravett (2004) and bibliographical references there as well as Scholz (2010: 30–39) and further references there.

7. I understand that some students might expect legal texts, but I still think that the content as well as the form, the bold prescriptions about utter death and the disregard for female agency couched in language that is *almost* easy to overlook since it is presented as "law," is disarming—especially when one is invited, and expected, to pause long enough to be able to pose contemporary questions to the texts.

8. As will become clear below, I am choosing the language of explicit and implicit intentionally, so as not to claim any one text is more or less violent than another. One might be seen as more obviously violent, but this does not mean that it is necessarily more violent.

9. For a reading that frames Deuteronomy 21 as a text about genocide and the gendered aspects of genocide see Steinberg (2018). See also Niditch (1993), 83–86 and Deborah L. Ellens, *Women in the Sex Texts of Leviticus and Deuteronomy: A Comparative Conceptual Analysis* (London and New York: T&T Clark, 2008).

10. See Scholz, *Sacred Witness*, 109–12.

11. Deut. 21:13 could be translated, "after that you may come to her and master her (u-ve`altah), and she shall be your wife."

12. See Robert Kawashima, "Could a Woman Say 'No' in Ancient Israel? On the Genealogy of Legal Status in Biblical Law and Literature" *AJS Review* 35, no. 1 (2011): 1–22; Robert Kawashima, "Gender and Law in the Hebrew Bible" in *The Oxford Encyclopedia of the Bible and Law*, edited by Brent Strawn, et al., 306–319. Oxford: Oxford University Press, 2015.

13. See Cheryl B. Anderson *Women, Ideology, and Violence: Critical Theory and the Construction of Gender in the Book of the Covenant and the Deuteronomic Law* (London: T&T Clark, 2004), 9.

14. Deut. 15: 12–17 is one of the epigraphs to Ta'Nehisi Coates's "The Case for Reparations" article. See Ta'Nehisi Coates, "The Case for Reparations," *The Atlantic*, June 2014, https://www.theatlantic.com/magazine/archive/2014/06/the-case-for-reparations/361631/.

15. In Exodus 21:5, a related text but with some key differences, the enslaved person is said to declare, "I love my master, and my wife and children; I do not wish to go free." Still, faced with the provision of his freedom without his wife and children, how much choice does the enslaved person have?

16. See Steinberg, "Social Death and Gendered Genocide," for an examination of just this question.
17. The extent to which women in biblical Israel could be seen as property is still debated. Kawashima writes, "Insofar as daughters constituted a type of property of the patriarchal household, marriage constituted, in effect, an exchange of goods between houses," "Gender and Law in the Hebrew Bible," 311. He also writes, "A man's power over his wife and children arguably constituted a type of limited ownership. Indeed, Exodus 20:17 provides what is, in effect, a list of the patriarch's belongings—house, wife, slave, ox, etc.—though an Israelite male cannot be said to have 'owned' his wife in the way that he owned an article of clothing, a beast of burden, etc." "Could a Woman Say 'No' in the Hebrew Bible?," 2. Lemos argues against equating women, or at least wives with property (T. M. Lemos, "Were Israelite Women Chattel: Shedding New Light on an Old Question," in *Worship, Women and War: Essays in Honor of Susan Niditch*, ed. John J. Collins, T. M. Lemos, and Saul Olyan, 227–42 (Providence, RI: Brown Judaic Studies, 2015). I do not, however, think there is much debate that marriage was understood as a transaction between men, whether or not women were conceived of as property; her consent was not deemed important enough, or relevant enough, to legislate.
18. Lemos writes, "Whether or not wives and daughters were the property of their husbands and fathers is a debated question that cannot be addressed at any length here" (T. M. Lemos, "Physical Violence and the Boundaries of Personhood in the Hebrew Bible," in *Hebrew Bible and Ancient Israel* 2, no. 500–31 (2013): 523). See also Carolyn Pressler, *The View of Women Found in the Deuteronomic Family Laws* (Berlin and New York: de Gruyter, 1993) and Harold C. Washington, "'Lest He Die in the Battle and Another Man Take Her': Violence and the Construction of Gender in the Laws of Deuteronomy 20–22," in *Gender and Law in the Hebrew Bible and the Ancient Near East*, eds. Victor H. Matthews, Bernard M. Levinson, and Tikva Frymer-Kensky, 185–213 (Sheffield: Sheffield Academic Press, 1998) in addition to Kawashima, "Could a Woman Say 'No' in Ancient Israel?" and "Gender and Law in the Hebrew Bible."
19. It seems possible that the social death for the enslaved Israelite who is set free after six years in Deut. 15, is more temporary than that of the captured woman in Deut. 21. In captivity her ethnicity and familial relations have been stripped from her, and even once she is discarded, this state remains. See Steinberg, "Social Death as Gendered Genocide." For the enslaved Israelite who does not leave after six years, and for the perpetually enslaved non-Israelite in Lev. 25, however their social death would be permanent.
20. See Orlando Patterson, *Slavery and Social Death: A Comparative Study* (Cambridge: Harvard University Press, 1982); Claudia Card, "Genocide and Social Death" *Hypatia* 18, no. 1 (Winter 2003): 63–79 and *Confronting Evils: Terrorism, Torture, and Genocide* (New York and Cambridge: Cambridge University Press, 2010); Jana Králová, "What Is Social Death?" *Contemporary Social Science* 10, no. 3 (2015): 235–48; and Steinberg (2018). Avery Gordon writes, "Social death refers to the process by which a person is socially negated or made a human non-person as the terms of their incorporation into a society: living, they nonetheless appear as if and are treated as if they were dead" (Avery Gordon, "Some Thoughts on Haunting and Futurity," *borderlands* 10, no. 2 (2011): 10.
21. See Králová, "What Is Social Death?" for the concept's earlier use, beginning in the 1960s, in the context of social processes surrounding death. Meredith Minister has pointed out that the use of the concept of "social death" would need to be further refined and analyzed for its potential applicability to certain French feminist writers, for example, Luce Irigiray and and Monique Wittig, for whom women are in many ways not a viable, living, category, rather a creation and projection of men's thinking and writing, in much of Western thought.
22. See Steinberg, "Social Death as Gendered Genocide," for a link between gender, contemporary genocide, biblical texts, and social death.
23. See also Card, "Genocide and Social Death," and Steinberg, "Social Death as Gendered Genocide."
24. Lemos asserts, "According to biblical texts, Israelites and Judeans entered into treaty relationships with foreigners and thus saw them as human beings who had the standing to be parties to such arrangements." ("Physical Violence and the Boundaries of Personhood in the

Hebrew Bible," 516.) It appears that Deuteronomy 7 denies this evidence of "personhood" for the seven nations it lists.

25. Card writes, "But in paradigmatic instance of genocide, such as the holocaust, there are always some survivors, even when there is clear evidence that the invention was to eliminate everyone in the group" ("Genocide and Social Death," 72). The biblical text might attest that there were indeed survivors to the prescribed genocide of these seven nations called for in Deut. 7 (cf. Deut. 20), since at least some of them, appear in biblical texts after the conquest of the land (e.g., Josh 16:10; Judges 1:27–33; II Samuel 24:7; I Kings 9:16; Obadiah 1:20). On the discontinuities among biblical references to Canaanites as well as the difficulties involved in fixing their identities, see Stone, "Queering the Canaanite."

26. Deuteronomy 20:13–15, for example, also prescribes the taking of children, both sons and daughters.

27. See Steinberg, "Social Death as Gendered Genocide." See also Niditch, *War in the Hebrew Bible*, 83–88.

28. See Alice Bach, "Introduction," especially the section "A Subversive Companion for Reading Ancient Texts," pp. xxiii–xxvi.

29. For the "ban as sacrifice" see Niditch, *War in the Hebrew Bible*, 28–55. It should be noted, however, that Niditch discusses Deuteronomy 7 in what she calls "the ban as God's justice."

30. The exception being the Perizzites, who are included here for other, less clear reasons.

31. Warrior "reads the Exodus stories with Canaanite eyes" (Robert Warrior, "Canaanites, Cowboys, and Indians: Deliverance, Conquest, and Liberation Theology Today" *Christianity and Crisis* 49, no. 12 (1989): 262. See also Edward Said, "Michael Walzer's 'Exodus and Revolution': A Canaanite Reading" *Grand Street* 5, no. 2 (1986): 86–106.

32. To some extent, death and the inability to thrive is also, according to the Bible, part of God's domain. See, for example, Deut. 28; Hosea 9:11. See Tikva Frymer-Kensky, *In the Wake of the Goddesses: Women, Culture and the Biblical Transformation of Pagan Myth* (New York: Free Press/Macmillan, 1992), 83–99. I note that Israel being "blessed above all people" would open up discussion about hierarchies between peoples and nations, even while the text extends God's blessings to Israel and Israel's animals. Further, that Israelite animals are blessed opens into discussions about why they are blessed—in order to benefit human Israel?

33. See Ken Stone, *Reading the Hebrew Bible with Animal Studies* (Stanford: Stanford University Press, 2017); Moore, *Divinanimality*; and Donna Haraway, *When Species Meet* (Minneapolis: University of Minnesota Press, 2008).

34. See Jacques Derrida, *The Animal That Therefore I Am* (New York: Fordham University Press, 2008).

35. Though I have to add that I don't find much of the analysis inaccurate or inconsistent on the topics of enslavement and rape insofar as the Bible locates authority, on the human level, with male Israelites of adult, patriarchal status.

36. Books I included in the course readings that are examples of broader, survey, studies include Avalos, *Slavery, Abolitionism, and the Ethics of Biblical Scholarship*; Niditch, *War in the Hebrew Bible;* Scholz, *Sacred Witness.* By survey I do not mean to indicate a lack of depth and nuance (with exception being Avalos). An example of a more focused, single text specific book that I included is Haynes, *Noah's Curse.*

37. Of course these binaries intersect, such that they are further refined, or might they also begin to break down by way of such multiplicity, through male non-Israelite enslaved, female Israelite slave, widowed (and thus "free") woman, etc.

38. See Tamar Kamionkowski, *Gender Reversal and Cosmic Chaos: A Study on the Book of Ezekiel* (London and New York: Sheffield Academic Press, 2003) and bibliographical references there.

BIBLIOGRAPHY

Anderson, Cheryl B. *Women, Ideology, and Violence: Critical Theory and the Construction of Gender in the Book of the Covenant and the Deuteronomic Law*. London: T&T Clark, 2004.

Avalos, Hector. *Slavery, Abolitionism, and the Ethics of Biblical Scholarship.* Sheffield: Sheffield Phoenix Press, 2011.
Bach, Alice. "Introduction." In *Women in the Hebrew Bible: A Reader.* Edited by Alice Bach. New York and London: Routledge, 1999, pp. xiii–xxvi.
Card, Claudia. "Genocide and Social Death." *Hypatia* 18, no. 1 (2003): 63–79.
———. *Confronting Evils: Terrorism, Torture, Genocide.* Cambridge and New York: Cambridge University Press, 2010.
Coates, Ta-Nehisi. "The Case for Reparations." *The Atlantic*, June 2014. https://www.theatlantic.com/magazine/archive/2014/06/the-case-for-reparations/361631/.
Cottrill, Amy. "Reading Textual Violence as 'Real' Violence in the Liberal Arts Context. In *Teaching the Bible in the Liberal Arts Classroom*, edited by Jane S. Webster and Glenn S. Holland, 192–198. Sheffield: Sheffield Phoenix Press, 2012.
Derrida, Jacques. *The Animal That Therefore I Am.* New York: Fordham University Press, 2008.
Ellens, Deborah L. *Women in the Sex Texts of Leviticus and Deuteronomy: A Comparative Conceptual Analysis.* London and New York: T&T Clark, 2008.
Everhart, Janet. "Dildos and Dismemberment: Reading Difficult Biblical Texts in the Undergraduate Classroom." In *Teaching the Bible in the Liberal Arts* Classroom, edited by Jane S. Webster and Glenn S. Holland, 184–91. Sheffield: Sheffield Phoenix Press, 2012.
Exum, Cheryl J. *Fragmented Women: Feminist (Sub)versions of Biblical Narratives.* Sheffield: Sheffield Academic Press, 1993.
Frymer-Kensky, Tikva. *In the Wake of the Goddesses: Women, Culture and the Biblical Transformation of Pagan Myth.* New York: Free Press/Macmillan, 1992.
Gordon, Avery. "Some Thoughts on Haunting and Futurity." *borderlands* 10, no. 2 (2011): 1–21.
Gravett, Sandie. "Reading Rape in the Hebrew Bible: A Consideration of Language." *Journal for the Study of the Old Testament* 28, no. 3 (2004): 279–99.
Haraway, Donna. *When Species Meet.* Minneapolis: University of Minnesota Press, 2008.
———. "Situated Knowledges: The Science Question in Feminism and the Privilege of Partial Perspective." *Feminist Studies* 14, no. 3 (1988): 575–99.
Harding, Sandra. *Whose Science, Whose Knowledge?: Thinking from Women's Lives.* Ithaca: Cornell University Press, 1991.
Haynes, Stephen. *Noah's Curse: The Biblical Justification of American Slavery.* Oxford and New York: Oxford University Press, 2002.
Kamionkowski, S. Tamar. *Gender Reversal and Cosmic Chaos: A Study on the Book of Ezekiel.* London and New York: Sheffield Academic Press, 2003.
Kawashima, Robert. "Could a Woman Say 'No' in Ancient Israel? On the Genealogy of Legal Status in Biblical Law and Literature." *AJS Review* 35, no. 1 (2011): 1–22.
———. "Gender and Law in the Hebrew Bible." In *The Oxford Encyclopedia of the Bible and Law*, edited by Brent Strawn, et al., 306–19. Oxford: Oxford University Press, 2015.
Koosed, Jennifer, editor. *The Bible and Posthumanism.* Atlanta: Society of Biblical Literature, 2014.
Králová, Jana. "What Is Social Death?" *Contemporary Social Science* 10, no. 3 (2015): 235–48.
Lemos, T. M. "Were Israelite Women Chattel: Shedding New Light on an Old Question." In *Worship, Women and War: Essays in Honor of Susan Niditch*, edited by John J. Collins, T.M. Lemos, and Saul Olyan, 227–42. Providence, RI: Brown Judaic Studies, 2015.
———. "Physical Violence and the Boundaries of Personhood in the Hebrew Bible." *Hebrew Bible and Ancient Israel* 2, no. 500-531 (2013): 500–31.
Moore, Stephen D., editor. *Divinanimality: Animal Theory, Creaturely Theology.* New York: Fordham University Press, 2014.
Niditch, Susan. *War in the Hebrew Bible: A Study in the Ethics of Violence.* Oxford and New York: Oxford University Press, 2016.
Patterson, Orlando. *Slavery and Social Death: A Comparative Study.* Cambridge: Harvard University Press, 1982.

Pressler, Carolyn. *The View of Women Found in the Deuteronomic Family Laws*. Berlin and New York: de Gruyter, 1993.
Said, Edward. "Michael Walzer's 'Exodus and Revolution': A Canaanite Reading." *Grand Street* 5, no. 2 (1986): 86–106.
Scholz, Susanne. *Sacred Witness: Rape in the Hebrew Bible*. Minneapolis: Fortress Press, 2010.
———. "Occupy Academic Bible Teaching." In *Teaching the Bible in the Liberal Arts Classroom*, edited by Jane S. Webster and Glenn S. Holland, 28–43. Sheffield: Sheffield Phoenix Press, 2012.
Schwartz, Regina M. *The Curse of Cain: The Violent Legacy of Biblical Monotheism*. Chicago: University of Chicago Press, 1997.
Steinberg, Naomi. "Social Death as Gendered Genocide: The Fate of Women and Children." *Biblical Interpretation* 26, no. 1 (2018): 23–42.
Stone, Ken. "Queering the Canaanite." In *The Sexual Theologian: Essays on Sex, God and Politics*, edited by Marcella Althaus-Reid and Lisa Isherwood, 110–34. London and New York: T&T Clark, 2004.
———. *Reading the Hebrew Bible with Animal Studies*. Stanford: Stanford University Press, 2017.
Trible, Phyllis. *Texts of Terror: Literary-Feminist Readings of Biblical Narratives*. Philadelphia: Fortress Press, 1984.
Warrior, Robert. "Canaanites, Cowboys, and Indians: Deliverance, Conquest, and Liberation Theology Today." *Christianity and Crisis* 49, no. 12 (1989): 261–65.
Washington, Harold C. "'Lest He Die in the Battle and Another Man Take Her': Violence and the Construction of Gender in the Laws of Deuteronomy 20–22." In *Gender and Law in the Hebrew Bible and the Ancient Near East*, edited by Victor H. Matthews, Bernard M. Levinson, and Tikva Frymer-Kensky, 185–213. Sheffield: Sheffield Academic Press, 1998.
Webster, Jane S. and Holland, Glenn S., editors. *Teaching the Bible in the Liberal Arts Classroom*. Sheffield: Sheffield Phoenix Press, 2012.
———. *Teaching the Bible in the Liberal Arts Classroom Volume Two*. Sheffield: Sheffield Phoenix Press, 2015.

Chapter Four

On #MosqueMeToo

Lessons for Nuancing and Better Implementing the Goals of #MeToo

Kirsten Boles

Like many women in the United States, when the #MeToo movement happened, I was already on board. As a scholar of feminist and queer theory—as well as a self-identifying feminist—I needed no convincing that habitual offenders of misogyny, sexual harassment, and sexual assault were due for a public reckoning. I was shocked at the audacity of Harvey Weinstein and Roy Price, disgusted at the unaccountability of Larry Nassar and Roy Moore, and offended at the arrogance of Kevin Spacey and Matt Lauer.[1] And as op-eds began to roll out questioning whether this had all gone too far and where this all would end, I rolled my eyes and scoffed at what I saw as patriarchy's inability to accept the truth as it choked on its last breath. This is a non-issue, I thought; everyone should be on the same page concerning consent, and if someone is not, that probably means they have their own #MeToo skeletons hiding in their closet.

It wasn't until Aziz Ansari was "MeToo'ed" after a "bad date" with a woman, that I realized the complexity of this cultural moment.[2] An anonymous woman wrote for Babe.net[3] how Ansari, though not violent, was pushy and didn't know when to stop "trying," an experience that left this woman feeling rather unsettled. She was unsure of whether such a scenario warranted a firm "no" because he hadn't technically done anything out-of-the-ordinary in terms of dating expectations. But she was embarrassed and uncomfortable as a result of the experience and felt that she should have had more options.

The accusation against Aziz Ansari struck me not only because I am a fan of his comedy and because he himself is a self-identifying feminist,[4] but because it complicated my previous assumptions about the #MeToo movement and its seemingly straightforward message about consent. The sticking point for the Aziz Ansari case was that *he hadn't done anything out of the ordinary*. What he did was what men in America do on dates all the time. Sometimes it works, and sometimes it doesn't, but generally such behavior is not painted as a violation of consent.

For me, this case demonstrated that even after the #MeToo movement, questions of consent still lingered. It reminded me of the—admittedly problematic—joke I have heard countless times and that makes its way around social media in various forms: "If he's cute, it's called 'flirting,' but if he's ugly or poor, it's called 'sexual harassment.'"[5] That is, I started to notice the ways that norms—here, norms of dating and norms concerning interactions between men and women—can complicate what consent means and when it is deemed necessary. Essentially, I started to notice within #MeToo discourse all of the ways that its objectives were not in fact straightforward, but were instead sometimes situational, sometimes contingent, sometimes blurry.

And so, since reading about the Ansari case, I have been thinking a lot about consent and the mission of #MeToo in general. The purpose of the #MeToo movement is to inspire large-scale social and institutional change, and the first step to doing that is to change individual minds. But how do we do that if sometimes the lessons of consent are nuanced and conditional?

Why and in what ways is consent sometimes difficult to understand? And more importantly, why and in what ways is consent sometimes difficult to teach? This is a conversation I have frequently with my students. I dedicate an entire class period of the "Violence Against Women" unit of my introductory Gender Studies course to the Ansari case, and it often provokes passionate conversation about what consent really means in different scenarios and how best to relay its importance. For instance, in my Introduction to Gender Studies class, when I begin this discussion, we all agree that rape and assault are horrible and should be prevented. But where things get messy is when we look at, for lack of a better word, less egregious cases of misconduct, like Ansari's. When does "consent" get muddled—for instance, in the context of dating, flirting, and even sex?[6] My students often highlight that there are sometimes cultural factors—such as notions of "proper" gender roles and assumptions about the rules of courtship—that play a role in muddying up "consent," and that can complicate what may have been previously clear delineations of "consent." When does teaching consent conflict with other social values? How do we navigate culture—and religion—when trying to teach and implement consent in our communities, especially our classroom and college communities? To what extent are the objectives of the #MeToo movement mediated by cultural—and often religious—norms, cues, and assumptions that make consent less of a settled concept and instead one in need of constant revisiting, rethinking, and renegotiating?

These were questions on my mind when I first heard and read about Muslim versions of the #MeToo movement since 2018. It is to these movements that I will attend in this chapter. That is, how can the work being done by the Muslim #MeToo movements help clarify what has perhaps not yet been worked out by the original #MeToo movement? How do they help the #MeToo movement recognize disparate contexts, and as a result, see more women? In what follows, I will explore these questions and how I use these ideas to ground my classroom conversations about consent, power, and sexual violence. I will also look at how the important work being done by Muslim #MeToo can be leveraged to augment and expand such conversations. Specifically, I will look at an example of a "Muslim #MeToo," #MosqueMeToo, to show how it and its followers are acknowledging and discussing the mediated ways consent can be understood, taught, and implemented. I will then discuss why it is so important to include the stories from #MosqueMeToo into the larger #MeToo movement—as central to its mission as opposed to derivative or secondary—to ensure that the #MeToo movement sees and hears all women and does not reenact some of the same mistakes of past feminist activism. Muslim women need to be able to see themselves in #MeToo discourse, but the question remains how best to do that, how best to include Muslim women in sexual violence discourse without also tokenizing them or singling them out as in particular need of such discourse *because* they are Muslim. As I will discuss, this is a complex endeavor with much historical baggage. But, to rephrase the words of Miriam Peskowitz,[7] dealing with complexity in the evolving production of sexual violence discourses allows us to better enact an intersectional and inclusive feminist politics in our activism and in our classrooms.

THE #METOO MOVEMENT

The #MeToo movement arose in the American collective consciousness in October of 2017, when actress Alyssa Milano tweeted about allegations against now-disgraced film producer and Miramax cofounder, Harvey Weinstein. But this was actually not the first breath of the #MeToo movement. The #MeToo movement was actually started in 2006 by Tarana Burke, a social activist, community organizer, and sexual assault survivor herself. Burke started the hashtag as a way of expressing solidarity with other survivors when perhaps the words to express that solidarity are too difficult to find.[8] It was not until Alyssa Milano's tweet went viral, however, that people began to pay attention to the hashtag in any meaningful way. The hashtag has since become a global phenomenon.

The purpose of #MeToo was to raise awareness about the prevalence and ubiquity of sexual assault and harassment and to inspire cultural, institutional, and maybe even eventually political, change. However, almost as soon as it arrived, #MeToo was met with harsh criticisms. Surely, some of these were to be expected: criticisms from both men and women that the movement had "gone too far" are unsurprising in a patriarchal context. Observers and commentators questioned "Where does it stop?" and "Is *any* man safe from revenge-hungry feminists?" These criticisms even inspired a response hashtag, #HimToo, meant to stand up for and defend innocent men afraid of being targeted and unjustly accused.[9]

But it was fellow feminists who delivered a more formidable critique of the #MeToo movement. Women and feminists of color have pointed out #MeToo's limitations when it came to inclusivity[10] and accessibility.[11] Some questioned whether the movement, despite being created by Burke, a black woman, had now become too white, too wealthy, too aligned with celebrity and entertainment industry culture. This shed a light on the potential illegibility of the movement for some women who perhaps don't have the cultural—or literal—capital to report sexual harassment in their job or in their personal life. Was this new movement only for middle- or upper-class, white women? *Whose* sexual assaults does society care about? *Which* bodies are we talking about when we talk about sexual assault and harassment? Who is left out? What does this newfound awareness of the prevalence of sexual assault reveal about our culture, and *really* how much are we willing to change? And to what extent are we willing to address the specific ways that sexual violence is also often indistinguishable from, overlapping with, and/or fueled by racism? Can the #MeToo movement be sensitive to the specific ways that sexual violence differs among different communities, particularly communities of color, and specifically for the purposes of this paper, among religiously or culturally minoritized groups?

MUSLIM #METOOS

It is in the context of such questions and critiques that the Islam-specific version of #MeToo mentioned above began to arise. There have been several episodes constituting the Muslim #MeToo story, and I will only outline some of the main headlines of these on-going developments to provide context for the upcoming discussion. The first episode in this movement was the allegations against Tariq Ramadan, an Islamic scholar and philosopher and Professor of Contemporary Islamic Studies at St. Anthony's College, Oxford.[12] In late 2017, Ramadan was accused of rape and assault by two French Muslim women,[13] and despite vehemently denying the allegations, took a leave from his position at Oxford University as a result. The allegations against Ramadan sparked discussion on social media as part of France's version of #MeToo, #BalanceTonPorc ("expose your pig").[14]

Another episode in the Muslim #MeToo story occurred in late September of 2018. As the Brett Kavanaugh hearings occupied almost all public discourse in the United States, Imam Zaid Shakir of Zaytuna College in Berkeley, California posted on Facebook in response to the hearings, citing a Qur'anic passage requiring four witness to prove sexual impropriety, and calling on Dr. Christine Blasey-Ford to produce such corroborating witnesses.[15] Unsurprisingly, Muslim women quickly responded on social media, decrying his post and condemning religious leaders who misunderstand and misrepresent the nature of sex assault and the experiences of assault survivors.[16] Imam Shakir later deleted his post and replaced it with an apology, but many women responding to the episode online insisted the only appropriate solution to misinformation on the part of Islamic leadership is to put more women in positions of leadership in Islamic institutions.[17]

And, the most recent (as of early 2019) Muslim #MeToo moment, #Masaktach in Morocco, was started in response to the sexual assault in the late summer of 2018 of a 17-year-old girl named Khadija who was kidnapped by 12 men and boys in her village. She was held for two months and during her capture was repeatedly raped and tortured. Her torture involved being burned by cigarettes and being tattooed all over her body.[18] Once freed, Khadija posted a video to social media describing her ordeal and urging other women who have experienced sexual assault to "never remain silent."[19] Responses were tagged with #Masaktach, which means "I will not keep silent," expressing solidarity with and support for Khadija and other women like her.[20]

The hashtag, shared or tweeted thousands of times,[21] soon became a formal organization of Moroccan women, adopting the name Masaktach, that works to end harassment and violence in Morocco. Masaktach organizes public events to raise awareness and prepare women and girls for protecting themselves against sexual violence. It also works to affect change in how Moroccan laws address violence against women.[22] And it seems to be having an impact. In September of 2018, Morocco finally passed a law banning violence against women, which had been in the works for five years.[23] While many Moroccan feminists criticized this new law for not going far enough to protect Moroccan women—specifically, in terms of marital rape—others have extolled this law as a much-needed accomplishment moving Moroccan women towards greater gender equality.[24]

Despite all of these interesting developments in the expansion and evolution of the #MeToo movement, the case I want to explore in detail here, that I find most compelling for conversations about navigating consent amidst complex social values and norms, is the hashtag #MosqueMeToo. #MosqueMeToo was started by Egyptian feminist author Mona Eltahawy. Eltahawy started this hashtag in response to a Facebook post written by a young Pakistani woman named Sabica Khan that was shared over 2000 times. Khan wrote in this Facebook post about being sexually harassed during Hajj in Saudi Arabia in 2018. Hajj is the annual ritual pilgrimage to Mecca, Saudi Arabia, the holiest city in Islam. Hajj is one of the five pillars of Islam, so it is required of all those who are physically and financially able to complete it. Performing Hajj can renew and revitalize the faith of practitioners, unite the Muslim *ummah*, and bring contemporary Muslims closer to their religious roots.

However, it can also be a breeding ground for sexual violence and harassment. During Hajj, participants make *tawaf*, one of the mandated rituals which entails praying while circling the *Ka'ba*—the most sacred site in Islam, whose significance is traced back thousands of years to the time of the first prophet, Ibrahim. During these circumambulations, thousands of people will shuffle around the *Ka'ba* in very close proximity due to the heavy crowding. It is in these very close quarters that many women experience being groped or grabbed, especially on their buttocks or on their breasts.[25]

This is what happened to Sabica Khan. According to her Facebook post, during her third *tawaf*, Khan felt someone's hand on her waist. She first thought this was just an innocent mistake, until it happened a second time. She then felt something "aggressively poking" her from behind.[26] She could not turn around to see who it was because the crowd was so dense and all moving in the same direction. When she felt someone later grab and pinch her buttocks, she grabbed the hand and threw it off without being able to turn around to see who was touching her. She said she felt violated and was petrified; she was unable to speak. She described her entire experience of this holy ritual as now "overshadowed by this horrible event."[27]

After Khan's post went viral on Facebook, women began sharing their own stories of sexual harassment and assault during Hajj. All of these stories were eerily similar to Khan's. Women described instances of men grabbing their buttocks, rubbing up against them, and poking them with their erect penises during *tawaf*. Some women also reported harassment outside of the mosque when they were visiting the holy city—for instance, taxi drivers flashing female passengers, shop owners groping young female patrons, and catcalls and harassment on the streets even when the woman was accompanied by a man.[28]

In response to conversation forming online, Eltahawy decided to share her own experience of being harassed and violated while performing Hajj in order to support and show solidarity with Khan and other women like her who maybe didn't yet have the courage to speak up. Eltahawy posted a series of tweets about being groped and sexually assaulted twice during Hajj in 1982 when she was fifteen years old.[29] She wrote about this experience in her 2015 book *Headscarves and Hymens: Why the Middle East Needs a Sexual Revolution*,[30] and in one of her tweets, she shared a picture of a passage from this book describing how she kept silent not only out of shame but also as a result of pressure from other Muslim women to not malign Islam.[31] Eltahawy tagged her tweets with #MosqueMeToo to organize the discussion, and in just a couple days, the thread had been liked or retweeted thousands of times.

A major theme of Eltahawy's, Khan's, and the thousands of other social media posts by other Muslim women was that sexual harassment and assault can happen anywhere, even in the most sacred of places. Women are vulnerable everywhere, even in the most conservative of attire. Eltahawy made this point in a tweet about her own experiences of harassment, writing, "Men sexually assault women everywhere—in sacred and sexual spaces,"[32] and "I was in hijab. The way you dress HAS NOTHING TO DO WITH SEXUAL ASSAULT! I wore hijab for 9 years and I lost count of how many times I was sexually assaulted while dressed that way. Men are responsible for sexual assault, not wardrobe."[33]

Besides being true and worth noting of sexual violence in general, this proved to be an important clarification in the development of this #MosqueMeToo conversation. As more and more people tweeted and added their voices to the conversation, some men joined in to use the harassment and assaults of the women as justification for patriarchal values and practices. One tweet by a Muslim man reads, "With this entire #MeToo [emoji] global epidemic on the rise. I am beginning to realise that ISLAM was right all along when it ordains gap between the 2 genders. So called modernism has brought us to a point where the line between flirting and harassment is insanely blurred."[34] Muslim women were quick to correct such misrepresentations of the facts by pointing out that such norms have no impact on preventing sexual violence, and that fault lies not with the religion or its practices but instead with the men who commit these acts. For example, a retweet and response to this man's tweet by a woman named Aisha Murtad said as much: "Gender segregation and Hijab don't prevent harassment. Some women get harassed in Mecca! #mosquemetoo."[35]

This gets at the heart of the issue being raised by #MosqueMeToo: women are not safe from sexual harassment and sexual assault even in the most holy of places. Even close proximity to what's most sacred cannot protect women from sexual violence. One #MosqueMeToo contributor described her experience performing pilgrimage as "something that should have been one of the best memories in my life and should have brought me closer to God just ruined me."[36] Compounding the loss of sacredness in these women's experiences of Hajj is the lack of institutional response by Saudi officials who many of these women felt should be protecting them. As Eltahawy pointed out in another tweet, "It's imperative to emphasize that I was sexually assaulted during Haj by ordinary man/fellow pilgrim AND also a #Saudi police officer. There is no safety in sacred spaces, from a fellow pilgrim ostensibly there for sacred ritual, from those ostensibly upholding the 'law.'"[37] The lack of response by both religious and law enforcement institutions left these women feeling ignored, alone, and disillusioned after what was supposed to be their most profound religious experience. It was, for many of them, the ultimate betrayal.

And in addition to feeling betrayed, many women expressed a profound feeling of shame. They felt that because this was a place where such things are not supposed to happen, the harassment or assault they experienced must have been their fault. In a kind of tragic irony, many expressed that it was actually *because* of the sanctity of the place that women felt even more ashamed of their assaults than they otherwise would have.[38] This was something Sabica Khan expressed in her original Facebook post about her experience of harassment at Hajj. She started her post by expressing her apologies to anyone whose "religious sentiments" were hurt, and she explained her silence after the assaults by saying she "knew no one would trust me, or nobody would take it seriously."[39] She only told her mother because she knew only her mother would believe her. Whether survivors of sexual violence will be believed or not is always a problem they face when choosing to speak up; but, as many of the #MosqueMeToo participants expressed, this problem seems to be extrapolated when it comes to holy sites:[40] who would believe something so awful, something so unholy, could happen in such a sacred space?

But breaking this silence and breaking this shame is exactly what Eltahawy aimed to accomplish with #MosqueMeToo. The hashtag and the conversations it started are about deconstructing and eliminating the taboos around sex and sexuality that cause shame in survivors of sexual violence. #MosqueMeToo's mission is to teach women that they do not have to be ashamed of their bodies nor their voices. In this, there is no difference between #MeToo and #MosqueMeToo. Both movements aim to undermine sexual shame and silence and foster open and honest conversation about sex and sexual violence in the hopes of eliminating unhealthy sexual relationships, practices, and attitudes. Eltahawy says as much when she writes, "Men sexually assault women everywhere—in sacred and sexual spaces. Women of all faiths find it especially difficult to speak out because of taboos and shame around sex. Fuck taboos and fuck shame. The shame belongs to the assaulter. #1 priority for me is women & girls."[41] So, #MosqueMeToo is first and foremost about calling out sexism, misogyny, and abuse in Islam and especially in its holiest of sites.

However, given the context within which conversations about Islam exist today, this is much harder than it should be. Islamophobia inevitably complicates the efforts by these women to critique aspects of Islam and the Muslim community. Some Muslim women fear that criticism of Muslim men will only fan the flames of Islamophobia. They fear that speaking out about their abuses in Muslim holy sites will give those with Islamophobic sentiments further reason to blame Islam for instances of sexual violence and misogyny within Muslim communities.[42] And this is what sets #MosqueMeToo apart from the white #MeToo movement: Muslim women participating in this public conversation must juggle the pressure to fight against, on the one hand, sexism, misogyny, and violence within their own communities and, on the other hand, the impulse from potential Islamophobes to read these critiques as affirmation of Islam's putative inherent misogyny. In other words, these women are faced with the double task of fighting patriarchy and sexist practices within their own religious communities, on the one hand, and Islamophobia from outside of their communities, on the other. This is what is commonly referred to in feminist theory as the "double bind" and what Eltahawy describes as being caught between a rock and a hard place: "Muslim women are caught between a rock and a hard place: between Islamophobes & racists who want to demonize all Muslim men and a community that wants to defend all Muslim men."[43]

The problem, Eltahawy articulates, is that when Muslim women are used as political footballs between two opposing sides, no one is actually thinking or caring about those women.[44] The only thing that matters is proving one's own side is right. The women caught in the middle are only acknowledged to the extent that they can be used as rhetorical tools. Islamophobia and misogyny are being carried out on the backs of Muslim survivors of sexual violence without any regard for their actual well-being or safety. Their experiences and stories get lost, swallowed up by political noise.

Muslim women being used as political ploys is unfortunately not necessarily a new phenomenon. Lila Abu-Lughod, for example, points out a similar phenomenon in her now canonical article, "Do Muslim Women Really Need Saving?" She describes how Afghan women were used by the George W. Bush administration as political pawns in justifying the 2003 Iraq War. The rhetorical moves used by Laura Bush and others in the media placed Muslim women at the center of a fight between the U.S. military, on the one hand, and the "Taliban-and-the-terrorists," on the other. One was either with the one or the other, and alliances were determined literally on the heads of Muslim women, as the burka took center stage in such debates. In other words, an East-West, Islam-Christianity proxy war was being carried out on the backs of Afghani women, and certainly not to their benefit.

SEEING MUSLIM WOMEN IN #METOO

This is why the hashtag #MosqueMeToo is so important: it not only helps bring to the surface the actual stories of the women who have experienced sexual violence, but it highlights the extra baggage that some women must carry when coming forward to share their stories of sexual violence. #MosqueMeToo shows that some women, whether because of their identity, their background, or perceptions about them, must labor more extensively for the same kind of recognition that should be equally accessible to all. It likewise shows that not all women experience this #MeToo moment the same way and with the same pressures. The double bind imposed on Muslim women who share their #MeToo stories means they must attend to additional considerations, additional sources of shame, and additional potential forms of social isolation that perhaps other women—especially the early women of the celebrity #MeToo movement—do not.

There has been little attention within the larger, celebrity-initiated #MeToo movement to the ways in which culture, and especially religion, influence whether and how the objectives of #MeToo are implemented and eventually realized. Much of the discussion around the #MeToo movement has been about implementing change; it has been—rightly, I think—focused on teaching people of all ages to prioritize consent, to let consent—not power, wealth, or status—dictate relations between people. But there has been little attention paid to the fact that *how* that goal can be achieved is inevitably culturally—and religiously—influenced. #MosqueMeToo highlights the inevitability of that kind of negotiation. It demonstrates that there are contingencies—such as, in this case, Islamophobia and a history of antagonism towards "Western" ideas among some Muslims as a result of colonialism, occupation, or war, for example—that complicate the efficacy and legibility of the #MeToo message. #MosqueMeToo's attention to the double bind faced by many women who report sexual assault demonstrates that the goals of #MeToo are not always as clear-cut or black-and-white as they have been presented, that sometimes implementing those goals takes mediation, careful cultural and religious mediation.

Not acknowledging the specific challenges that some women face reporting sexual assault could potentially exclude or minimize their stories. And leaving out these stories would confirm one of the primary criticisms of the #MeToo movement: that #MeToo is too much of a white, straight, Western, rich women's movement, that it is too closely saddled to privilege to be legible to all women. Teaching and understanding consent are processes that are inevitably mediated through cultural, and often religious, knowledges that can either enhance or inhibit the efficacy of those lessons. Not attending to these cultural and religious specificities will not only limit the number of people reached, but more importantly, it could impose a kind of "one-size-fits-all" message onto disparate communities and circumstances. And "one-size-fits-all" usually ends up meaning "the-dominant-size-fits-all." In other words, inattention to additional pressures faced by Muslim women who report sexual violence could marginalize or neglect Muslim women's voices within the #MeToo movement.

Marginalizing Muslim women's voices within a larger women's movement runs the risk of recreating or reinforcing other existing forms of dominance. For instance, it could end up reenacting what Leila Ahmed has called "colonial feminism," or the using of the language of feminism in the service of colonialism or other systems of domination.[45] There is a historical legacy of redirecting feminist critiques, whose primary aim is the liberation of women, to delegitimize the culture, and undermine the agency, of the people of colonized countries.[46] The United States used the language of women's liberation to decry all of Islam and justify military intervention into Afghanistan. But examples of colonial feminism can be found much earlier. Ahmed, in her book, *Women and Gender in Islam*, discusses they ways in which concern for the liberation of Muslim women—and particularly the de-veiling of Muslim women—in British-occupied Egypt was often a thinly veiled—excuse the pun—effort to "modernize" or "Westernize" Egyptian culture. In essence, colonial feminism is a form of domination and violence that disguises itself as advocacy. It seemingly concerns itself with the liberation and rights of Muslim women without ever attending to the realities of those Muslim women's experiences.

Moreover, I think many, myself included, would say that these recent Muslim iterations of #MeToo offer one answer to the inclusivity problems of #MeToo. They are useful for extending the conversation started by #MeToo into additional spheres of cultural and religious experience. But then I wonder to what extent an overreliance on culturally-specific or religiously-specific versions of #MeToo as that solution then enable and leave unchallenged the ongoing problems with #MeToo that perhaps ought to be addressed. In other words, do these Islam-specific #MeToo's allow for the ghettoizing of Muslim women's experience within conversations about sexual violence and perhaps prevent needed interventions within the larger—largely white—#MeToo movement?

Let me be clear: I in no way see these Muslim-specific versions of #MeToo as problematic and think they make a needed and necessary space for women to share their voices in what they feel is their own community. But my question is more, why isn't #MeToo that space for these women, and what does that say about how feminist activism has approached this new mission of teaching and implementing "consent" as a guide for better human relations? Have efforts towards gender equality still not shaken its historical tendency to make secondary or peripheral "Other" women and centralize only the privileged, only those for whom it is easier to speak, for whom it easier to be heard, for whom it is perhaps easier to include? Rather than critiquing #MosqueMeToo and other hashtags like it, I instead wonder to what extent their existence in the first place reveals lasting and intractable problems of inclusivity in conversations about sexual violence and consent.

In other words, I wonder to what extent the fact that these iterations exist shows that there are still issues of inclusivity and accessibility to be worked out. Do these hashtags and the subsequent movements and discussions they inspire help facilitate Muslim women seeing themselves in conversations about sexual violence and consent in a way that nuances such conversations everywhere, or do they *enable* the non-inclusivity and inaccessibility of the earlier #MeToo movement? Does #MeToo's attention to—but not absorption of—these Muslim women's stories of sexual violence call attention to the ways that feminism has not gotten over some of its colonial remnants?

MOSQUE #METOO AND THE CLASSROOM

And how do questions of absorbing or including get worked out the classroom? That is, how do educators avoid reproducing colonial paradigms in their pedagogy? As mentioned, I teach the #MeToo moment in my introductory gender and sexuality course, and I also incorporate a unit on women, gender, and sexuality in the Abrahamic religions near the end of this class. Do conversations about #MosqueMeToo fall under the purview of a #MeToo unit, or are they better placed in a "women/gender/sex and Abrahamic religions" unit? That is, how do institutions and students "see" Muslim women, as Muslims first or as women first? One of the unique benefits of #MosqueMeToo is its intersectionality, that it identifies the complex identity-specific challenges of dealing with sexual violence and its prevention. But as a result, the case of #MosqueMeToo also complicates the very categories that facilitate the teaching of it. #MosqueMeToo and the discourses it inspires challenge the very disciplinary parameters on which teaching such a case might rely—for instance, Gender/Sexuality Studies, Religious Studies, and even already interdisciplinary genres such as Women's Studies in Religion. Its inherent intersectionality makes these parameters seem arbitrary, forced, even outdated. While all disciplines teach intersectionality as a concept, are our lessons and course structure really that intersectional? Or are we bound by existing paradigms that force us to organize topics—and people—into old boxes? We teach "intersectionality" because cases like #MosqueMeToo necessitate it, but how do we teach *intersectionally* in a way that does those cases justice? How do we actually *perform* intersectionality in our pedagogies? How do we *demonstrate* intersectionality in our syllabi?

Clearly, Muslim women, like all women, need to be able to "see" themselves in #MeToo discourse. And clearly, Muslim students, like all students, need to see themselves in the curriculums informed by #MeToo activism. I think this point is fairly obvious. But how we do that is a question that still remains, that is still being worked out on the ground, in conversations online, on the news, and of course, in classrooms just like mine.

And in these conversations, I wonder to what extent there exists a tension between, on the one hand, Muslim women needing to see themselves within discourses about sexual violence, and on the other hand, the fact that Muslim women's bodies have been historically an overburdened place of anxiety within such discourses. By that I mean, specifically *because* of the tendency for Muslim women's bodies to be used as political pawns, often placed at the fault lines of cultural differences, as discussed earlier, there is a tendency to over-imbue Muslim women's bodies with meaning and significance. There is a tendency to overburden Muslim women's bodies as places of sexual anxiety and violence, to presume that Muslim women's bodies are problematic bodies or bodies that endure more trauma than other bodies, simply by virtue of Islam being presumed more threatening to them.

This is something I observe not only from pundits, but also from my own peers and students. When I tell people that I study gender and sexuality in the context of Islam and within discourses about Islam in the United States, the most common reaction I get is excited relief. "Oh, thank God," some have said to me, "that is *so* needed! Those women have it the worst." Or, "Oh, that's so important! They kill gay people in those countries . . . " It is always "those"—"those women," "those countries"—a rhetorical framing that distances the speaker from any wrongdoing and eschews any self-reflection on how women or the LGBTQ community are treated in the United States. Depending on who it is and how comfortable I am with offending them, I usually say something to the sort of, "Well, it's actually that reaction right there that I study. I am curious about the impulse on the part of some Americans to be so concerned with the sexuality and bodies of Muslims *in particular* . . ."

My students, too, are often interested in the affairs of Muslim women and what Islam "really says" about women and the LGBTQ community—however, my students at least approach the subject with genuine curiosity and always try to frame their questions in careful and self-reflexive ways, unlike people much older, who, in my opinion, should know better. On the one hand, my students are hesitant to make sweeping generalizations about an entire identity, especially one with which they often admit unfamiliarity. But, on the other hand, they also try to reconcile what they have seen and heard on the news and from their own parents about Muslim women and their putative oppression at the hands of their men and their culture. Surely, such a ubiquitous consensus about the misogynistic abuse Muslim women endure at the hands of Muslim men can't be a coincidence. Surely, not *everyone* could be misinformed. But this, I try to explain to my students, is an example of how power works its way into our understandings of our world and of one another. I ask them to think not only about the context within which they learned such things—most of my students were too young to really know anything other than a post-9/11 context, so I always do my best to convey just how much that moment contributed to current understandings and representations of Islam—but also about the implications of such questions. I try to explain that even how we frame our questions is important, that no matter how genuine, no matter how well-intentioned, such questions are not necessarily *neutral*, not necessarily untouched by power. Because no one is immune to the dog-whistle of ideology, we are all invited, one way or another, to see difference as distance, as deficit, to see those dissimilar from us as "other."

Deconstructing, dismantling, and discouraging this type of thinking is a lesson my students and I constantly revisit throughout the semester. I admit to them that ideology works on me just as it works on them, and the onus is on all of us to strive to be better when we encounter "difference." Just as I tell my students that patriarchy is a water we all swim in, so too are other power imbalances implicit and ubiquitous in the cultural products with which we engage every day.

Being aware of the problems of this type of thinking echoes Edward Said and his groundbreaking work *Orientalism*. In it, Said details how the "Orient" was constructed as both exotic and sensual, on the one hand, and barbaric, depraved, and backwards, on the other hand, both in contradistinction to the "Occident," or the West, which was civilized, rational, and moral.[47] Sexuality in the "Orient" was represented as a place of anxiety, as both desired and feared, as both sensual and repressed. This was often exemplified in art or literature by the image of the Muslim harem, the epitome of both the Western colonizer's desirous gaze and the putative barbarism of the sexist Muslim man. The harem—and by extension, the occupant of the harem, the Muslim woman's body—was often portrayed in terms of its inaccessibility. To the Western (male) imagination, Muslim women's bodies symbolized both titillation and apprehension. Since *Orientalism*, theorists such as Lila Abu-Lughod, Leila Ahmed, Ziba Mir-Hosseini, Fatima Mernissa, Deniz Kandiyoti, and Maryam Khalid have written about the different ways that fascination with and apprehension of Muslim women's bodies manifests in contemporary media, pop culture, and political discourse.[48]

So, there is a historical legacy of overburdening Muslim women's bodies when it comes to issues of misogyny, sexual violence, and women's liberation across cultures and across religions. While I think it is obvious that Muslim women indeed do need to "see" themselves in conversations about consent and violence prevention, I question how best to do that without also overburdening Muslim women bodies as *in particular* need of being seen, *in particular* need of liberation from sexual violence over other women. That is, #MeToo discourse—in activist circles as well as in classrooms such as mine—must include Muslim women without that inclusion being symptomatic of their *being* Muslim. It must include Muslim women without simultaneously tokenizing, essentializing, or encumbering them with undue signification or symbolism.

CONCLUSION: BLURRING LINES,[49] EXPANDING CONVERSATIONS

So now, to return to the case—and the classroom conversations—with which I started, what both the Aziz Ansari case and #MosqueMeToo show us is that the lessons of #MeToo are mobile and in need of constant negotiation and renegotiation, that notions of consent and the ways that one teaches consent are culturally—and religiously—mediated. As we move forward in this #MeToo moment and continue to think about the many facets and many faces of #MeToo—whether white, black, Muslim, Latinx, Asian, etc.—we need our conversations about sexual violence and about consent to mirror the flexibility and mobility that constitute our lived experiences. This will not only ensure no women fall through the cracks of discourse but will also better teach our next generations of students to *see* more bodies—including their own—in feminism and in feminist curricula.

As mentioned, my analysis of this topic evolved out of conversations I had with my students about sexual violence, about consent, and about the messiness that can sometimes complicate how we enact the objectives of #MeToo. What we concluded from discussing the Aziz Ansari case is that more open and honest conversation about consent and its sometimes blurred lines—without shaming women for desires outside of consent and acknowledging the role both men and women play in constructing flirting and dating culture—will lead to better understandings about how to inspire others to embrace consent as a moral guide. I land on similar conclusions when I think about what #MosqueMeToo can ameliorate within the original #MeToo movement. I want to have fuller, more nuanced conversations with my classes, and I want our global dialogue about this subject matter to also be swinging, large, and flexible. I don't necessarily have all of the answers on how best to accomplish this—these are questions I am currently working out in real time in my classes and within my syllabi. But inattention to such questions—question of categorization, canonization, representation, legibility, and self-reflection—will move our discourse and our pedagogy nowhere. If we don't ask such questions, we risk recreating the same problematic paradigms that have thwarted past feminist activism; we risk undermining what progress the #MeToo movement has already made.

NOTES

1. KT Hawker and Chicago Tribune Staff, "#MeToo: A Timeline of Events," *Chicago Tribune*, January 11, 2018, https://www.chicagotribune.com/lifestyles/ct-me-too-timeline-20171208-htmlstory.html.
2. Megan Garber, "Aziz Ansari and the Paradox of 'No,'" *The Atlantic*, January 16, 2018, https://www.theatlantic.com/entertainment/archive/2018/01/aziz-ansari-and-the-paradox-of-no/550556/.
3. Katy Way, "I went on a date with Aziz Ansari. It turned into the worst night of my life," *Babe.net*, January 13, 2018, https://babe.net/2018/01/13/aziz-ansari-28355.
4. Way, "I went on a date with Aziz Ansari. It turned into the worst night of my life."
5. "What men don't understand when they complain, 'It's only creepy if the guy's hot,'" *The Happy Talent*, August 29, 2018, http://www.thehappytalent.com/blog/what-men-dont-understand-when-they-complain-its-only-creepy-if-the-guy-isnt-hot.
6. Julia Serano, "Why Nice Guys Finish Last," *Women's Lives: Multicultural Perspectives*, 6th ed., edited by Gwyn Kirk and Margo Okazawa-Rey (New York: McGraw-Hill, 2013), 189–95.
7. Miriam Peskowitz, "What's in a Name? Exploring the Dimensions of What 'Feminist Studies in Religion' Means," *Women, Gender, Religion: A Reader*, ed. Elizabeth A. Castelli (New York: Palgrave, 2001), 32.
8. Abby Olheiser, "The woman behind 'MeToo' knew the power of the phrase when she created it—10 years ago," *The Washington Post*, October 19, 2017, https://www.washingtonpost.com/news/the-intersect/wp/2017/10/19/the-woman-behind-me-too-knew-the-power-of-the-phrase-when-she-created-it-10-years-ago/?utm_term=.70b5747302d2.
9. Stephanie McNeal, "This mom said her son was 'afraid to date' because of feminists and now everyone's trolling her," *Buzzfeed News*, October 9, 2018, https://www.buzzfeednews.com/article/stephaniemcneal/this-guys-mom-accidentally-turned-him-into-a-hilarious-meme.
10. Sophie Chou, "Millions say #MeToo. But not everyone is heard equally," *Public Radio International*, January 23, 2018, https://www.pri.org/stories/2018-01-23/millions-say-metoo-not-everyone-heard-equally.
11. Kyli Rodriguez-Cayro, "The 'Me Too' hashtag isn't as inclusive as it could be, but here's how you can help change that," *Bustle*, October 20, 2017, https://www.bustle.com/p/the-me-too-hashtag-isnt-as-inclusive-as-it-could-be-but-heres-how-you-can-help-change-that-2955147.
12. "Professor Tariq Ramadan," *St. Anthony's College, University of Oxford*, n.d., accessed January 2, 2019, http://www.sant.ox.ac.uk/people/tariq-ramadan.
13. Florence Dixon, "Explainer: The Tariq Ramadan Affair," *The New Arab*, September 18, 2018, https://www.alaraby.co.uk/english/indepth/2018/9/18/explainer-the-tariq-ramadan-affair.
14. Jalal Baig, "The Perils of #MeToo as a Muslim," *The Atlantic*, December 21, 2017, https://www.theatlantic.com/international/archive/2017/12/tariq-ramadan-metoo/548642/. There is a long history of associating in France the symbol of "the pig" with sexual misconduct by men. Not only does it connote the vulgarity of violent and uncontrolled male lust, but it also references a rumored private nickname for Harvey Weinstein—"The Pig" at the Cannes Film Festival. For more on this history and the links between "pig" and sexual violence within French thought and culture, see Misgav Har-Peled, "#BalanceTonPorc: the story behind pigs and lust," *The Conversation*, April 26, 2018, http://theconversation.com/balanceTonporc-the-story-behind-pigs-and-lust-92491.
15. Dilshad Ali, "Muslim #MeToo isn't just a man problem. It's also a male-led theology prob...," *Religion News Service*, October 26, 2018, https://religionnews.com/2018/10/26/muslim-metoo-doesnt-have-a-man-problem-it-has-a-male-theology-problem/.
16. Ali, "Muslim #MeToo isn't just a man problem. It's also a male-led theology prob..."
17. Ali, "Muslim #MeToo isn't just a man problem. It's also a male-led theology prob. . ."
18. Anais Bremond & Rebecca Ratcliffe, "Morocco rape victim urges women: never remain silent," *The Guardian*, November 26, 2018, https://www.theguardian.com/global-development/2018/nov/26/morocco-victim-khadija-masaktach.

19. Bremond and Ratcliffe, "Morocco rape victim urges women: never remain silent."
20. Bremond and Ratcliffe, "Morocco rape victim urges women: never remain silent."
21. Josh Babb, "#Masaktach Brings Attention to Sexual Harassment, Assault in Morocco," *Moroccan World News*, October 17, 2018, https://www.moroccoworldnews.com/2018/10/255576/masaktach-brings-attention-to-sexual-harassment-assault-in-morocco/.
22. Babb, "#Masaktach Brings Attention to Sexual Harassment, Assault in Morocco."
23. Siobhán O'Grady, "Why activists aren't happy with Morocco's new anti-sexual-harassment laws," *Washington Post*, September 13, 2018, https://www.washingtonpost.com/world/2018/09/13/why-activists-arent-happy-with-moroccos-new-anti-sexual-harassment-laws/?utm_term=.d3e7f5c28239.
24. O'Grady, "Why activists aren't happy with Morocco's new anti-sexual-harassment laws."
25. Malaka Gharib, "#MosqueMeToo Gives Muslim Women A Voice About Sexual Misconduct At Mecca," *National Public Radio*, February 26, 2018, https://www.npr.org/sections/goatsandsoda/2018/02/26/588855132/-mosquemetoo-gives-muslim-women-a-voice-about-sexual-misconduct-at-mecca.
26. Rose Troup Buchanan, "These women are sharing stories of being sexually harassed during pilgrimage in Saudi Arabia," *Buzzfeed News*, February 7, 2018, https://www.buzzfeed.com/rosebuchanan/muslim-women-are-speak-out-about-being-sexually-harassed.
27. Buchanan, "These women are sharing stories of being sexually harassed during pilgrimage in Saudi Arabia."
28. Buchanan, "These women are sharing stories of being sexually harassed during pilgrimage in Saudi Arabia."
29. Mona Eltahawy, Twitter Post, February 5, 2018, 2:43pm, accessed December 20, 2018, https://twitter.com/monaeltahawy/status/960645178020323329.
30. Eltahawy, Twitter Post, February 5, 2018, 2:43pm.
31. Mona Eltahawy, Twitter Post, February 5, 2018, 2:45pm, accessed December 20, 2018, https://twitter.com/monaeltahawy/status/960645516500635648.
32. Mona Eltahawy, Twitter Post, February 5, 2018, 2:53pm, accessed December 20, 2018, https://twitter.com/monaeltahawy/status/960647473994895361.
33. Mona Eltahawy, Twitter Post, February 5, 2018, 3:22pm, accessed December 20, 2018, https://twitter.com/monaeltahawy/status/960654844066516992. Emphasis in original.
34. Aisha Murtad, Twitter Post, April 20, 2018, 5:03am, accessed December 26, 2018, https://twitter.com/UmmAlMumineen/status/987300692485459970
35. Murtad, Twitter Post, April 20, 2018, 5:03am.
36. ExMuslimWoman (@exmuslimwoman), Twitter Post, November 22, 2018, 6:26am, accessed December 26, 2018, https://twitter.com/exmuslimwoman/status/1065612427721678848
37. Mona Eltahawy, Twitter Post, February 5, 2018, 3:10pm, accessed December 20, 2018, https://twitter.com/monaeltahawy/status/960651936352686083
38. Aymann Ismail, "#MosqueMeToo puts Muslim women 'between a rock and a hard place,'" *Slate*, February 14, 2018, https://slate.com/news-and-politics/2018/02/mosquemetoo-exposes-how-hard-it-is-for-muslim-women-to-speak-up-about-sexual-violence.html.
39. Buchanan, "These women are sharing stories of being sexually harassed during pilgrimage in Saudi Arabia."
40. Gharib, "#MosqueMeToo Gives Muslim Women A Voice About Sexual Misconduct At Mecca."
41. Eltahawy, Twitter Post, February 5, 2018, 2:53pm.
42. Gharib, "#MosqueMeToo Gives Muslim Women A Voice About Sexual Misconduct At Mecca."
43. Mona Eltahawy, Twitter Post, February 5, 2018, 2:56pm, accessed December 20, 2018, https://twitter.com/monaeltahawy/status/960648250398212097.
44. Ismail, "#MosqueMeToo puts Muslim women 'between a rock and a hard place.'"
45. Leila Ahmed, *Women and Gender in Islam* (New Haven: Yale University Press, 1993), 151.
46. A perfect example is Abu-Lughod's discussion of Afghan women, mentioned earlier.

47. Edward W. Said, *Orientalism* (Toronto, ON: Vintage Books Ed., 1979).
48. Lila Abu-Lughod, "Review: 'Orientalism' and Middle East Feminist Studies," *Feminist Studies*, 27, no. 1 (Spring, 2001): 101–13 and Maryam Khalid, "Gender, orientalism and representations of the 'Other' in the War on Terror," *Global Change, Peace & Security*: formerly *Pacifica Review: Peace, Security & Global Change* (2011), 23, no. 1: 15–29.
49. This section title is in part paying homage to an important essay by Roxane Gay that I teach alongside the Aziz Ansari #MeToo case. (Roxane Gay, "Blurred Lines, Indeed," *Bad Feminist: Essays* (New York: Harper Perennial, 2014).) "Blurred Lines" is also a 2013 song by Robin Thicke that was widely criticized for promoting rape culture.

BIBLIOGRAPHY

Abu-Lughod, Lila. "Review: 'Orientalism' and Middle East Feminist Studies." *Feminist Studies*, Vol. 27, No. 1 (Spring, 2001), 101–13.
Ahmed, Leila. *Women and Gender in Islam*. New Haven: Yale University Press, 1993.
Ali, Dilshad. "Muslim #MeToo isn't just a man problem. It's also a male-led theology prob . . ." *Religion News Service*. October 26, 2018. Accessed December 26, 2018. https://religionnews.com/2018/10/26/muslim-metoo-doesnt-have-a-man-problem-it-has-a-male-theology-problem/.
Babb, Josh. "#Masaktach Brings Attention to Sexual Harassment, Assault in Morocco." *Moroccan World News*. October 17, 2018. Accessed December 26, 2018. https://www.moroccoworldnews.com/2018/10/255576/masaktach-brings-attention-to-sexual-harassment-assault-in-morocco/.
Baig, Jalal. "The Perils of #MeToo as a Muslim." *The Atlantic*. December 21, 2017. Accessed December 20, 2018. https://www.theatlantic.com/international/archive/2017/12/tariq-ramadan-metoo/548642/.
Bremond, Anais & Rebecca Ratcliffe. "Morocco rape victim urges women: never remain silent." *The Guardian*. November 26, 2018. Accessed December 26, 2018. https://www.theguardian.com/global-development/2018/nov/26/morocco-victim-khadija-masaktach.
Buchanan, Rose Troup. "These women are sharing stories of being sexually harassed during pilgrimage in Saudi Arabia." *Buzzfeed News*. February 7, 2018. Accessed December 20, 2018. https://www.buzzfeed.com/rosebuchanan/muslim-women-are-speak-out-about-being-sexually-harassed.
Chou, Sophie. "Millions say #MeToo. But not everyone is heard equally." *Public Radio International*. January 23, 2018. Accessed January 12, 2019. https://www.pri.org/stories/2018-01-23/millions-say-metoo-not-everyone-heard-equally.
Dixon, Florence. "Explainer: The Tariq Ramadan Affair." *The New Arab*. September 18, 2018. Accessed January 18, 2019. https://www.alaraby.co.uk/english/indepth/2018/9/18/explainer-the-tariq-ramadan-affair.
Eltahawy, Mona. Twitter Post. February 5, 2018, 2:43pm. Accessed December 20, 2018. https://twitter.com/monaeltahawy/status/960645178020323329.
———. Twitter Post. February 5, 2018, 2:45pm. Accessed December 20, 2018. https://twitter.com/monaeltahawy/status/960645516500635648.
———. Twitter Post. February 5, 2018, 2:53pm. Accessed December 20, 2018. https://twitter.com/monaeltahawy/status/960647473994895361.
———. Twitter Post. February 5, 2018, 2:56pm. Accessed December 20, 2018. https://twitter.com/monaeltahawy/status/960648250398212097.
———. Twitter Post. February 5, 2018, 3:10pm. https://twitter.com/monaeltahawy/status/960651936352686083.
———. Twitter Post. February 5, 2018, 3:22pm. Accessed December 20, 2018. https://twitter.com/monaeltahawy/status/960654844066516992.
ExMuslimWoman (@exmuslimwoman). Twitter Post. November 22, 2018, 6:26am. Accessed December 26, 2018. https://twitter.com/exmuslimwoman/status/1065612427721678848.

Garber, Megan. "Aziz Ansari and the Paradox of 'No.'" *The Atlantic*. January 16, 2018. Accessed October 18, 2018. https://www.theatlantic.com/entertainment/archive/2018/01/aziz-ansari-and-the-paradox-of-no/550556/.

Gay, Roxane. "Blurred Lines, Indeed." *Bad Feminist: Essays*. New York: Harper Perennial, 2014.

Gharib, Malaka. "#MosqueMeToo Gives Muslim Women A Voice About Sexual Misconduct At Mecca." *National Public Radio*. February 26, 2018. Accessed December 20, 2018. https://www.npr.org/sections/goatsandsoda/2018/02/26/588855132/-mosquemetoo-gives-muslim-women-a-voice-about-sexual-misconduct-at-mecca.

Har-Peled, Misgav. "#BalanceTonPorc: the story behind pigs and lust." *The Conversation*. April 26, 2018. Access January 18, 2019. http://theconversation.com/balancetonporc-the-story-behind-pigs-and-lust-92491.

Hawker, KT and Chicago Tribune Staff. "#MeToo: A Timeline of Events." *Chicago Tribune*. January 11, 2019. Accessed January 10, 2019. https://www.chicagotribune.com/lifestyles/ct-me-too-timeline-20171208-htmlstory.html.

Ismail, Aymann. "#MosqueMeToo puts Muslim women 'between a rock and a hard place.'" *Slate*. February 14, 2018. Accessed December 20, 2018. https://slate.com/news-and-politics/2018/02/mosquemetoo-exposes-how-hard-it-is-for-muslim-women-to-speak-up-about-sexual-violence.html.

Khalid, Maryam. "Gender, orientalism and representations of the 'Other' in the War on Terror." *Global Change, Peace & Security*: formerly *Pacifica Review: Peace, Security & Global Change* (2011), 23:1, 15–29.

McNeal, Stephanie. "This mom said her son was 'afraid to date' because of feminists and now everyone's trolling her." *Buzzfeed News*. October 9, 2018. Accessed January 12, 2019. https://www.buzzfeednews.com/article/stephaniemcneal/this-guys-mom-accidentally-turned-him-into-a-hilarious-meme.

Murtad, Aisha. Twitter Post. April 20, 2018, 5:03am. Accessed December 26, 2018. https://twitter.com/UmmAlMumineen/status/987300692485459970.

O'Grady, Siobhán. "Why activists aren't happy with Morocco's new anti-sexual-harassment laws." *Washington Post*. September 13, 2018. Accessed December 26, 2018. https://www.washingtonpost.com/world/2018/09/13/why-activists-arent-happy-with-moroccos-new-anti-sexual-harassment-laws/?utm_term=.d3e7f5c28239.

Olheiser, Abby. "The woman behind 'MeToo' knew the power of the phrase when she created it—10 years ago." *The Washington Post*. October 19, 2017. Accessed January 12, 2019. https://www.washingtonpost.com/news/the-intersect/wp/2017/10/19/the-woman-behind-me-too-knew-the-power-of-the-phrase-when-she-created-it-10-years-ago/?utm_term=.70b5747302d2.

Peskowitz, Miriam. "What's in a Name? Exploring the Dimensions of What 'Feminist Studies in Religion' Means." *Women, Gender, Religion: A Reader*, ed. Elizabeth A. Castelli. New York: Palgrave, 2001.

"Professor Tariq Ramadan." *St. Anthony's College, University of Oxford*. n.d. Accessed January 2, 2019. http://www.sant.ox.ac.uk/people/tariq-ramadan.

Rodriguez-Cayro, Kyli. "The 'Me Too' hashtag isn't as inclusive as it could be, but here's how you can help change that." *Bustle*. October 20, 2017. Accessed January 12, 2019. https://www.bustle.com/p/the-me-too-hashtag-isnt-as-inclusive-as-it-could-be-but-heres-how-you-can-help-change-that-2955147.

Said, Edward. *Orientalism*. Toronto, ON: Vintage Books Ed., 1979.

Serano, Julia. "Why Nice Guys Finish Last." *Women's Lives: Multicultural Perspectives*, 6th ed., edited by Gwyn Kirk and Margo Okazawa-Rey. New York: McGraw-Hill, 2013.

Way, Katy. "I went on a date with Aziz Ansari. It turned into the worst night of my life." *Babe.net*. January 13, 2018. Accessed January 12, 2019. https://babe.net/2018/01/13/aziz-ansari-28355.

"What men don't understand when they complain, 'It's only creepy if the guy's hot." *The Happy Talent*. August 29, 2018. Accessed January 12, 2019. http://www.thehappytalent.com/blog/what-men-dont-understand-when-they-complain-its-only-creepy-if-the-guy-isnt-hot.

Chapter Five

Judges 19 and Non-Con

Sado-Kantian Aesthetics of Violence in the Tale of an Unnamed Woman

Minenhle Nomalungelo Khumalo

This is an essay about rape and representation. It is also intended to be an essay about rape culture and pedagogy, and as such, it is also an essay about events; that of sexual violence and that of learning/teaching. Affect theorist Eugenie Brinkema has argued that "[t]he question of rape is always the question of an event. The questioning of an event. The event as a question mark to which no answer can be finally, with finality, appended."[1] Accordingly, this essay is concerned with the questioning of the Judges 19 rape event. Judges 19, a narrative that has been subject to much academic scrutiny, offers the story of an unnamed woman who is the concubine of a Levite. She initially leaves her husband to return to her father's house but is later retrieved by the Levite. On the way back to her husband's home, she is gang raped by the men of Gibeah during an overnight stay there, and consequently dismembered by her husband upon arrival at his home.

In relation to the above, I suggest that the question of rape should be understood as a pedagogical question. Hence, my reading of Judges 19 is not limited to narrated eventuation, but proceeds to speculate about the mechanic and epistemic informants of the narrative phenomena and ultimately speculates on how we might go about constructing critical pedagogies of resistance to the fatal objecthood that (in)forms Judges 19. For the purposes of this essay, the lines of inquiry that are taken up for Judges 19 do not question whether or not the event has occurred. A gang-rape has unquestionably taken place within the narrative: "the man seized his concubine and brought her out to them; and they knew her and abused her all night until the morning"

(Judges 19:25). Yet, we are not allowed to view the incident in any palpable sense. Thus, questioning Judges 19 places readers/hearers in the predicament of making meaning of an event we cannot fully know, and in turn, demands pedagogical strategies that facilitate learning and teaching out of limitation.

Although my reading does not exclude interactions with biblical scholarship, because the interests of this paper are also pedagogical, the hermeneutical framework used to read Judges 19 extends beyond the methodological concerns and apparatuses of exegesis. My approach does not only read Judges 19, it also reflects on the implications of reading as well as teaching with and/or about rape representation, a reflection that has—albeit fortuitous—manifested itself as notably Lacanian in its framework. My reading of Judges 19 understands the text to be a *rape-narrative*. That is, a narrative which is not only concerned with telling and representing rape, but is produced through and is productive of rape culture.[2] The unnamed woman through which the narrative takes its shape is scarcely *visible* in the events leading up to her rape, completely *in*visible during her rape and alarmingly *di*visible after her rape. The body through which the sexual violence(s) and subsequent murder are represented is almost completely hidden from the reader/hearer, to the extent that, even the precise moment of her death, despite the explicit narration of her dismemberment, is severed from our gaze.[3] The rape scene is shut out along with the woman on the other side of an old man's door (Judges 19:25). Unexpectedly, we are given a brief picture of the severity of her ordeal as we are told that she falls to touch the threshold of the house (19:26). And in this liminal moment there is no doubt that *the thing*, as the text will call it, has happened. But what is the exact nature of this *thing*? The story takes no pause for any questioning, however, as the door is swung open by her master. He demands for her get up and continue on their journey, but, she is unresponsive. With that, her body is hauled back to the Levite's home, and she is cut into twelve pieces (19:27–29).

Now, it is not without irony that the attentions of this essay are split, as I read Judges 19 with inquiries that cut across concerns with rape, representation, rape culture, popular culture, pedagogy, learning, and teaching (amongst other things). But there is no joke there. As a black, queer woman, and an immigrant to the United States, I am unfortunately familiar with the severities of seeking post-secondary education. All too often have I encountered the sexual as well as economic, political, and ideological violences of higher education systems in the United States. In light of this, my reading of Judges 19 is (in)formed by pedagogical approaches that are primarily interested with and invested in bodies on the ground. Literally! As such, a question that also motivates this essay, albeit incompletely addressed, is borrowed from Gerald West: "What does it mean to have our work nurtured by and in the service of the poor and marginalized, but yet to have the academy as a secondary dialogue partner?"[4] In part, the response to this question is my commitment to pragmatic pursuits of critical pedagogical hermeneutics. Because of this, my essay is also committed to "actively and overtly betray the hidden transcript—the undisclosed interests and agendas—of the white, middle-class, male biblical studies industry."[5] As Cheryl Anderson's "Biblical Interpretation as Violence: Genesis 19 and Judges 19 in the Context of HIV and AIDS" has helped me to articulate, much of biblical scholarship—especially within Christian frameworks of understanding—knowingly or unknowingly holds its allegiances to a *mythical norm.* This, in Anderson's words, "constructs distinctions between the dominant group and others: those who are not white (black), not heterosexual (homosexual), and not male (female). Furthermore, because those who reflect the attitudes of the mythical norm hold privileged position, those who are "Other" necessarily hold a subordinate position in society."[6] What this means for this essay and its attempt to betray the "hidden transcript," is a critical attention to the ways in which most approaches to Judges 19, even those that overtly expose and challenge the text's misogyny, fail to adequately resist the epistemic mechanisms of the textual norm of the biblical narrative. That is, scholarly readings of the unnamed woman in Judges 19, in my opinion, have not sufficiently departed from modes of knowing her and the narration of her rape that are directly shaped by the phallocentrism of the narrative in its reduction of her subjective agency to objecthood. Thus, I will show that a primary focus on the violence that *is* depicted in the text and a failure to more intently engage with the violence that *is not* depicted in the story is symptomatic of engagements with rape, rape representation, and rape culture that are dictated by a masculine gaze.

QUESTIONING THE TEXT: *DAFUQ DID I JUST READ?*

How does one speak/read/write about a raped body that is made accessible only to its abusers? What does it mean to read or write about rape without the rape? What is the nature of the Judges 19 rape event? And what is the nature of my desire to read, write, learn and teach about this event? This *thing*, as the text calls it. How is the value of bodies allocated when this *thing* has happened? How are the events surrounding the *thing* made visible or invisible? What epistemic apparatuses produce the frameworks of understanding used to engage with and respond to the *thing*? And what does it mean to inhabit a (literary) world that is (in)formed through and by rape(d)-things?

My questioning of this biblical event is an anxious activity. On the one hand, my reading conforms to the feminist convictions and observations of Phyllis Trible (1984), Mieke Bal (1989), and Cheryl Exum (1993) (amongst others), all of whom have emphatically highlighted the blatant pursuit of male interests, at the expense of female interests, displayed in this narrative.[7]

It concurs with the assertions of Susanne Scholz (2010) and Alice A. Keefe (1991) that rape in the Hebrew Bible is (often) directly related to the outbreak of war and is used as a textual indication of "larger social chaos."[8] This essay also feels a solidarity with the hermeneutical agendas of Koala Jones-Warsaw (1994), and Patrick Cheng (2002) which focalize and give representation to the lived experiences of African-American Womanist and Queer Asian-American communities in their readings of the narrative.[9] Yet, on the other hand, my reading departs from these indispensable approaches to the text in a significant way. This departure is rooted in a methodological maneuver that is not only attentive to the excessive violence of the Judges 19 narrative but also gives critical consideration to the evasion of violent depiction in this story—particularly in the narration of the rape moment(s). This methodological maneuver is shaped by my critical pedagogical approach to interpretation in that it understands the reader/hearer to be involved in processes of identifying and challenging inadequate representations of the self and other in addition to commenting on the nature and function of such representation. Thus, while most scholars who read Judges 19 share James Harding's assumption that this story is an "exceptionally graphic account of the violent death of the Levite's concubine, a victim of sexual violence wholly without voice, and almost wholly without agency,"[10] this essay argues that Judges 19 also avoids the violence inflicted on the unnamed woman. And with this reading of textual avoidance of violent depiction, I also suggest an alternate understanding of the unnamed woman's subjectivity. Specifically, I argue that she is not without voice or agency as Harding suggests above, rather the narrative and its genre fails and/or refuses to recognize and/or represent her voice and agency.[11]

As several of the scholars mentioned above might agree, the fact that Judges 19 only offers an attenuated description of the woman's rape may function to suggest that her rape is less important than the homosocial bonding it facilitates. It can be seen to indicate to the reader/hearer that they ought to be less interested in the rapists, the raped woman, and her subsequent dismemberment. That we are merely required to see the event constituted by the double atrocity only to the extent that it is an occurrence previously unseen in Israel; the thing that threatens to disrupt the male political ambition of the Israelite nation.[12] This is heightened by the fact that the text, as Ken Stone has already observed, is almost entirely "free of evaluative statements from the narrator. The overall tenor of the story is generally recognized as negative but explicit judgements about who is considered to have acted appropriately or inappropriately, and upon what bases, are nearly absent from the text."[13] Nevertheless, even a glimpse of a rape event is difficult to unsee. Encountering it—even briefly—can stamp its mental image in our minds in a manner that lingers. It sticks with us and can impel us to visualize (even fantasize) about the rape for ourselves. This impulse that comes from the occluded representation of the woman's rape in Judges 19 has engendered this reading and has driven me to follow lines of questioning of the rape event with the use of a visual aid in the form of the pornographic genre known as Non-Con. Non-Con is a form of fan-fiction pornography that portrays the sexual assault of (predominantly female) characters taken from popular media. What has emerged as a more widespread and easily accessible form of Non-Con is Studio FOW's depictions of the capture and rape of protagonists from video games such as *Tomb Raider*, *Bioshock*, *Dead or Alive*, and *Arkham Knight*. Thus, the excessively violent yet diminutive, detail-deficient rape depiction in Judges 19 will be read *with* the elaborate, detail-obsessed depiction of the rape of *Dead or Alive* protagonist, Kasumi, in Studio FOW's production of *Kunoichi: Broken Princess* (henceforth, *Broken Princess*).

By reading Judges 19 with Non-Con, I intend to illustrate how the representation of sexual violence in the biblical narrative is dependent on violent depiction that is constructed through nexuses of mimicking, exceeding, as well as evading the physical (and psychological) effects of rape. The move to read rape representation in the biblical text with rape representation in popular culture is risky—and, in the case of *Broken Princess*, not likely a risk one ought to take in a classroom.[14] What Judges has not shown me I have sought elsewhere. I have returned with what I have found and I have crudely inserted it into my hermeneutical framework as I revisit the scene of the biblical crime. Taking my lead from artistic representations of the rape of the unnamed woman down through the ages coupled with the narrative's longtime salacious status as a "text of terror"[15] in the Hebrew Bible, I have made the explicit choice to read Judges 19 primarily as rape fantasy. By reading Judges 19 as rape fantasy I perform an avoidance of so-called real rape (that is the physical rape of material bodies). And by reading the narrative in tandem with Non-Con I heighten that avoidance.[16] Yet, as Stone's 1995 reading of Judges 19 notes, many readings of this text bypass significant questions in the interpretation of the narrative by making use of singular methodological approaches. He further asserts that, "the restriction of vision which our methodological decisions necessarily create can be particularly damaging to our understanding of the story."[17] Stone's critique is especially relevant to this essay because it opens up the discussion of whether academia or even pedagogy, alone, is sufficient to construct a resistant response to rape in (biblical) literature and culture. While recent scholarly readings of Judges 19 have moved towards more interdisciplinary modes of analysis (see Ng 2007, Masenya 2012, Helen 2013, Kuja 2016, Anderson 2016, Edenburg 2016) my reading of Judges 19 contends that the violence depicted in this narrative is still predominantly viewed as entirely and singularly excessive and graphic. As a result, the text has not been adequately addressed in its function as rape fantasy. Thus, I make use of Non-Con in this chapter as a way of learning and teaching the text's nature as a rape fantasy. To this end, the inclusion of Non-Con serves as a scopic tool used to discuss the desire for and dynamics of rape representation, to speculate on the narrative devices used to re-produce and re-present rape events, as well as to expose and critique the problematics of rape representation. The use of Non-Con to read Judges 19 grounds this essay in an approach that can be likened to Judith Fetterly's reading of American literature in *Resisting Reader* (1977), in that it begins with a recognition that biblical studies as a field is dominated by (white) male perspectives and proceeds to make use of reading strategies that are constructed as a form of resistance to normative white male scripts. According to Maaike Meijer, "Fetterly's resistance takes the form of arming women with different ways of reading the very same books."[18] For Carter Shelley, that means "1) Name the text's sexist subtext. 2) Expose the text's contradictory statements. 3) Undermine the text's pretensions to authority. 4) Recognize the text's fake claim to universality."[19] As this essay seeks to read Judges 19 differently, expose the phallocentrism of the text, and challenge normative representations of the self, it will also work towards constructing politico-pedagogical strategies for recognizing power and agency in those who bear the burden of objecthood.

The choice to read Judges 19 with Non-Con brings up the question of how the distinction between the narrative presentation of "real rape" and rape fantasy is made. The easy answer to this question for *Broken Princess* is that it is more readily identifiable as fantasy by virtue of its virtual medium. *No humans were harmed in the making of this video.* Or so the makers of *Broken Princess* would claim.[20] As noted above, the subgenre of pornography made by Studio FOW is most commonly referred to as Non-Con, which, as *Kotaku* writer Patricia Hernandez explains, "is short for 'non-consent.' As in, rape. The term 'non-con' could be considered a deflection, a way to call the genre something other than rape."[21] Yet, Hernandez also notes that, "some fans bristle at the mention of rape, even if that [i]s technically what is being depicted. But, in the eyes of a fan, it [i]s not as clear-cut. For fans of the genre, the characters in question could be interpreted as 'passionate'—forced sex becomes something admirable, a sign of love, or anticipating the desires of your partner."[22] Furthermore, the use of Computer Generated Images in Studio FOW's animation of Kasumi's rapes allows for a realism that on the one hand is excessive, but, on the other hand, is also evasive in its depictions. The animators of *Broken Princess* omit displays of blood or gore and exclude visible bodily abrasions, bruising, vaginal tearing/laceration and other material signs of physical traumas that are associated with material rape. There is the occasional use of graffiti-like markings on victims' bodies as well as handprints that function as indicators of the number of times Kasumi has been raped and the duration of the assault (often lasting days). However, the portrayal of the sexual brutality is rendered primarily through the use of a realistic female body that is penetrated by larger-than-life penises, belonging to demon-like male figures, which result in phallic distortions of Kasumi's bodily orifices.[23] We are shown copious ejaculations on the part of the rapists that fills the victim's belly and overflow out of her vagina. Kasumi's rape inexplicably functions to summon a (demonic) power, the Arch Fiend, which those who conspire in her rape exploit in order to succeed in the battles they intend to engage in the latter portions of the narrative's plot. Therefore, it can be said that the representation of rape in the *Broken Princess* narrative is *not* designed to reproduce the material features of rape as a physical event that a woman experiences so much as to extract select features of material rape and accentuate them in service of the narrative desire and pleasure of the (predominantly male) audience. While Non-Con shows an express interest in realistically representing rape as an event, it also actively de-humanizes and de-personalizes rape events. The rapes in *Broken Princess*—even though they require the realistic female body—are more specifically presented as a phallocentric spectacle and any tolls that serial rape take on Kasumi's body are only measured in the number of "loads taken." To be clear, *Broken Princess* is a rape-narrative about animated dicks that measure their power in forced sex. When Kasumi is shown to have no concern left for her own well-being, when her body has been so thoroughly abused that she is consumed by and completely at the disposal of the desires of her rapist and is even shown to take pleasure in her rape, she is *broken*. With this, Kasumi, now the Broken Princess, becomes the body that is symbolically sacrificed in order to resurrect the "Arch-Fiend"—the seemingly unstoppable masculine force that will battle and take possession of her ninja clan. Kasumi is represented only in relation to that which allows her body to be consumable and, once she is spent, the Non-Con saga quickly begins to prepare itself for the sequel; *Kunoichi Part 2: Fall of the Shrinemaiden*—the account of the abduction and rape of a shrinemaiden, Mimoji.[24]

While Judges 19–21 has interesting plot parallels to the ways the Non-Con films develop, this essay will focus specifically on the similarities in the ways in which the stories are told. Like *Broken Princess*, Judges 19 presents the reader/hearer with excess and evasion. As Stuart Lasine has noted, the display of hospitality shown by the woman's father towards her husband is performed in excess (19:3–9). The hostility of the men of Gibeah toward the old man's guest is gratuitous (19:22–25). The old man's willingness to sacrifice his virgin daughter and the unnamed woman is absurd (19:24)—although not entirely unheard of in the Hebrew Bible: witness Lot's and Jephthah's daughters (Genesis 19 and Judges 11). The seemingly arbitrary acceptance of the unnamed woman as sacrifice by the mob is inexplicable (19:25). The Levite's apparent amnesia regarding the event of the previous night when he opens the door the next day is outrageous. And his dismemberment of the woman whom he cruelly abandoned to the mob is doubly atrocious

(19:28).[25] As Ryan Kuja highlights, "Instead of being seen as a human being, as a female, as a daughter, the unnamed woman was objectified by males and was stripped of her humanity."[26] Yet, part of this objectification is a product of literary representation. Even if this story were based on a true event, the unnamed woman is necessarily constructed and contrived as a literary character, presumably by a man who does not experience the material threat of rape in a way that a woman would. Hers is a story-world, non-material body that cannot physically experience rape.[27] And thus, functionally, not so different from a CGI animated body. In addition to this, the de-personalizing, de-humanizing narrative mechanisms that animate the Non-Con saga, *Broken Princess*, are no less active in the tale of the Levites's *Non-Con-cubine*. As noted before, this nameless woman is scarcely visible in the narrative. The text leaves us with no doubt that she was raped and abused but refuses the reader/hearer any physical details related to her ordeal. Her rape event goes on to be named only as a "thing" in the narrative, an unspecified violation with an indefinite victim.[28] Although we see the woman lying at the threshold the next morning, any physical trauma specifically associated with rape, as in the CGI saga, is not represented. The narrative of Judges 19, which is centered by the raped woman, represents her experience only as a thing that allows others—the Levite and the virgin daughter—to escape rape. Both the unnamed woman and Kasumi are raped-things for rape-narratives that swiftly move on to abduction and more rape after attempts at tribal vengeance (Judges 21:20–23). Like *Broken Princess*, Judges 19 is a narrative concerned with phallocentric spectacles dependent on disposable female bodies. The Levite's *Non-Con-cubine*, like Kasumi, is represented only as a penetrable and expendable object, however, for the unnamed woman in Judges 19, objecthood is fatal.[29]

Madipoane Masenya Ngwan'a Mphahlele asserts that the unnamed woman is made invisible not only "by her lack of name, but also by her silence."[30] Indeed, the voice of the unnamed woman is never represented, a fact that is heightened by textual obscuring of her fatal moment(s).[31] As Masenya continues to speculate, "This was probably an imposed voicelessness. Silenced all the way through, even when she was thrown out to the rapists! This was clearly not silence by choice. Being surrounded by foreigners to her sex, thus a stranger in a patriarchal setting, the (strange) male narrator chose to deprive her of a voice even in the context of what can be designated an event akin to serial murder."[32] Furthermore, as Stone points out, the Levite "never speaks to her during the entire transaction, apparently plans to leave without her in the morning, and simply orders her to get up when he finds her on the doorstep."[33] She was not asked if she wanted to leave when they began the journey from her father's house (19:9). She was not consulted when the decision to go to Gibeah was made (19:11–12). The Levite does not invite her to consider whether she is comfortable to enter the old man's home

(19:18–20). And he certainly takes no time to make any requests before he brings her out to the predatory mob (19:25). Additionally, the brutality of her experience is only rendered through indications of the duration of her ordeal. While we can read her fall at the threshold of the door as a textual indication of the severity of her ordeal and that the woman may very well have been unresponsive as a result of her physical and/or psychological trauma, we do not know the extent nor the nature of any injury she may have suffered. Kuja—drawing on the work of Trible—argues that the "use of language describing her physical position emphasizes her stark powerlessness and immense degree of pain."[34] And while this is a reasonable conjecture to make, it is a detail absent in the text. The absence of any explicit depiction of the injury she suffers means that the reader/hearer, like Kuja, constructs most of the detail about the rape event from inference. That is, those who are capable of empathy imagine what she might have endured and those who have similar experiences of sexual assault recall and relate details from their experience in place of the absented descriptions. Arguably, this text narrates the rape event in a manner that expressly requires the reader/hearer to imagine the grisly particularities of her rape event themselves in order to engage with it. With the use of both excess and evasion of mimetic depiction, the biblical narrative—like *Broken Princess*—creates an unbalanced world in which events appear so bizarre in relation to one another that the reader/hearer may be persuaded to believe that such accounts could not possibly have any bearing on material reality. This form of representation, as seen with Judges 19 and *Broken Princess*, is what allows rape events to enter into the realm of the imaginary. It is what marks it as remote from material reality, in part or in whole, and as such it is what makes rape *fantastic*, what makes this *rape fantasy*.

#MENARETRASH: SEXUAL VIOLENCE IN THE MAKINGS OF NATIONAL CULTURE

But what happens when rape fantasy also functions as founding fantasy? When sexual violation is the foundation of the nation? In Judges 19, rape is depicted as the unrepresentable thing that all of Israel, no less than the reader/hearer, do not actually witness but are nevertheless forced to face, in part, in her body part(s). This story and the events narrated present a fatal disruption of subjective agency and identity that also function as a means to construct and assert subjective agency and identity. The future that the Judges text foresees, the days when Israel shall have a divinely appointed king, is grounded in the unseen event of the unnamed woman's rape during Israel's days without a monarch. The very same raped and dismembered body that marks the chaos infecting the Israelite communities is parceled out to all of

Israel, and paradoxically becomes that which incites the tribes to act as a unified body. To be clear, the text says:

> When he had entered the house, he took a knife and seized his concubine and divided her into twelve pieces, limb by limb, and sent her throughout all the territory of Israel. Then he commanded the men whom he sent, saying, 'Thus shall you say to all the Israelites, "Has such a thing ever happened since the day that the Israelites came up from the land of Egypt until this day? Consider it, take counsel, and speak out." 'Then all the Israelites came out . . . and the congregation assembled as one body before the Lord at Mizpah . . .' 'Tell us, how did this criminal act come about?' The Levite, the husband of the woman who was murdered, answered, 'I came to Gibeah that belongs to Benjamin, I and my concubine, to spend the night. The lords of Gibeah rose up against me, and surrounded the house at night. They intended to kill me, and they raped my concubine until she died. Then I took my concubine and cut her into pieces, and sent her throughout the whole extent of Israel's territory; for they have committed a vile outrage in Israel. So now, you Israelites, all of you, give your advice and counsel here and now.' All the people got up as one, saying, 'We will not any of us go to our tents, nor will any of us return to our houses. But now this is what we will do to Gibeah: we will go up against it by lot. We will take ten men of a hundred throughout all the tribes of Israel, and a hundred of a thousand, and a thousand of ten thousand, to bring provisions for the troops, who are going to repay Gibeah of Benjamin for all the disgrace that they have done in Israel.' So all the men of Israel gathered against the city, united as one. (19:29–20:11)

It is important to remember what Scholz and Keefe highlight in their readings of rape-narratives in the Hebrew Bible: that for Judges19—as in 2 Samuel 13 and Genesis 34—phallocentric epistemic perspective take precedence in the ways in which rape is represented and responded to in the text.[35]

After the initial horror, there are understandable questions but, more notably, there are ambitions. "Rape authorizes revenge," but revenge breeds revolution, and revolution will ultimately move the Judges 19 plot toward the monarchy.[36] As such, the rape fantasy that is the tale of the Levite's *Non-Con-cubine* can be seen not only as a product of but also as productive of ancient Israelite culture. As Scholz and Keefe highlight, it is a culture for which rape is concomitant with the political life of the communities. In this case, the desire for and question of rape is only relevant in relation to the desire for and question of masculine and/or national power. The rape as a crime perpetrated against the woman is circumvented by the men in the text and it is converted into an answer to the question of what inspires men to (re)form and fight for national allegiances. The unnamed woman's rape and dismemberment initiates an Israelite "brotherhood of guilt." It is no longer, and indeed never was a story about the rape of a woman—but rather a rape fantasy that displays the ways in which female bodies and their experiences are transferred and appropriated by masculine imaginations and are "used, abused, consumed, swapped, broken and discarded" to fuel the political desires of the text.[37] Israel is not just plagued with rape, it is re-made through it—and those who refuse the brotherhood of guilt that has been initiated by the rape of the unnamed woman are cut-off and are re-made, yet again, in abduction, rape, and murder.[38] The threat of rape to the Levite as well as the rape and murder of the unnamed woman in Judges 19 is the textual strategy for the justification of Israelite patriarchy as not only appropriate but necessary for survival.[39] Through the rape and murder of the unnamed woman, toxic masculinity upgrades itself to the sovereignties of biopower. Hence, I insist that the questioning of the rape event in Judges 19 cannot limit itself to questioning of the occluded rape moment(s). The use of rape fantasy in this story issues the casting call for Israel's necropolitics; it is used to further normalize what Achille Mbembe describes as "the generalized instrumentalization of human existence and the material destruction of human bodies and populations" in Israelite politics.[40]

IPSA DIXIT QUOD DIXIT: RESISTING FATAL OBJECTHOOD(S)

Arguably, fantasy, as a genre, functions outside the conventional boundaries and rules of reality, and thus is always, already in the business of *abjection*, the business of simultaneously setting and violating borders. Yet, once fantasy concerns itself with representing rape, and in the case of Judges 19, death and war, abjection is overlaid with abjection. Judges 19 and *Broken Princess*'s blatant disrespect for bodily borders, rules of hospitality and laws on physical violation, as Julia Kristeva's assertions suggests, is exactly that with which the abject is concerned.[41] The use of rape fantasy as founding fantasy in Judges is seen as a portrayal of the abject as defined by Kristeva as that which "at once represents the threat that meaning is breaking down and constitutes our reaction to such a breakdown."[42] To be clear, it is not solely the text's interest in representing rape that constitutes the abjection in Judges 19; it is also the seemingly paradoxical express disinterest in the raped woman that places this story in the realm of the abject. The excess and evasion of material reality shown in these narratives draws reader/hearer/viewer into an uncanny space where we must imagine omitted violence(s) ourselves. And yet, both narratives still dare us to find pleasure in them. The makers of *Broken Princess* assume more straightforwardly that there is pleasure to be found in its representation of rape. In a 2015 interview about the production of their early Non-Con films, Studio FOW founder, Dark Crow, suggests that if one does not take pleasure in the violent pornographic display of the Non-Con saga then there may be pleasure to be found in the knowledge that this film, according to his estimation, provides a safe outlet for sexually violent desire to be expressed and explored. And if not there, he suggests there is possibility for finding pleasure in the creative activity of the reconstructing and repurposing of the video game CGI bodies and their voices for the context of this pornographic film.[43] Correspondingly, within the wider context of Judges 17–21 we are repeatedly told that, "In those days there was no king in Israel; everyone did what was pleasing in their own eyes" (Judges 17:6, 21:25). (*Everyone? Even this unnamed woman and the many other violated women?*) Arguably, we are invited in the larger narrative context to take pleasure in the knowledge that this woman's violation, murder, and dismemberment will contribute to the undoing of the situation that did her in, the situation of everyone doing what was pleasing in his rapacious eyes in the absence of a disciplining monarch. Still, by giving rise to the occasion where we begin to consider our own pleasures in relation to this narrative, the text gives rise to the occasion where we ask ourselves, can we do the unthinkable? Can we find pleasure in the *grotesque*? Can we eff the ineffable? Can we fuck the fuckable? As such, Judges 19, like *Broken Princess*, presents itself as a "horrible beauty," where beauty is not a mere object within dualistic moral constructions of, but is constituted by "the ugly and the pretty, the grotesque and the ordinary," the disgusting and the pleasurable, visible and invisible.[44] To appropriate the words of Bülent Diken and Carsten Bagge Laustsen, the violence in Judges 19 as a representation of abjection is not constituted by "a pole in a binary distinction but indistinction itself."[45]

In the biblical narrative, rape *is* represented, but, it is presented as a literary separation that does not grant visibility to the event. It is presented as "an absence or gap that is both product and source of textual anxiety, contradiction, [and] censorship."[46] Reading Judges 19 in conjunction with Non-Con, then, allows us to see in the biblical text the representation of a topsy-turvy world, as Lasine calls it, that appears to be ruled by something akin to Lacan's modified Sadean maxim, "I have the right over [*je droit de jouir de*] your body, anyone can say to me, and I will exercise this right, without any limit stopping me in the capriciousness of the exaction that I might have the taste to satiate."[47] Lacan modifies the Sadean maxim of the right of enjoyment in a way that highlights its relationship to the Kantian ethical imperative. Moral logic according to Lacan's modified Sadean maxim is ruled only by enjoyment, or, in the case of the biblical text, pleasure. Indeed, for Judges 17–19, the narrated moral logic, *hayyāšār*, "what is right," is also "what is pleasing." While this libertinage is homosocially allocated in Judges 19, the evasion of violent depiction in the narration of a violent event nevertheless challenges all its readers to participate in its topsy-turvy world. Escaping the exposure to its terrifying sublimity and the effects of its homosocial liberties becomes difficult to do. And our moral-ethical questioning of the Judges 19 event then also presents us with the question of our own pleasures. We are faced with the question of whether or not we take pleasure in rape and its representation, even if it is a pleasure in reading, writing, learning, and teaching about rape representation in order to see its undoing. Assuming this text should indeed be read with and as rape fantasy (as I have) if or when we reach the end of this narrative, we find ourselves in a condition where the homosocial violence portrayed in the story has "left us without leaving us alone."[48] Judges 19's seemingly unlimited power to terrorize with hidden horror draw us in. And as we get caught up in the crises of the literary world, we become involved in what is not yet "an ultimate resistance to but an unveiling out of the abject."[49] Yet, what does this unveiling of abjection do? What does it offer? As witnessed by the discussion above, it appears as though the text itself only offers us the masculine gaze and the ability to gaze on its masculine spectacles.

When this is pedagogically posed, we are forced to ask, then, what do or what can we *actually* learn/teach by talking, reading, and writing about rape representation in our publications and in our classrooms? That is, if we define our knowledge and power to question rape and rape culture in relation to our capacity to read and understand texts such as Judges 19, do we make ourselves complicit in Israel's brotherhood of guilt? I will linger, here, in what may be a scandalous drama of my own making. *If* what I am considering is not exclusively the imaginary consequences of my reading of Judges 19 as rape fantasy with the use of Non-Con, then what is at stake is not only our ability to identify the ways in which this text has exercised a power to strip a woman of "life itself" but also the capacity to see the ways it has "attempted to capture 'resistance itself.'"[50] Whether we are outraged, entertained, or both, the text's terrifying sublimity demands our participation and response. If our responses are interested in resistance, then I firmly hold that we have not resisted the rape event or rape culture just by reading the text. We have, at best, come to know the maimed and unnamed in a different way than she is known in the text, but even then only to the extent that the men who have taken on the task of representing her and her rape allow.[51] Even though the rape event is difficult to unsee, the representation of rape is not necessarily the recognition of rape, and the recognition of rape is not yet a resistance to rape! Pedagogically speaking, the act of issuing outraged rejection of the narrative's violence does not do enough to learn/teach resistance to rape and rape culture. Such a response fails to recognize the ways in which the violence of sexual abuse is transferred and appropriated through erasure. Consequently, we remain in a position where we mimic the textual power and privilege allocated to men in our expressed desire for something different to what is presented. Once we begin to reject and separate ourselves from the narrative world, we re-constitute the abjection of an abject text. The excessive and evasive narrative mechanisms help to construct a world where masculinity, masculine power and desire, and the masculine gaze are near inescapable. Material concerns with rapists and victims of rape are made less interesting than political desire.[52] Yet, to subvert this dynamic, so long as we fail to adequately recognize and resist rape and rape culture, we are impelled to make use of similar mechanisms and epistemic apparatuses in order to attempt to make toxic masculinity and its abusive power less interesting.

Insisting on the conjunction of intentional attempts to identify and resist the epistemic apparatuses of rape culture means that we must learn to combat the dangers of the failure of recognition in representation. I want to stress that, the point is not to issue an attack to non-mimetic modes of representation, like fantasy. Rather it is point out the ways in which the combination of the excess and evasion of material expectation, *here*, is deployed as a failure and/or refusal to recognize or a misrecognition of the humanity of the other and the ways in which this kind of representation enables (sexual) violence. I suggest that careful, close-reading of rape representation in and out of the classroom can help us to learn the ways in which combatting inadequate and objectifying images and imaginings of the self and more especially that of the other can be a matter of life and death. I further insist that the undergraduate classroom is one of the spaces in which "the conversation that we are" can take place. (Not quite the conversation between man and the gods that Heidegger suggests—although that is not excluded—but the conversation between self and other, between bodies with and without power.)[53]

CONCLUSION

I am persuaded that the Judges 19(–21) narrative presents women as a *surviving object*—not individual women, but "womanhood" in entirety. For, when one woman dies in the story world, as a result of male callousness, there will always be other women to rape and abuse. Women constitute the objecthood(s) that is used as the "other" over and against which masculinity constructs itself into a singular distinguishable (national-monarchic) subjective identity. Yet, if Trible is correct that "[o]ur task is to make the journey alongside the concubine: to be her companion in a literary and hermeneutical enterprise," our investigations of rape and rape culture in and out of the classroom must privilege the unnamed woman as epistemic authority.[54] Which means we must betray the text's representation of her whenever we can, whatever way we can!

Judges 19:27–28 says, "And when her master got up in the morning and opened the doors of the house, and he went out to go on his way, and behold, his concubine fallen at the door of the house, with her hands on the threshold. And he said to her, 'Get up, we are going.' But there was no answer. So the man took her onto the donkey; and the man got up and went to his home." The unnamed woman, by necessity of the genre, must not be represented as having a voice of her own that can be heeded. And her agency cannot work for her own subjective expression. So then we must ask, why does the Levite stop to address her in this moment? As noted above, she was not consulted at any point in the text. Why would he not simply take hold of her and do whatever he wants with her, as he has done before? Her consent is never required prior to this and her compliance in preceding scenarios is not only implied but is, to some degree, expected. What is the point of his verbal demands, now? Has the text betrayed its own fantasy of her objecthood? As a move to resist the notion of her complete powerlessness and lack of agency, I argue that the moment with no answer, here, does more work than has been previously acknowledged and many commentators have too hastily moved on from this moment. I suggest that we read this portion of the text as an indication that her body, fallen at the threshold, demands a response. This paper chooses to see it as the consequence of an action by an objectified woman who has now made herself an obstacle in the way of her abuser. I argue that her body on the ground, touching the threshold, is an act of demanding recognition and thus an act of silent resistance. As I show above, Judges 19, as a rape fantasy, is dependent on an unresponsive female body that is rendered as a commodity for masculine political exchanges. The text uses objecthood, configured through exceeding and evading mimetic realism, establishes narrative apparatuses that make use of women and their experiences as raw material for the pursuits of male political agendas.[55] Although the physical consequence of her rape(s) is subject to conjecture, the consequence of her movement to fall and touch the threshold is clear. The Levite must first address her and her body before he can move on with his own desires and agendas.

The resistance is subtle but it is discernable nevertheless. Although the woman does not or cannot verbally respond, Judges 19, read as a rape fantasy, has already invited the reader/hearer to participate and respond to the rape event and thus offer the opportunity and responsibility to participate in her act of resistance and response to her demand for recognition with attentive care to silenced voices rather than acceptance of absented subjective agency. To be sure, then, if reading Judges 19 with Non-Con has taught us that the failure and/or refusal to recognize or the misrecognition of the humanity of the other is capable of producing and (re)presenting fatal objecthood, then, I hold to the claim that the learning/teaching experience facilitated by reading texts like Judges 19 is the site/sight in and through which the battle for recognition continues to rage.[56]

NOTES

1. Eugenie Brinkema, "The Fault Lines of Vision: Rashomon and The Man Who Left His Will on Film," in *Rape in Art Cinema*, ed. Dominique Russell (New York: Continuum, 2010), 27.
2. Brinkema, "The Fault Lines of Vision," 31.
3. Andrew Hock Soon NG, "Revisiting Judges 19: A Gothic Perspective," *Journal for the Study of the Old Testament* 32 (2007): 204.
4. Gerald West, "Reading From this Place," rev of *Reading from this Place: Social Location and Biblical Interpretation*, ed. Fernando F. Segovia and Mary Ann Tolbert, *Journal of Theology for Southern Africa* 103 (1999): 96.
5. West, "Reading from this Place," 95.
6. Cheryl Anderson, "Biblical Interpretation as Violence: Genesis 19 and Judges 19 in the Context of HIV and AIDS," in *La Violencia and the Hebrew Bible: The Politics and Histories of Biblical Hermeneutics on the American Continent*, ed. Susanne Scholz (Atlanta: SBL Press, 2016), 126.
7. Koala Jones-Warsaw, "Towards a Womanist Hermeneutic: A Reading of Judges 19–21," *Journal of the I.T.C.* (1994): 9, 11, 18; Mieke Bal, "Introduction" in *Anti-Covenant: Counter-Reading Women's Lives in the Hebrew Bible*, ed. Mieke Bal (Sheffield: The Almond Press, 1989); Cheryl J. Exum, *Fragmented Women: Feminist (Sub)versions of Biblical Narrative*. (Bloomsbury: T&T Clark, 1993), 182.
8. Alice A. Keefe, "Rapes of Women/Wars of Men." *Semeia 61* (1991), 90; Frank M. Yamada, *Configurations of Rape in the Hebrew Bible: A Literary Analysis of Three Rape Stories* (New: York, Peter Lang, 2008).
9. Patrick S. Cheng, "Multiplicity and Judges 19: Constructing a Queer Asian Pacific American Biblical Hermeneutic," *Semeia* 90 (2002): 199–20.
10. James Harding, "Homophobia and Masculine Domination in Judges 19–21," *The Bible and Critical Theory* 12 (2016): 41.
11. For a detailed discussion of the distinction and contextual implications of the difference between the politics of representation and the politics of recognition see TreaAndrea M. Russworm, *Blackness is Burning*: Civil Rights, Popular Culture, and the Problem of Recognition (Detroit: Wayne State University Press, 2016).
12. Eileen Julien, "Rape, Repression, and Narrative Form," in *Le Devoir de violence* and *La Vie et demie*," in *Rape and Representation*, ed. Lynn A. Higgins and Brenda R. Silver (New York: Columbia University Press, 1991), 164–45,169.
13. Ken Stone, "Gender and Homosexuality in Judges 19: Subject-Honor, Object-Shame?," *Journal for the Study of the Old Testament* 67 (1995): 90.
14. This is not to suggest that the use of rape representation in popular culture is altogether inappropriate in a classroom setting. However, while Non-Con pornography is making a significant contribution to the comparative analysis that forms the foundations of this essay's pedagogical exploration, its presentation of rape is overdetermined in the visual format and its use in a classroom would be an exercise of graphic excess that is likely more distracting than helpful for undergraduate learners. Pedagogically speaking, it is its contribution to the recognition of what is at play in the biblical text that takes priority. As such, the Non-Con, in my opinion, serves the classroom best as a preparatory scopic tool for the critical pedagogue by lending its stark visuals and visibility to the act of recognizing the nature of the biblical text so as to prepare instructors to facilitate engagements with the biblical text that are attentive to the ways in which the text can be seen to function as rape fantasy.
15. Phyllis Trible, *Texts of Terror: Literary-Feminist Readings of Biblical Narratives* (Philadelphia: Fortress Press, 1997).
16. This is a problem that has been highlighted to some extent by Exum when her reading of Judges 19 makes the distinction between "real" sexual/gendered violence and the violence suffered by women in biblical literature. Exum correctly observes that Judges 19 "perpetuate[s] ways of looking at women that encourage objectification and violence." Based on this, Harding will suggest that for readings of Judges 19, then, "the question is whether these forms of violence in connection with the biblical narrative are any less real." Yet, reading Judges 19 with

Non-Con assists me in illustrating the ways in which the narrative is less interested in material reality than we are. I argue that this story is not only interested in telling stories about what people do but is also interested in what storytelling can do to and/or for people. In turn, this chapter is interested in what reading and writing about biblical texts that represent rape can do to and/or for the learning/teaching about rape culture. This is done through an analysis of how this disinterest in direct mimetic representation of that which is understood to be real rape functions in Judges 19 if it is to be read as rape fantasy.

17. Stone, "Gender and Homosexuality in Judges 19," 88–89.

18. Maaike Meijer, "A Manual for self-defence: Feminist literary theory," in *Women's Studies and Culture: A Feminist Introduction*, ed. Rosemarie Buikema and Anneke Smelik (London and New Jersey: Zed Books, 1993), 27.

19. Carter Shelley, "A Widow Without Wiles: Proclaiming the Parable of the Persistent Widow (Lk. 18.2–5)," in *The Lost Coin: Parables of Women, Work and Wisdom*, ed. Mary Ann Beavis (New York: Sheffield Academic Press, 2002), 83.

20. Because *Broken Princess* is a fan made pornography spinoff of the *Dead or Alive* (*DOA*) video games, an understanding of the game's plot and how the Non-Con spinoff builds on this plot may be necessary for context. The premise of the *DOA* video games is relatively simple. There is a martial arts tournament in which the best global competitors compete in varying location across the world. Kasumi, a Kunoichi (female ninja), the protagonist of the *Broken Princess* fan-fiction, is one of the initial characters in the video game. She competes and wins in the Dead or Alive tournament, however, leaving her strict ninja community to fight in the Dead or Alive tournament relegates her to an "outsider" position that makes her vulnerable to attacks on multiple fronts. Allegedly, the Dead or Alive tournament organizers have a secret agenda called the "Omega project," which is a plan to create the ultimate fighter. In the Non-Con spinoff, the now vulnerable Kasumi is captured by a secret organization, presumably the equivalent to the tournament organizers, and it is through the rapes of Kasumi as well as other unidentified women that "Omega," who *Broken Princess* refers to as the "Arch Fiend" is summoned.

21. Patricia Hernandez, "The People Who Make Brutal Video Game Porn," *Kotaku*, last modified March 11, 2015, https://kotaku.com/the-people-who-make-brutal-video-game-porn-1690892332.

22. Hernandez, "The People Who Make Brutal Video Game Porn."

23. Hernanadez, "The People Who Make Brutal Video Game Porn."

24. Mimoji is captured after an attempt to avenge Kasumi and her clan. Although the connection between Kasumi and Mimoji is never made explicitly clear in the video game, the Non-Con spin-off suggests that they are from the same clan that has been resisting the DOA tournament organizers efforts to actualize the Omega project. What is noteworthy about the plot's movement to the rapes of Mimoji is the similarities (although apparently coincidental) to Judges's plot progression to the abduction and rape of the maidens of Shiloh. Although there is no indication that the Non-Con plot is based on Judges 19–21, it is striking that the characterization of objectified women in both stories consists of women who initially leave their domesticity (although they never fully exit male-dominated spaces) and abducted women, identified as maidens, whose rape is seen as a remedy for the threat of male extinction.

25. Keefe, "Rapes of Women/Wars of Men," 92; Stuart Lasine, "Guest and Host in Judges 19: Lot's hospitality in an inverted world," *Journal for the Study of Old Testament* 29 (1984): 37, 42, 45.

26. Ryan Kuja, "Remembering the Body: Misogyny through the Lens of Judges 19," *Feminist Theology* 21, no. 1 (2016): 92.

27. Exum, "Fragmented Women," 170–71; Don M. Hudson, "Living in a land of Epithets: Anonymity in Judges 19–21," *Journal for the Study of the Old Testament* 62 (1994): 50, 54.

28. Exum, "Fragmented Women," 185–86.

29. Anne Michele Tapp, "An Ideology of Expendability: Virgin Daughter Sacrifice," in *Anti-Covenant: Counter-Reading Women's Lives in the Hebrew Bible*, ed. Mieke Bal (Sheffield: The Almond Press, 1989), 163–64.

30. Madipoane Masenya, "Without a voice, with a violated body: Re-reading Judges 19 to challenge gender violence in sacred texts," *Missionalia* 40 (2012): 214.

31. Masenya, 210.
32. Masenya, 214.
33. Stone, "Gender and Homosexuality in Judges 19," 93.
34. Kuja, "Remembering the Body," 92.
35. Bülent Diken and Carsten Bagge Laustsen, "Becoming Abject: Rape as a Weapon of War," *Body and Society* 11 (2005): 112.
36. Coppelia Kahn, "*Lucrece:* The Sexual Politics of Subjectivity" in *Rape and Representation*, ed. Lynn A. Higgins and Brenda R Silver (New York: Columbia University Press, 1991), 141; Keefe, "Rapes of Women/Wars of Men," 92–93.
37. Caroline Blyth, "Lost In The 'Post': Rape Culture And Postfeminism In Admen And Eve," *The Bible and Critical Theory* 10 (2014): 4.
38. Diken and Bagge Laustsen, "Becoming Abject," 125.
39. Judith Fetterly, *The Resisting Reader: A Feminist Approach to American Fiction* (Bloomington: Indiana University Press, 1978), 178.
40. Achille Mbembe, "Necropolitics," *Public Culture* 15 (2003): 14.
41. Julia Kristeva, *Powers of Horror: An Essay on Abjection,* trans. Leon S. Roudiez (New York: Columbia University Press, 1982), 4.
42. Kristeva, 4.
43. raze, "Interview with Studio FOW-interview," *Lewd Gamer*, last modified September 9, 2015, https://www.lewdgamer.com/2015/09/05/interview-with-studio-fow.
44. Alex Garcia-Rivera, *A Wounded Innocence: Sketches for a theology of art* (Minnesota: The Liturgical Press, 2003), ix.
45. Diken and Bagge Laustsen, "Becoming Abject," 133.
46. Lynn Higgins and Brenda R. Silver, "Introduction," in *Rape and Representation* ed. Lynn A. Higgins and Brenda R. Silver (Columbia University Press: New York, 1991), 3.
47. Jacques Lacan, "Kant with Sade," *The MIT Press* 51 (1989): 58; Lasine, "Guest and Host in Judges 19," 39.
48. Kristeva, *Powers of Horror,* 208.
49. Kristeva, 208.
50. Jasbir K. Puar, "The 'Right' to Maim: Disablement and Inhumanist Biopolitics in Palestine," *Borderlands* 14 (2015): 5.
51. Russworm, *Blackness is Burning,* 22–24.
52. Julien, "Rape, Repression, and Narrative Form," 169.
53. Brice R. Wachterhauser, *Hermeneutics and Modern Philosophy* (Albany: State University of New York Press, 1986), 203.
54. Trible, *Texts of Terror,* 66.
55. Gayle Rubin, "The Traffic in Women," in *Literary Theory: An Anthology*, ed. Julie Rivken and Michael Ryan (Oxford: Wiley Blackwell, 2017), 902.
56. Russworm, *Blackness is Burning,* 24.

BIBLIOGRAPHY

Anderson, Cheryl. "Biblical Interpretation as Violence: Genesis 19 and Judges 19 in the Context of HIV and AIDS." In *La Violencia and the Hebrew Bible: The Politics and Histories of Biblical Hermeneutics on the American Continent,* edited by Susanne Scholz and Pablo R. Andiñach, 121–36. Atlanta: SBL Press, 2016.

Bal, Mieke. "Introduction." In *Anti-Covenant: Counter-Reading Women's Lives in the Hebrew Bible*, edited by Mieke Bal, 11–34. Sheffield: The Almond Press, 1989.

Blyth, Caroline. "'Lost In the "Post": Rape Culture and Postfeminism in Admen and Eve." *The Bible and Critical Theory* 10 (2014): 1–10.

Brinkema, Eugenie. "The Fault Lines of Vision: Rashomon and The Man Who Left His Will on Film." In *Rape in Art Cinema*, edited by Dominique Russell, 27–40. New York: Continuum, 2010.

Cheng, Patrick S. "Multiplicity and Judges 19: Constructing a Queer Asian Pacific American Biblical Hermeneutic." *Semeia* 90 (2002): 119–33.

Diken, Bülent and Bagge Laustsen, Carsten. " Becoming Abject: Rape as a Weapon of War." *Body and Society* 11 (2005): 111–28.
Edenburg, Cynthia. *Dismembering the Whole: Composition and Purpose of Judges 19–21*. Atlanta: SBL Press, 2016.
Exum, J. Cheryl. *Fragmented Women: Feminist (Sub)versions of Biblical Narrative*. Bloomsbury: T&T Clark, 1993.
Fetterly, Judith. *The Resisting Reader: A Feminist Approach to American Fiction*. Bloomington: Indiana University Press, 1978.
Garcia-Rivera, Alex. *A Wounded Innocence: Sketches for a theology of art*. Minnesota: The Liturgical Press, 2003.
Harding, James. "Homophobia and Masculine Domination in Judges 19–21." *The Bible and Critical Theory* 12 (2016): 41–74.
Helen, Chukka Sweety. "Voicing the silenced: A re-reading of Judges 19." *Religion and Society* 58 (2013): 97–106.
Hernandez, Patricia. "The People Who Make Brutal Video Game Porn." *Kotaku*. Last modified March 11, 2015. https://kotaku.com/the-people-who-make-brutal-video-game-porn-1690892332.
Higgins Lynn and Silver, Brenda R. "Introduction: Re-reading Rape." In *Rape and Representation*, edited by Lynn A. Higgins and Brenda R. Silver, 1–14. Columbia University Press: New York, 1991.
Hudson, Don M. "Living in a land of Epithets: Anonymity in Judges 19–21." *Journal for the Study of the Old Testament* 62 (1994): 46–66.
Jones-Warsaw, Koala. "Towards a Womanist Hermeneutic: A Reading of Judges 19–21." *Journal of the I.T.C.* (1994): 18–35.
Julien, Eileen. "Rape, Repression, and Narrative Form in *Le Devoir de violence* and *La Vie et demie*." In *Rape and Representation*, edited by Lynn A. Higgins and Brenda R Silver, 160–181. New York: Columbia University Press, 1991.
Kahn, Coppelia. "*Lucrece*: The Sexual Politics of Subjectivity." In *Rape and Representation* edited by Lynn A. Higgins and Brenda R Silver, 141–59. New York: Columbia University Press, 1991.
Kant, Immanuel. *Observations on the Feeling of the Beautiful and Sublime*. Translated by John T. Goldthwait. Berkeley and Los Angeles: University of California Press, 1965.
Keefe, Alice A. "Rapes of Women/Wars of Men." *Semeia* 61 (1991): 79–97.
Kristeva, Julia. *Powers of Horror: An Essay on Abjection*. Translated by Leon S. Roudiez. New York: Columbia University Press, 1982.
Kuja, Ryan. "Remembering the Body: Misogyny through the Lens of Judges 19." *Feminist Theology* 21, no. 1 (2016): 89–95.
Lacan, Jacques. "Kant with Sade," *The MIT Press* 51 (1989): 55–75.
Lasine, Stuart. "Guest and Host in Judges 19: Lot's hospitality in an inverted world." *Journal for the Study of Old Testament* 29 (1984): 37–58.
Masenya, Madipoane. "Without a voice, with a violated body: Re-reading Judges 19 to challenge gender violence in sacred texts." *Missionalia* 40 (2012): 205–14.
Mbembe, Achille. "Necropolitics." *Public Culture* 15 (2003): 11–40.
Meijer, Maaike. "A Manual for self-defence: Feminist literary theory." In *Women's Studies and Culture: A Feminist Introduction*, edited by Rosemarie Buikema and Anneke Smelik, 26–39. London and New Jersey: Zed Books, 1993.
Ng, Andrew Hock Soon. "Revisiting Judges 19: A Gothic Perspective." *Journal for the Study of the Old Testament* 32 (2007): 199–215.
Puar, Jasbir, K. "The 'Right' to Maim: Disablement and Inhumanist Biopolitics in Palestine." *Borderlands* 14 (2015): 1–27.
raze. "Interview with Studio FOW-interview." *Lewd Gamer*. Last modified September 9, 2015. https://www.lewdgamer.com/2015/09/05/interview-with-studio-fow.
Rubin, Gayle. "The Traffic in Women." In *Literary Theory: An Anthology*, edited by Julie Rivken and Michael Ryan, 901–24. Oxford: Wiley Blackwell, 2017.
Russworm, TreaAndrea M. *Blackness is Burning*: Civil Rights, Popular Culture, and the Problem of Recognition. Detroit: Wayne State University Press, 2016.

Shelley, Carter. "A Widow without Wiles: Proclaiming the Parable of the Persistent Widow (Lk. 18.2–5)." In *The Lost Coin: Parables of Women, Work and Wisdom*, edited by Mary Ann Beavis, 53–61. New York: Sheffield Academic Press, 2002.

Stone, Ken. "Gender and Homosexuality in Judges 19: Subject-Honor, Object-Shame?" *Journal for the Study of the Old Testament* 67 (1995): 87–107.

Susanne Scholz. Sacred Witness: Rape in the Hebrew Bible . Minneapolis: Fortress, 2010.

Tapp, Anne Michele "An Ideology of Expendability: Virgin Daughter Sacrifice." In *Anti-Covenant: Counter-Reading Women's Lives in the Hebrew Bible*, edited by Mieke Bal, 157–74. Sheffield: The Almond Press, 1989.

Trible, Phyllis. *Texts of Terror: Literary-Feminist Readings of Biblical Narratives*. Philadelphia: Fortress Press, 1997.

Wachterhauser, Brice, R. *Hermeneutics and Modern Philosophy*. Albany: State University of New York Press, 1986.

West, Gerald. "Reading from this Place." Review of *Reading from this Place: Social Location and Biblical. Interpretation Journal of Theology for Southern Africa* 103 (1999): 94–100.

Yamada, Frank M. *Configurations of Rape in the Hebrew Bible: A Literary Analysis of Three Rape Stories*. New: York, Peter Lang, 2008.

Chapter Six

To Confess the Fundamental Marian Dogma

Postulating the Doctrine of Mary's Reproductive Justice

Jeremy Posadas

Every December, children's nativity plays are staged in myriad Christian congregations throughout the world. In them, children are dressed as shepherds and angels, Mary and Joseph, and other characters drawn from the biblical books of Luke and Matthew. The goal is for these adorable performers to convey points that are regarded within the congregation as the essential meaning and significance of the birth of Jesus, in simplified language that can be understood even at a young age. In most of these nativity plays, there's a moment that passes quickly at the beginning, with an exchange between two children that goes something like this (from a script originally written for performance in a Protestant congregation committed to gender justice):

Angel: Hail, Mary! God is with you!

Mary: Wow! What does that mean?

Angel: Well in *your* case, it means that you will have a baby, and he will be Christ the Lord.

Mary: But that's impossible!

Angel: Nothing is impossible with God. The baby will be a child of the Holy Spirit. He will be called the Son of God and the Prince of Peace. He will teach people how to love each other, save them from sin, and give them life everlasting.

Mary: Does God really love me that much?

Angel: God loves all his children, past, present, and future. But you are special, because you have been chosen to bring his message to Earth.

Mary: *If God wants me to do this*, then that's what I'll do.[1] [emphasis added]

Most of the children performing and watching this scene likely do not know the details about how babies are conceived nor the proper form of obtaining sexual consent. But long before they understand those details, they are shown one version of how sexual intimacy and impregnation can work, in a context presented as the most important pregnancy in human history: namely, a male God has decided he wants to impregnate a woman and wants her to bear that child, he informs her of that decision, and the woman says she will do it because it's what he wants. In other words, for a brief moment during what is, for most children, the most emotionally invested time of their religious year, their consciousness is formed according to a basic logic of sexual and reproductive coercion, which lies at the heart of rape culture.

Recognizing the patriarchal violence that is germinated in such a seemingly delightful moment as a nativity play, this chapter proceeds from the conviction that Christian churches' authoritative teachings about Mary are so structured that they enlist Christians, from a very early age, in the perpetuation of rape culture. And because the doctrinal edifice that Christian hierarchs have built around Mary for two millennia is inherently complicit in rape culture, this chapter proposes that it must be re-constructed on an entirely new foundation. Just as Christians in centuries past have declared certain ideas about Mary—that Mary is the "Mother of God," that Mary was a virgin when she gave birth to Jesus, and so on—to be dogma, or divinely revealed truth, so this chapter invites all Christians, working through the various organs of polity that govern the several churches, to declare a divine truth that has been revealed to us: *the reproductive justice of Mary*.[2] This is proposed as the fundamental principle in accordance with which other Christian teachings about and practices relating to Mary shall be conformed and, as necessary, re-formulated.

This chapter is manifestly an essay in the constructive, normative articulation of Christian theology: a statement of what Christians ought to think and do. Within a volume intended as an instance of religious studies, the chapter is offered as one illustration of what it can look like when religious practitioners take seriously the insights of religious studies of rape culture and seek to transform their religious traditions on the basis of them. In this way, it is a form of applying religious studies. Of course, the practicing interior of religious traditions is not the only, or even a necessary, venue for "applied religious studies," and for those students of religion who are not interested specifically in transforming Christian rape culture, the chapter can at least be useful for making a contrast between projects of empirical description and those of normative construction. In addition, the final section includes some consideration of congregations as learning communities, and while congregations and classrooms are quite different in their pedagogical purposes, congregational practices that disrupt rape culture in the consciousness of religious practitioners may suggest some useful analogues, *mutatis mutandis*, for disrupting rape culture in the consciousness of students in religious studies courses.

The chapter's method, broadly speaking, is the "see-judge-act" model (sometimes referred to as the "pastoral cycle"), originally developed by Catholic theologian Joseph Cardijn and informing the work of many liberationist Christian communities.[3] It begins by diagnosing how hierarchal Christianity's authoritative teaching about Mary has the effect of forming Christians' consciousness in patterns that underlie rape culture. It then describes how the framework known as reproductive justice, when applied across the entire domain of social reproduction, offers a vision of a social order that labors to consistently disrupt rape culture and toxic masculinity and secure equitable possibilities of liveliness for all. This framework is the basis for judging that a new fundamental Marian doctrine—the doctrine of Mary's reproductive justice—is necessary, and it is proposed in the third section. The chapter then concludes by exploring how the church[4] can act by ratifying this doctrine as authoritative teaching and manifesting it in Christian practice. The chapter assumes as an interpretive axiom that sexual violence, reproductive coercion, and other violations of reproductive justice are incompatible with Christian teaching. And it shares theologian Elizabeth Johnson's conviction that "the living remembrance of this woman can function positively to inspire the struggle for God's compassionate and liberating justice" and, with her, it seeks "a theology of Mary that will promote the flourishing of women and thereby all the relationships and communities of which they are a part."[5]

CHRISTIANITY'S TEACHING ABOUT MARY IS COMPLICIT IN RAPE CULTURE

We must begin by recognizing how the core ideas about Mary that dominate Christian thought and practice are fundamentally structured through concepts that uphold rape culture. Although Mary has figured so extensively in Christian life—in both elite theologizing and popular devotion—that it may appear inaccurate to refer to *the* authoritative teaching in Christianity[6] about Mary, nevertheless, there are several themes that pervade the myriad Christian claims about Mary and form a core made coherent by the logic of rape culture. Furthermore, such themes have been reinforced for two millennia, to the degree that they can be said to operate as the widespread "common sense" of the church concerning Mary, against which feminist interpretations must struggle. Chief among them are "[s]trong emphasis on Mary's obedience, virginity, and primary importance as a mother":[7] Mary is, to cite one of her frequently used appellations, the "Blessed Virgin Mother" precisely because she is the "Obedient Virgin Mother."[8] Indeed, even when scholars try to demonstrate the multiplicity of interpretations of Mary, they inadvertently demonstrate how the vast majority of interpretations rely on seeing Mary through the prism of obedience, virginity (sexlessness conflated with moral purity), and motherhood.[9]

Feminist theologians have cogently critiqued this dominant doctrinal framework because of its many misogynistic underpinnings and effects. As Johnson writes, "the marian symbol became that of an idealized woman, created as an act of men's definition of women [. . .] that satisfied the needs of a monastic or ecclesiastical male psyche more adequately than it served women's spiritual search of social capabilities."[10] Feminist theologian Hilda Buhay explicates how Christianity's authoritative teaching about Mary "puts a premium on submission, blind obedience, and passivity" in women; "Mary then, when imitated, becomes an extremely useful means of domesticating women and other oppressed people."[11] Mental health practitioners Rosa Gil and Carmen Vazquez, analyzing Latina/o engagements with Mary, have identified a code of femininity that has analogues throughout Christian traditions: "*marianismo* [. . .] teaches women to live a life of self-sacrifice in order to please men," including the injunctions to "not forget that sex is for making babies, not for pleasure" nor to "criticize him for [. . .] verbal and physical abuse."[12] One of the roots of the church's complicity in rape culture is the fact that, as feminist Orthodox theologian Elisabeth Behr-Sigel writes, the authoritative teaching about Mary offers "the vision of an ideal woman" that can "go hand in hand with the way in which actual women might be despised or devalued in societies where patriarchal norms prevail[]."[13]

In solidarity with these critiques, I want to consider how Christianity's core teachings about Mary foster a mindset that is resonant with rape culture, starting with the consciousness of children who grow up in the church and have lots of exposure to it.[14] Year after year these children are encouraged to understand Mary first of all as "the Virgin."[15] Likely even before they are told how sex works, they are encouraged to perceive Mary first of all in terms of sex—and not Mary's own self-understanding of her sexuality, but her sexual status as determined by others. The message repeatedly conveyed is that it is proper to *perceive* girls/women first of all as sexual objects and to *value* them based on whether or not they have remained "pure." (And the primary ritual context in which this message is conveyed—Christmas—is, for a Christian child, the most clearly marked religious ritual and frequently the most emotionally meaningful.) Moreover, there is no man whose virginity is, in Christian practice, explicitly marked and celebrated; Jesus could correctly be referred to as "the Virgin Jesus" or "Christ the Virgin," but in contemporary practice he never is. This is an early theological legitimation of a sexual double-standard in which only female sexuality needs to be controlled.

Along with Mary's virginity, the other aspect about Mary that Christian children are most familiar with and that is inculcated in their minds for the longest time is the fact that Mary gave birth to Jesus. Again, it is not Mary's own self-understanding of motherhood (which would, presumably, cover many different elements and activities of mothering in which Mary engaged) that is celebrated, but her gestation and birthing of Jesus. Thus, to the degree that the woman lifted up as Christianity's ideal of femininity is recognized as sexually active at all, it is only in the act of childbearing: the image of a completely sexless woman is instantly replaced by that of a woman experiencing one of the common results of sex. Mary's basic theological significance—the reason Christian children are supposed to care about Mary at all—is because she became pregnant and gave birth to a child. (And even if Mary is assigned further roles such as intercessor or healer, these are derived solely as a consequence of her role as the one who obediently gave birth to Jesus.) This legitimizes, in the minds of Christian children, the idea that girls/women do not have value other than as sexual objects and childbearers, as well as an unattainable standard of being simultaneously sexless and procreatively fruitful. Even if it is not the express intent of Christianity's authoritative teaching about Mary to found rape culture, it nonetheless creates a background that renders some of the fundamental principles of rape culture morally acceptable, even natural.

One major aspect of Christianity's authoritative teaching about Mary that explicitly contributes to rape culture is the event known as the Annunciation (Luke 1:26–38), which raises the issue of consent. After an exchange in which the angel Gabriel declares that Mary will bear a child and Mary poses two questions to clarify the situation, Luke portrays her saying: "Here am I, the servant of the Lord; let it be with me according to your word" (1:38, NRSV). This is generally treated as an unambiguous confirmation that Mary gave her free consent to bearing Jesus.[16] Yet feminist scholars have drawn attention to the fact that, as Johnson puts it, "[t]raditional demands for conformity to patriarchal order [. . .] make women shudder before this text and reject it as dangerous to physical and psychological health as well as to a liberating spirituality."[17] In light of this, there have been several attempts at recuperating this text by demonstrating the ways Mary created agency for herself.[18] These certainly expand the range of how the text can be interpreted, but there are several constitutive elements of the text that continue to reinforce rape culture. These elements mean that, even in the best light, this text on its own cannot offer a model of consent that is necessary to eradicate rape culture.

Most fundamentally, this is not an interaction between equals who are mutually sharing vulnerability. Mary doesn't even speak directly with God, but with a messenger from God. At no point does the text suggest that God has divested himself (the masculine pronoun here is intentional) of divine power. In the power-structure within which God and Mary encounter one another, God remains the superior throughout. What Mary consents to, therefore, is not her own vision of and for her life, but a male superior's vision of her life, which that superior announced he wanted for her. Even if Mary enthusiastically liked God's plan, it is still a plan that *God* came up with, not she: this is absolutely *not* a vision of God respectfully asking Mary what she wants for her own life and how she wanted God to support her in realizing it and then honoring her wishes. Furthermore, did Mary really feel like she had legitimate options besides simply saying yes? Did she feel empowered to decline God's request or to propose alternatives? For if she *didn't* feel like she had other options, then her response is more like a concession in the face of superior force than a meaningful, non-coerced choice.

In addition, here we run into the major problem that Mary's story is always told on the basis of the foregone conclusion that she will, in fact, bear Jesus. When children hear the story, they know at the outset that there's only one way this story can end—and that ending is indubitably the greatest possible ending of all. In other words, even in hearing the story, listeners participate mentally in a scenario of pressuring Mary to bear Jesus. I call this phenomenon "christological sexual and reproductive coercion": Christian beliefs about the necessity and goodness of Christ's birth lead Christians to actively participate in a scenario in which Mary's sexual and reproductive self-determination is never taken seriously into account. After all, if Mary is "the linchpin in the economy of salvation,"[19] then it's inconceivable to Christians that she would or even could say no. If Mary terminated her pregnancy, Jesus would never have been born, the Word would not have become flesh, and the salvific resistance (and/or resurrection) of Christ would not have occurred. Therefore, in order for humans to be saved, Mary *must* give birth to Jesus. Christological sexual and reproductive coercion occurs when Christian theology puts Christians themselves in the mindset of pressuring Mary sexually and reproductively, imposing on her their own desires and judgments about what is morally best.[20]

To sum up: I contend that all the interpretive recuperations that might allow one to describe Mary's response as consent still do not add up to consent as we mean that term in feminist sexual violence prevention. A woman reporting a sexual encounter with the same fact-pattern as Mary's story would, in the world of sexual violence prevention, be regarded as having been a victim of sexual coercion (as well as reproductive coercion).[21] So long as the power-structure underlying this story retains the elements I've noted, no amount of agency can be interpretively recuperated for Mary that is sufficient to make the current authoritative teaching about Mary consistent with the eradication of rape culture. The church must proclaim a new truth about Mary if it wants to form its children into people who resist rape culture.

In light of this, I propose that Christians define a new dogma and proclaim a new confession regarding Mary, one that unambiguously contests rape culture in the church's teaching about Mary and commits and forms Christians to disrupt rape culture in both church and society. However, before describing some possible parameters for such a new dogma and confession, it is necessary to establish the theoretical framework that can serve as their foundation.

A NEW MARIAN DOCTRINE MUST BE FOUNDED ON REPRODUCTIVE JUSTICE

If the church is to break its complicity with rape culture, then it must reconstruct its authoritative teaching about Mary. But in order to do so, rape culture must be understood in relationship to reproductive justice, because rape culture must be replaced with *something*, after all. Reproductive justice (in its broadest sense) is, I argue, the best way to characterize the gender and sexual order of a world from which rape culture has been eliminated. Christians' goal in re-founding the church's teachings about Mary is not only the diminution of rape culture, but the ongoing promotion of reproductive justice. An overview of the reproductive justice framework will make clear how it contributes to undoing the very foundations of rape culture.

The reproductive justice framework was first developed in the mid-1990s by activist women of color who found that the reproductive choice framework that dominates white feminist activism (as well as the reproductive health framework privileged by clinical providers) did not adequately address the challenges women of color endure nor respond to the particular forms of reproductive oppression faced by women of color.[22] For, at various times throughout U.S. history, women of color have not only been forced to bear children against their will but have also been sterilized without their consent. Moreover, they have been widely denied access to the economic and social resources necessary to provide for the full development of their children's capacities. Thus, in its most frequent formulation, reproductive justice guarantees "(1) the right *not* to have a child; (2) the right to *have* a child; and

(3) the right to *parent* children in safe and healthy environments. In addition, reproductive justice demands sexual autonomy and gender freedom for every human being."[23]

Two additional formulations illustrate the power of reproductive justice as a moral vision: it is "rooted in the belief that individuals and communities should have the resources and power to make sustainable and liberatory decisions about their bodies, genders, sexualities, and lives" and will be achieved when all people, especially women and girls, "have the economic, social and political power and resources to make healthy decisions about our bodies, sexuality and reproduction for ourselves, our families and our communities in all areas of our lives."[24] These definitions make clear that rape and all forms of sexual and intimate-partner violence are violations of reproductive justice and, moreover, that sexual violence and reproductive coercion are part of a single matrix of reproductive injustice: both deny self-determination over one's body, gender, and sexuality.

These definitions, however, also imply a critique of toxic masculinity, which is a primary engine of rape culture. Toxic masculinity imposes normative pressures on boys and men to, among other things, avoid appearing "weak" in the eyes of other people, especially other males; suppress emotional connection with others as well as with themselves; express themselves primarily through physical force, often including possession; and emphasize the pursuit of things that involve danger to themselves and others.[25] It is the overwhelmingly dominant culturally approved script for masculinity, making it very difficult to escape as boys grow into men. It is, moreover, one of the things that drives rape culture, which is built on the assumption of men's entitlement to use women's bodies and of the acceptability of violence as a means to get sex: both of these have deep roots in toxic masculinity.

Being raised in toxic masculinity involves denying the gender freedom of boys, because they are restricted in how they can inhabit their bodies through gender. In addition, because toxic masculinity incentivizes actions that are harmful to self and others, it is a constriction of the social power necessary for boys and men to make liberatory and healthy decisions for one's body, one's family, and one's community; it pressures boys to violate their well-being and that of others. In other words, boys who are raised in a society where the dictates of toxic masculinity are imposed on their genders, bodies, sexualities, and lives are experiencing a form of reproductive injustice. Now, to be clear, when some of those boys then commit sexual or reproductive violence or coercion, and some of those boys support or tacitly permit it, they are themselves perpetrating reproductive injustice, for which they must be held accountable. My point is *absolutely not* to excuse such perpetration by pointing out how toxic masculinity is socially enforced. Rather, I want to acknowledge that the path to becoming a violator of reproductive justice (in the form of sexual violence) begins in most instances with having one's own reproductive justice violated (at a minimum in the form of having toxic masculinity imposed without one's consent). Reproductive justice, then, seeks to liberate *all* people from various forms of sexual and reproductive oppression. Boys and men have a direct stake in creating a society where everyone guarantees everyone else's capacity to "make sustainable and liberatory decisions about their bodies, genders, sexualities, and lives."[26]

Thus far we have been considering reproductive justice as it pertains to sexual activity, gender performance, and biological reproduction. But reproductive justice also addresses the conditions in and resources with which parents raise their children. One of its key insights is that the choice to have and raise a child is a desire not simply for the child to be born, but to sustain the child through the complete development of the child's capacities. Indeed, as a key manifesto of reproductive justice, authored by the organization Asian Communities for Reproductive Justice, recognizes, "[r]eproduction encompasses both the biological and social processes related to conception, birth, nurturing and raising of children as participants in society."[27] Yet, as theorists of social reproduction have argued, social reproduction extends well beyond child-rearing—central though that is—to encompass such things as "caring for the old, maintaining households, building communities and sustaining the shared meanings, affective dispositions and horizons of value that underpin social cooperation."[28] Social reproduction consists of all the activities by which people keep their bodies and their communities living, from one day and one generation to the next. Although all people (and society as a whole) depend on social reproduction, throughout Western history the work of social reproduction (which we can call social-reproductive labor, that is, reproductive labor in its broadest sense) has been profoundly gender-unequal, falling mostly on women to do.

In response to such inequalities, we can expand the notion of reproductive justice across the full array of social reproduction. So in addition to (and consistent with) the preceding principles, reproductive justice is realized to the degree that the tasks necessary to keep bodies and communities living, from one day and one generation to the next, are equitably shared by all people and everyone can equitably participate in decisions about how these tasks are allocated and structured.[29] Now, this principle does put each individual under an obligation to contribute their fair share of the social-reproductive labor that is needed for everyone to equitably survive—reproductive justice means that no one is free to freeload on others' social-reproductive labor, which would be exploitation. That is why it is necessary to ensure that everyone is able to participate in decisions that affect their social-reproductive labor. Moreover, no collective decision can override each individual's above-named rights to self-determination over their body, gender, sexual activity, and biological reproduction. Ultimately, reproductive justice is a vision of everyone contributing their fair share to creating the conditions and structures that secure everyone's bodily integrity and allow everyone to equitably pursue and enjoy liveliness.[30] How, then, can the church tell Mary's story in a way that manifests this vision?

RE-CONSTRUCTING CHRISTIANITY'S AUTHORITATIVE TEACHING ABOUT MARY

Given the pernicious depths of Christian complicity with rape culture, of which one key enabler is Christianity's authoritative teaching about Mary, it is necessary for the whole Christian church to adopt a new authoritative teaching. It is time for the Body of Christ in all times and places to define as dogma and confess a new doctrine: the Fundamental (or Zeroth) Marian Dogma—the Fundamental Confession Concerning Mary—namely, the doctrine of Mary's reproductive justice. By "fundamental" and "zeroth" I mean a set of principles that set the normative parameters for Christian teachings about Mary. The most basic of these, I submit, is that Christians must relate to and interact with Mary in ways that achieve and promote reproductive justice for her and for all people and, therefore, that all Christian explanations and interpretations of Mary must unconditionally promote reproductive justice for her and for all people. When Christians explain what Mary and God did, Mary's relationship with Jesus, and Mary's relationship with Christians, we must do so on the assumption that these things are meant to promote reproductive justice. Reproductive justice, and not Mary's virginity, obedience, or motherhood, must become the conceptual center of all that Christians think and say regarding Mary. What is being proposed here is that Christians, through the authorities of the several churches, ratify, as a revealed sacred truth, that reproductive justice is the fundamental condition and intended consequence of Mary's actions in relation to God, Jesus, humankind, and the whole of Creation.

Before elaborating some of the implications of this proposed doctrine of Mary's reproductive justice, it may be helpful to acknowledge two things. First, this doctrine is itself built on the presumption that God desires and is committed to reproductive justice for everyone. As noted at the outset, this is assumed as an axiom in this chapter; whether Christians ought to assume this about God is a matter that would have to be adjudicated elsewhere. It is certainly the case that many Christians, particularly male hierarchs, have often explained God's actions in ways that do not promote reproductive justice, but this fact does not eliminate God's own desire for and commitment to it. Second, many of the ideas here are novel imaginings that are not contained in the Bible and, moreover, seem to run counter to the plain meaning of the biblical texts concerning Mary, read as literary constructions within their historical social-cultural contexts. Yet what is being proposed here is not a declaration that the doctrine of Mary's reproductive justice can be deduced from scripture through rational analysis alone, but that it is a revealed truth—moreover, a revealed truth that ought to serve as the lens through which all Christian accounts of Mary (those articulated in scripture no less than those articulated in doctrine, and practice) shall be interpreted. In ratifying this as a revealed truth, Christians will necessarily be recognizing the possibility that the human writers and editors of the Gospels were so shaped by the norms of patriarchy in their social-cultural context that they were unable to reduce this truth to words adequate to clearly and adequately communicate it within our own social-cultural context.[31] What is being proposed here is that, in light of this, Christians declare: "We believe, as an act of faith, that the truth God would have us enact is that reproductive justice is the fundamental condition and intended consequence of Mary's actions in relation to God, Jesus, humankind, and the whole of Creation."[32]

So what other principles inhere in this new doctrine? In the remainder of this section I offer a series of possible elements that I believe are consistent with the reproductive justice framework (in its fullest sense), but I do so in a spirit of inviting Christians everywhere to ecumenically take up the task of articulating this new doctrine. This is not the final word, but a word of invitation to expansive dialogue. Collectively listening to the voices of all victims of reproductive injustice and in them hearing God remind Christians of the magnificent possibilities that God and Mary imagined together, Christians will learn how to offer a more truthful and faithful account about Mary. The following are some things that, I propose, can give a form to that account that aligns with reproductive justice.

Christians must proclaim as sacred truth that Mary's actions arise first of all from her own desires for her life—in other words, the principle of Mary's self-determination.[33] Mary acts based on her own sense of how she wanted to live in the world. Perceiving the injustices that structured her society, she longs for equity and liveliness, celebrated in the traditions of her ancestors. Her interactions with God do not consist of God telling her what to desire, but rather God and Mary discovering that they shared a desire that could be realized together: a desire to create a new kind of human community, devoted to ensuring that all people, with the Earth, can enjoy liveliness. Together they imagine many aspects of how to create this kind of community and what it would be like, delighting in the possibilities. And one of those possibilities that Mary imagines is bringing forth new life from within herself. Mary wants to expand her own liveliness through bearing a child. There are any number of reasons that Mary decides to try this out, but the point is that *she* decides it, based on what she wants for her own life. And she asks God to partner with her in realizing this desire.

This leads to another principle: God and Mary become mutually vulnerable with one another. Like Mary, God also wants to expand God's own liveliness, to experience being alive in a new way—as a flesh-and-blood human being. But God cannot do this by godself, because flesh-and-blood humans begin life being born from humans who are able to bear children. Thus, God needs Mary, depends on Mary, yet God does not simply impose God's desire on Mary. Rather, having listened to Mary's desires for her own life and liveliness, God imagines a way that God could support Mary in achieving one of her desires and, simultaneously, be supported by Mary in achieving one of God's own desires for God's own life and liveliness. God suggests this as one way for them to mutually support each other's desires.

And Mary is fully free to say no—and God would have honored her decision and celebrated that she made the decision for herself. This is the crucible for transforming a situation of coercion into one of genuine consent. In the words of feminist theologian Gabriella Lettini: "We have to believe that Mary did have a choice in this version of the story. A choice not to be pregnant. A choice not to carry out the pregnancy. [. . .] To understand God as a benevolent being in this story, we must believe that Mary somehow had a choice to bring forth more life. She must have been more than an empty and passive vessel [. . .] ."[34] Christians must proclaim that Mary was unconditionally free to reject God's proposal and that God would have fully respected Mary's decision; anything less is *a priori* denying Mary access to reproductive justice.[35] And because Christians tell Mary's story already knowing that she didn't reject God's idea, it is necessary to emphasize with extra rigor that, even if she had rejected it, God would have responded with respect and continued partnering with Mary to build the community they'd been imagining. God, in other words, would have responded with openness to finding ways of achieving their respective desires that were mutually chosen and allowed them to mutually support one another. Christians must make it perfectly clear that God did not respond in any way with anger or otherwise negatively and especially not with punishment or reprisal, for even a scintilla of such negative response would legitimize the sexual and reproductive coercion of Mary and, thereby, of girls and women in general.

As part of emphasizing explicitly that Mary could have said no, Christians must declare and embrace the possibility that God entrusted Mary with the option of terminating her pregnancy at any point. Again, forcing a pregnant person to continue a pregnancy to term is a species of sexual and reproductive coercion, at the heart of rape culture. Guaranteeing reproductive justice for Mary means ensuring not only that she was *not* coerced into conceiving Jesus, but just as much that she was not coerced into gestating and carrying Jesus to term. This idea likely evokes an aghast reaction on the part of most Christians: does reproductive justice mean Mary was perfectly free to terminate God in her womb?! The fear this raises is that, if Mary terminated her pregnancy, it would thereby terminate the *Heilsgeschichte* and wreck the economy of salvation. Again, this is christological sexual/

reproductive coercion, leading Christians to participate in pressuring Mary to not refuse God's sexual advances and reproductive demands.

But Christians must proclaim: if Mary had terminated her pregnancy, God would have been able to be born of another woman (or any pregnancy-capable human) who enthusiastically wanted to bear God as part of her own pursuit of liveliness.[36] Although God, in order to exist in the form of a particular human, needed to be born from *a* particular human, there is no reason that only Mary and no one else could have been that particular human. (In other words, the necessity of God being born from a particular human does not entail the necessity of God being born specifically from the particular human Mary.) The mystery of the Incarnation means that, in some unique sense, Mary infused God's being into the prenate (the term used by feminist Christian ethicist Rebecca Todd Peters[37]) she was gestating in her womb. But if Mary had decided to terminate this process, God's being would not thereby have been destroyed or harmed, because God's being is not a finite substance. Eliminating the christological coerciveness in the Christian understanding of Mary shifts the moral gravity: instead of Mary being celebrated as a reward for giving in to God's demand—thereby doing what Christians want her to do—Mary is celebrated for upholding reproductive justice and making the choice that makes the most sense to her, given her assessment of her situation.

Thus far we have explored how Christianity's authoritative teaching about Mary must be re-formulated so as to support Mary's pursuit of reproductive justice in biological reproduction. This also requires valuing Mary for all of the contributions she made rather than reducing her simply to her contributions through her womb. For this we must look to reproductive justice's broader horizon of social reproduction, which allows us to see that Mary's contributions to the Christ-event did not stop at the point of giving birth. Rather, Mary's social-reproductive labor is the first part of the Christ-event itself. And it is not through Mary's obedience and submissiveness to a male (God) that Mary does these things, but through self-determined, powerful, creative, and persistent action.

To begin with, we can characterize Mary as the initiator of the community that formed Jesus. This community, at the outset, included Mary, God, and Joseph. Mary was the initiator of this community because it is her free consent that brings it into existence.[38] Mary and Joseph, in the context of extended family and village life, did the exhausting activities that guaranteed day-to-day subsistence for Jesus and their other children. Moreover, we can suppose that they sustained a social world in which Jesus was exposed to relations of care by which people created liveliness with one another, which required emotional as well as physical effort. These labors take on additional significance if one follows Rita Nakashima Brock's re-interpretation of the Christ-event as the power that emerges relationally out of the whole "Christa/

Community":[39] Mary gathers the first instance of Christa/Community in which Jesus will participate. And later, after Jesus's death, the church that arose in his name would define itself in part through rituals of bathing and teaching (i.e., baptism) and feeding one another (eucharist)—actions whose life-giving power Jesus first experienced through Mary.

In addition, Mary revealed to Jesus the vision that she and God had been imagining together. Rather than assuming that God just implanted these ideas directly in Jesus's mind, Christians should recognize that Mary had a necessary role as the primary influence on and guide for Jesus's moral formation. Mary was Jesus's most important teacher; she taught Jesus the meaning of justice and cultivated in him a passion for its pursuit. She tuned Jesus's moral sensibilities toward the oppression all around them and articulated an alternative order in which everyone shares in liveliness created together. And she figured out how to convey these things in a way that stuck with Jesus all of his life and definitively stamped Jesus's actions. Certainly others, in both official and informal roles, may have been important teachers of Jesus. But it is Mary who defined the foundational terms for understanding and the framework for integrating others' teaching. Insofar as Christians conceive of Jesus as the Word, Mary is, on the basis of her labors, rightly to be revered as the Shaper of the Word (perhaps: the Wordsmith of God).

Having been taught by Mary, Jesus pursued a ministry that centered on social-reproductive activities that promoted reproductive justice. Teaching and healing, the things he is most frequently portrayed doing in the canonical gospels, are definitive elements of social reproduction. His acts of healing, moreover, were intended not only to relieve physical discomfort, but to restore social bonds between the person with the illness and the rest of the community.[40] Similarly, Jesus's meal practices sought to establish social bonds across lines of exclusion and the hierarchies that defined the Roman Empire.[41] Thus, Jesus's ministry can be understood as joining in his parents' social-reproductive project of creating a community where all mutually sustain the conditions for one another to equitably pursue liveliness.[42] The story of Mary raising Jesus to be a man who cares about everyone and whose focus is on helping build a community of mutual liveliness can teach Christian children a masculinity that lives and acts in disruption of rape culture.

THE DOCTRINE OF MARY'S REPRODUCTIVE JUSTICE AS PRACTICAL THEOLOGY

The theological shift I have outlined would mark a radical change in Christian teaching about Mary. But it is the direction in which the church must move if it is to contribute to the eradication of rape culture rather than operating as one of its most dedicated agents. In this final section, I want to explore what it could concretely look like for the church to make such a shift, considering doctrine and then practice. In the realm of doctrine—that is, what Christians officially proclaim and teach—I am calling for the definition of the Fundamental (or Zeroth) Marian Dogma, the Fundamental Confession Concerning Mary, but, again, the principles offered above are meant as a contribution to collective discernment about what should be encompassed within it. The first step must be for Christians committed to ending rape culture to earnestly proceed with ecumenical conversation about how to reformulate Christian teaching concerning Mary.

In referring to it as a Fundamental Marian Dogma, I am recognizing how major teachings about Mary have achieved official authoritative status within the Catholic tradition: by being defined as such either by a general council of bishops or, in modern times, by the pope. In most Protestant traditions, the analogous process would be the adoption of a new written confession concerning Mary.[43] But is it is necessary to have these ideas enshrined in a formal document at all? What's the point, particularly given vast diversity of perspectives available in the era of theological postmodernity? I contend that it is necessary for three reasons. First, Christianity's authoritative teaching about Mary, which actively promotes rape culture and reproductive injustice, cannot be dislodged *as* the authoritative teaching about Mary until a new teaching is declared to be authoritative over (or instead of) it. Second, official statements of doctrine are the mechanism that has the widest impact on how authorized teachers of the church, from pastors to Sunday school teachers to theologians, form Christian consciousness concerning Mary, and thereby shape in no small part Christian consciousness concerning gender. And third, the very process of getting new dogma defined or a new confessional statement adopted—even though, in this case, it will likely be the work of a century or more—can be a way of creating a new culture that venerates and vindicates reproductive justice and diminishes the church's complicity in rape culture.

As noted earlier, the doctrinal statement I have in mind would be the underlying norm to which other teachings about Mary would need to be conformed. While the principles suggested here could be seen as an expansion of the near-universally accepted doctrine of Mary as *Theotokos* (God-Bearer / Mother of God), the even more near-universally accepted doctrine of Mary's virginity is, of course, much less compatible with a doctrine of Mary that is unconditionally committed to eradicating rape culture and establishing reproductive justice. For the insistence that Mary must have been a virgin in order to have borne Christ is, on its face, a foreclosing of Mary's sexual and reproductive self-determination.[44] Moreover, it draws Christians into participating in the control of Mary's sexuality and thereby forms them for rape culture. Some feminist theologians have pursued wholly reconstructing the notion of virginity so that it is about bodily integrity preserved from sexual violence rather than preserving a woman's body from any sexual contact.[45] But if Mary's virginity cannot be reconstructed in a way that makes it totally opposed to rape culture and promotive of reproductive justice, then it will have to be abandoned.[46]

Yet changes in doctrinal standards do not automatically transform the life of the church simply by virtue of being adopted by vote or promulgated; they can only do so if they are turned into on-the-ground religious practices such as of worship, religious education, and spiritual formation. Indeed, the adoption of a doctrinal standard that re-interprets the story of Mary as an unconditional vindication of reproductive justice and rejection of rape culture would create a new impetus for teaching about these things. Rather than simply being "special interest" topics that a congregation may or may not want to address, once it is clear that they are necessary for rightly understanding the incarnation of Christ and the ministry of Jesus—and therefore lie at the very heart of Christian faith—then congregations must teach them in order to adequately proclaim the Christian faith. The most important practical implication of this is that congregations will have a positive responsibility to teach their children about and form them to struggle for the realization of reproductive justice and the eradication of rape culture. Curricula will need to be developed for use in Sunday school across the age-span. Resources will need to be developed for parents to talk to their children about these things. These are, after all, the central tasks of building any kind of culture—in this case, a culture of reproductive justice to oppose rape culture.

Along with doctrine, the second major area for transformation is in liturgical practices. Since a congregation's regular Sunday worship is, in general, one of the activities that definitively instantiates and reinforces its theological commitments, the kind of changes we are imagining here must be incorporated into such worship in order to effect deep change in Christianity. Moreover, worship is particularly implicated in changes to the church's teaching about Mary because worship is the primary mechanism through which this teaching is performatively inculcated. I am focusing my proposal on the portion of the year when Mary's role is near-universally foregrounded, even in congregations that do not structure their worship according to the traditional liturgical calendar, namely, the weeks immediately before and after Christmas (commonly designated the liturgical seasons of Advent and Christmas).

The traditional affective focus of Advent has been on hope-filled expectation, anticipating the birth of Jesus. Mary's decision-making process and consent are, in most communities, simply taken for granted. But the focus can be shifted to one of renewing individual and collective commitments to pursue the same shared vision of reproductive justice that drew Mary and God together and inspired them to create new possibilities of liveliness for all people. For example, each of the four Sundays could have a different sub-theme related to reproductive justice: (1) eliminating all forms of coercion in biological reproduction; (2) eliminating all forms of sexual violence; (3) ensuring that all parents have adequate resources to raise their children in safety and wellness; and (4) ensuring gender justice in the full and equitable participation of all people in society. The worship service could include a brief rite of proclaiming the vision of reproductive justice in that sub-theme and naming how that form of justice is denied to many people around the world today. Anticipating the birth of Jesus can explicitly be connected to the continuing struggle to realize reproductive justice for all people today.

Then, the Christmas eve and Christmas morning services can include an affirmation of commitment to realize reproductive justice. Yes, at first this would likely feel completely out of place for most congregations, but this just confirms of how removed the celebration of Mary's reproductive labor is from the desire for all people to live in reproductive justice that motivated Mary in the first place. The birth of Jesus, in the conditions of reproductive justice that, I've argued, Mary and God ensured were in place, is precisely when Christians should most clearly state their intention to create a world where reproductive justice is the condition in which all children are born and where all people are able to equitably create liveliness together.

Now, because there are twelve days between Christmas and the Feast of the Epiphany, there is always at least one "Sunday after Christmas" in the traditional liturgical calendar. This first Sunday after Christmas can be dedicated to celebrating the full range of Mary's efforts to pursue reproductive justice—for the purpose of both recognizing her necessary role in establishing a new sacred path (i.e., the Way of Christ) and not reducing Mary merely to the role of gestator of Jesus. Mary as one who imagined with God new possibilities of all people to enjoy liveliness, Mary as the one who achieved mutual consent with God in a unique way (but who was in no way coerced into it), and Mary as the founder of Christ's community are all examples of roles of Mary that can be venerated on this day.

In addition to Advent and Christmas, two other traditional Marian holy days can be transformed so as to commit the church to realizing reproductive justice and eradicating rape culture. March 25 (nine months before Christmas) is the Feast of the Annunciation, presenting a prime opportunity to proclaim and celebrate that Mary could have said no to God and God would have fully honored this choice. August 15 is, in Catholic and Anglican traditions, the Feast of the Assumption, based on the belief that at the end of Mary's life, her body was transported directly into heaven and did not suffer any earthly decay. This day can be a day of solemn remembrance of all victims of sexual and reproductive coercion and violence. Rather than focusing on the integrity solely of Mary's body, this day can affirm God's desire to safeguard *everyone's* bodily integrity from any form of sexual or reproductive coercion or violence.

The church's public witness for reproductive justice must, of course, extend beyond statements of doctrine and practices of worship to action in solidarity with all victims of reproductive justice and with organizations that work to realize reproductive justice in society, in all its forms. But the doctrine of the reproductive justice of Mary, which I have proposed the whole church ought to confess in word and deed, is a necessary foundation for such public witness. One of the purposes of publicly confessing Christian faith is to clarify or correct matters that, left unaddressed, would impair the church's basic competence to invite all people to create a new community of universal justice. The vastness of reproductive injustice—including but not limited to sexual violence, reproductive coercion, sexism, misogyny, femicide, heteronormativity, homophobia and transphobia, toxic masculinity, and much else—combined with Christianity's deep enmeshment with structures that perpetuate such injustice is just such a situation. Christians must, therefore, boldly proclaim and enact the sacredness of reproductive justice, so as to join Mary in giving genuine consent to the mutual pursuit of equitable liveliness for all.

NOTES

1. Gwynne Watkins, *Wow! A New Nativity Play for Kids*, 2 (New York: Beat by Beat Press, 2013). Watkins originally wrote this play for performance at First Presbyterian Church of Brooklyn, New York, a congregation known for its commitment to gender and sexual justice.

2. I dedicate this chapter to my colleagues, friends, and feminist collaborators Dr. Lisa M. Brown, Dr. Erin Copple Smith, Dr. Randi Lynn Tanglen, and Dr. Thomas Blake, who have shaped my thinking in these matters through generous conversation and the example of their courageous teaching.

3. See Consejo Episcopal Latinoamericano, *Concluding Document of the Fifth General Conference* (Bogotá, Colombia: CELAM, 2007); Australian Catholic Social Justice Council, *Reading the Signs of the Times: See, Judge, Act*, accessed June 14, 2018, http://www.socialjustice.catholic.org.au/files/Social-Teaching/Reading_the_Signs_of_the_Times.pdf.

4. Although it is disfavored, after the contextual turn in Christian theology, to speak of "the church" as a unitary thing, I have decided to retain that old language out of my conviction that eradicating rape culture and realizing reproductive justice is a task that must be universally taken up by all Christians, in every Christian tradition. Moreover, I want to make clear that eradicating rape culture and realizing reproductive justice are not "special interests" only of women in Christianity—they are the collective responsibility of the whole church, *qua* the church.

5. Elizabeth Johnson, *Truly Our Sister: A Theology of Mary in the Communion of Saints* (New York: Continuum, 2003), xiv.

6. Throughout this chapter, I use the phrase "Christianity's authoritative teaching" as shorthand for doctrines as they have been promulgated by Christian hierarchs and imposed over the centuries.

7. Johnson, *Truly Our Sister*, 7.

8. Surveys of the history of Christian teaching about Mary demonstrate the depth and persistence of these themes. See, for example, Tina Beattie, "Mary in Patristic Theology" in *Mary: The Complete Resource*, eds. Sarah Jane Boss and Tina Beattie, 75–105 (New York:

Continuum, 2004); and Tim Perry and Daniel Kendall, *The Blessed Virgin Mary* (Grand Rapids, MI: Eerdmans, 2013).

9. For example, Christopher O'Donnell taxonomizes Christian theologies about Mary into seven "models," six of which are variations on the obedience-virginity-motherhood theme: Mother of God, Icon of the Church (on account of her obedience and purity), Temple/Spouse of the Holy Spirit (obedient, giving her virginity to no man, *Panagia* ("All-Holy," on account of her obedience), Servant and Disciple, and Spiritual Mother. (The seventh model is the feminist one of Mary as a historical woman, struggling against injustice.) Christopher O'Donnell, "Models in Mariology," in *Mary for Time and Eternity: Essays on Mary and Ecumenism*, eds. William McLoughlin and Jill Pinnock, 65–89 (Herefordshire, UK: Gracewing, 2007).

10. Johnson, *Truly Our Sister*, 7.

11. Hilda Buhay, "Who Is Mary?," in *Women and Religion: A Collection of Essays, Personal Histories, and Contextualized Liturgies*, ed. Mary John Mananzan, 59–78 (Manila: St. Scholastica's College, 1992), 55.

12. Rosa Maria Gil and Carmen Inoa Vazquez, *The Maria Paradox: How Latinas Can Merge Old World Traditions with New World Self-Esteem* (New York: Putnam, 1996), 266, 8.

13. Elisabeth Behr-Sigel, "Mary and Women," *Sobornost: Eastern Churches Review* 23 (2001): 25.

14. In particular, I am concerned about how boys are formed into men, the group by whom sexual violence is predominantly enacted. See Jackson Katz, *The Macho Paradox: Why Some Men Hurt Women and How All Men Can Help* (Naperville, IL: Sourcebooks, 2006) and Michael Kimmel, *Guyland: The Perilous World Where Boys Become Men* (New York: Harper, 2009).

15. Because there is such great variety in how prominently Mary is featured in the theological practices of Christian congregations, some Christian children will have had lots of exposure to the aspects I discuss here, while for others it is more marginal. What I want us to focus on is how Christianity's core teaching shapes the gender/sexual consciousness of those children who *do* have lots of exposure to it as they are raised in Christianity.

16. See Johnson's discussion of this in *Truly Our Sister*, 254–58.

17. Johnson, *Truly Our Sister*, 255.

18. See, for example, Ana María Bidegain, "Women and the Theology of Liberation," in *Through Her Eyes: Women's Theology from Latin America*, ed. Elsa Tamez, 15–36 (Maryknoll, NY: Orbis, 1989); Hyun Kyung Chung, *Struggle to Be the Sun Again: Introducing Asian Women's Theology* (Maryknoll, NY: Orbis, 1990); Diana Hayes, *And Still We Rise: An Introduction to Black Liberation Theology* (New York: Paulist Press, 1996).

19. Richard Price, "Theotokos: The Title and Its Significance in Doctrine and Devotion," in *Mary: The Complete Resource*, ed. Sarah Jane Boss, 56–73 (New York: Continuum, 2004), 69. Price situates this understanding of Mary's role within the fifth-century christological debates.

20. The horror of such christological sexual/reproductive coercion is greatly magnified if Jane Schaberg is correct that the canonical gospels' accounts of Mary are motivated by anxiety over the "illegitimacy" of the historical Mary's pregnancy, possibly on account of rape. If that's the case, it means some of the earliest layers of Christian tradition responded to sexual violence in a way that begets yet more sexual violence. See Jane Schaberg, *The Illegitimacy of Jesus: A Feminist Theological Interpretation of the Infancy Narratives* (New York: Crossroad, 1990) and Jorunn Økland, "'The Historical Mary' and Dea Creatrix: A Historical-Critical Contribution to Feminist Theological Reflection," in *A Feminist Companion to Mariology*, ed. Amy-Jill Levine with Maria Mayo Robbins, 147–63 (Cleveland, OH: Pilgrim Press, 2005).

21. See, for instance, the definition by the U.S. Centers for Disease Control and Prevention (emphasis added): "Sexual coercion is defined as unwanted sexual penetration that occurs after a person is pressured in a nonphysical way [. . .] includ[ing] being worn down by someone who repeatedly asked for sex or showed they were unhappy; feeling pressured by being lied to, being told promises that were untrue, having someone threaten to end a relationship or spread rumors; and *sexual pressure due to someone using their influence or authority*." National Intimate Partner and Sexual Violence Survey.

22. Loretta Ross and Rickie Solinger, *Reproductive Justice: An Introduction* (Berkeley: University of California Press, 2017), 63–73.

23. Ross and Solinger, *Reproductive Justice*, 9.

24. SPARK Reproductive Justice, "What Is Reproductive Justice?," accessed March 30, 2018, http://www.sparkrj.org/about/whatisreprojustice; Asian Communities for Reproductive Justice, *A New Vision for Advancing Our Movement for Reproductive Health, Reproductive Rights, and Reproductive Justice* (Oakland, CA: Asian Communities for Reproductive Justice, 2005), 4.

25. See Douglas Schrock and Michael Schwalbe, "Men, Masculinity, and Manhood Acts," *Annual Review of Sociology* 35 (2009): 277–95; Jennifer Siebel Newsom, dir. *The Mask You Live In* (San Francisco: The Representation Project, 2014).

26. SPARK Reproductive Justice, "What Is Reproductive Justice?"

27. Asian Communities for Reproductive Justice, *A New Vision*, 2.

28. Nancy Fraser, "Contradictions of Care and Capital," *New Left Review* 100 (July/August 2016): 101. For a comprehensive overview of social reproduction, see Tithi Bhattacharya, ed. *Social Reproduction Theory: Remapping Class, Recentering Oppression* (London: Pluto Press, 2017).

29. In formulating this I've been influenced by feminist political theorist Joan Tronto, who analyzes the politics of care and offers a normative political theory of it, most fully in her *Caring Democracy: Markets, Equality, and Justice* (New York: NYU Press, 2013).

30. Note that, if *everyone* were equitably involved in social reproduction, it would offer a much wider range of acceptable ways for boys and men to perform gender, thereby disrupting toxic masculinity at its core.

31. For Catholics, this would involve invoking the teaching authority of the church to declare that this doctrine is revealed through sacred tradition, which is coequal with sacred scripture. For Protestants, this would involve finding that Mary's reproductive justice is an essential component of the witness of the Gospel, which is the canon-within-the-canon by which scripture itself is to be interpreted. Mary's reproductive justice can be understood as inherent to the Gospel because it is Mary's reproductive agency that is the very mechanism by which God becomes incarnate as a human being.

32. It must be admitted that one of the two theological ideas about Mary that are near-universally accepted (at least within Catholic, Orthodox, and Protestant Christianity)—that Mary is the "Mother of God" (*Theotokos*) is not self-evident or plain deducible from scripture, but was affirmed as a revealed truth by the Third Ecumenical Council, the Council of Ephesus, in 431. Price, "Theotokos," 60–63.

33. Sharon Jacob offers an extensive engagement with the Marian narrative through the lens of reproductive justice (and based on compelling ethnographic work) in *Reading Mary alongside Surrogate Indian Mothers*. While Jacob and I share many commitments regarding reproductive justice, she offers a seriously different account of choice: "[. . .] but what if the freedom to choose promises an independence contingent on one's enslavement? Mary, read through the living bodies of Indian surrogates, reflects a mother who resists the attempts to polarize her actions/choices into binary categories. She is a victimized hero who *willingly choses to be used* by both God and her people. See Sharon Jacob, *Reading Mary alongside Indian Surrogate Mothers: Violent Love, Oppressive Liberation, and Infancy Narratives* (New York: Palgrave Macmillan, 2015), xxiii (emphasis in original).

34. Gabriella Lettini, "What If Mary Did Not Have a Choice?," *The Huffington Post*, Dec. 16, 2013, https://www.huffingtonpost.com/gabriella-lettini-phd/what-if-mary-did-not-have_b_4445635.html.

35. I do not here address the issue of whether a concept of God's omniscience, by which God would have known that Mary would say yes, is compatible with complete non-coercion of Mary. I doubt that it is, but analyzing this is beyond the scope of this chapter and must be addressed in subsequent work.

36. I here assume as authoritative and rely on Rebecca Todd Peters's theo-ethical account of pregnancy and abortion, in *Trust Women: A Progressive Christian Argument for Reproductive Justice* (Boston: Beacon, 2018).

37. Peters, *Trust Women*.

38. We have no record of how Mary and Joseph came to be betrothed. Even in a patriarchal society such as first-century Galilee, it is certainly plausible that Joseph approached Mary with

deep respect for her self-determination rather than forcing himself upon her, however unique this would have made him relative to the norms of their society. This is the possibility that Christians must emphasize.

39. Rita Nakashima Brock, *Journeys by Heart: A Christology of Erotic Power* (Eugene, OR: Wipf & Stock, 1988), 52–55.

40. See John Dominic Crossan, *Jesus: A Revolutionary Biography* (New York: HarperOne, 1995).

41. See Richard Horsley, *Jesus and the Politics of Roman Palestine* (Columbia, SC: University of South Carolina Press, 2014).

42. See Elizabeth Schüssler Fiorenza, *Jesus: Miriam's Child, Sophia's Prophet: Critical Issues in Feminist Christology* (New York: Continuum, 2004) and Howard Thurman, *Jesus and the Disinherited* (Nashville: Abingdon-Cokesbury, 1949).

43. Such a document would, therefore, have to overcome not only centuries-old Protestant suspicion that to elevate the role of Mary is to take away from the unique power of Christ. The roles of Mary on which I have focused do not wholly avoid this problem, but they are not incompatible with the Protestant *solus Christus* principle. For the challenges of Protestant engagements with Mary, see Gaventa and Rigby's introduction in *Blessed One: Protestant Perspectives on Mary* (Louisville, KY: Westminster John Knox Press, 2002), 1–6; as well as, in the same volume, Miller-McLemore, "'Pondering All These Things,'" 100–105.

44. The survey, in Perry and Kendall, of classical (male) theological voices odiously appropriating Mary's virginity vividly illustrates how embedded in rape culture the doctrine is.

45. See, for example, Chung, *Struggle to Be the Sun Again*; Marianne Katoppo, *Compassionate and Free: An Asian Woman's Theology* (Maryknoll, NY: Orbis, 1981); Catharina Halkes, "Mary in My Life," in *Mary: Yesterday, Today, Tomorrow*, eds. Edward Schillebeeckx and Catharina Halkes (New York: Crossroad, 1993).

46. There remain two other dogmas that are authoritative in Catholic but not Protestant traditions. The Immaculate Conception of Mary is only necessary insofar as the drive to control Mary's sexuality is maintained; but it can be re-constructed in a way that is consistent with eradicating rape culture and promoting reproductive justice (e.g., from the very beginning of Mary's life, Mary was committed to reproductive justice). The Assumption of Mary is less tied to control of Mary's sexuality, and it can be similarly re-constructed.

BIBLIOGRAPHY

Asian Communities for Reproductive Justice. *A New Vision for Advancing Our Movement for Reproductive Health, Reproductive Rights, and Reproductive Justice.* Oakland, CA: Asian Communities for Reproductive Justice, 2005.

Australian Catholic Social Justice Council. *Reading the Signs of the Times: See, Judge, Act.* Accessed June 14, 2018. http://www.socialjustice.catholic.org.au/files/Social-Teaching/Reading_the_Signs_of_the_Times.pdf.

Beattie, Tina. "Mary in Patristic Theology." In *Mary: The Complete Resource*, edited by Sarah Jane Boss and Tina Beattie, 75–105. New York: Continuum, 2004.

Behr-Sigel, Elisabeth. "Mary and Women." *Sobornost: Eastern Churches Review* 23 (2001): 23–39.

Bhattacharya, Tithi, editor. *Social Reproduction Theory: Remapping Class, Recentering Oppression.* London: Pluto Press, 2017.

Bidegain, Ana María. "Women and the Theology of Liberation." In *Through Her Eyes: Women's Theology from Latin America*, edited by Elsa Tamez, 15–36. Maryknoll, NY: Orbis, 1989.

Boss, Sarah Jane, ed. *Mary: The Complete Resource.* London: Continuum, 2007.

Brock, Rita Nakashima. *Journeys by Heart: A Christology of Erotic Power.* Eugene, OR: Wipf & Stock, 1988.

Buhay, Hilda. "Who Is Mary?" In *Women and Religion: A Collection of Essays, Personal Histories, and Contextualized Liturgies*, edited by Mary John Mananzan, 59–78. Manila: St. Scholastica's College, 1992.

Chung, Hyun Kyung. *Struggle to Be the Sun Again: Introducing Asian Women's Theology*. Maryknoll, NY: Orbis, 1990.

Consejo Episcopal Latinoamericano (CELAM) [Latin American Episcopal Council]. *Concluding Document of the Fifth General Conference* [commonly referred to as the *Aparecida Document*]. Official English translation. Bogotá, Colombia: CELAM, 2007.

Crossan, John Dominic. *Jesus: A Revolutionary Biography*. New York: HarperOne, 1995.

Fraser, Nancy. "Contradictions of Care and Capital," *New Left Review* 100 (July/August 2016): 99–117.

Gaventa, Beverly Roberts, and Cynthia Rigby, eds. *Blessed One: Protestant Perspectives on Mary*. Louisville, KY: Westminster John Knox Press, 2002.

Gil, Rosa Maria, and Carmen Inoa Vazquez. *The Maria Paradox: How Latinas Can Merge Old World Traditions with New World Self-Esteem*. New York: Putnam, 1996.

Halkes, Catharina. "Mary in My Life." In *Mary: Yesterday, Today, Tomorrow*, edited by Edward Schillebeeckx and Catharina Halkes, 47–81. New York: Crossroad, 1993.

Hayes, Diana. *And Still We Rise: An Introduction to Black Liberation Theology*. New York: Paulist Press, 1996.

Horsley, Richard. *Jesus and the Politics of Roman Palestine*. Columbia, SC: University of South Carolina Press, 2014.

Jacob, Sharon. *Reading Mary alongside Indian Surrogate Mothers: Violent Love, Oppressive Liberation, and Infancy Narratives*. New York: Palgrave Macmillan, 2015.

Johnson, Elizabeth. *Truly Our Sister: A Theology of Mary in the Communion of Saints*. New York: Continuum, 2003.

Katoppo, Marianne. *Compassionate and Free: An Asian Woman's Theology*. Maryknoll, NY: Orbis, 1981.

Katz, Jackson. *The Macho Paradox: Why Some Men Hurt Women and How All Men Can Help*. Naperville, IL: Sourcebooks, 2006.

Kimmel, Michael. *Guyland: The Perilous World Where Boys Become Men*. New York: Harper, 2009.

Lettini, Gabriella. "What If Mary Did Not Have a Choice?" *The Huffington Post*, Dec. 16, 2013. https://www.huffingtonpost.com/gabriella-lettini-phd/what-if-mary-did-not-have_b_4445635.html.

Miller-McLemore, Bonnie. "'Pondering All These Things': Mary and Motherhood." In Gaventa and Rigby, *Blessed One*, 97–114.

Newsom, Jennifer Siebel, director. *The Mask You Live In*. San Francisco: The Representation Project, 2014.

O'Donnell, Christopher. "Models in Mariology." In *Mary for Time and Eternity: Essays on Mary and Ecumenism*, edited by William McLoughlin and Jill Pinnock, 65–89. Herefordshire, UK: Gracewing, 2007.

Økland, Jorunn. "'The Historical Mary' and Dea Creatrix: A Historical-Critical Contribution to Feminist Theological Reflection." In *A Feminist Companion to Mariology*, edited by Amy-Jill Levine with Maria Mayo Robbins, 147–63. Cleveland, OH: Pilgrim Press, 2005.

Perry, Tim, and Daniel Kendall, *The Blessed Virgin Mary*. Grand Rapids, MI: Eerdmans, 2013.

Peters, Rebecca Todd. *Trust Women: A Progressive Christian Argument for Reproductive Justice*. Boston: Beacon, 2018.

Price, Richard. "Theotokos: The Title and Its Significance in Doctrine and Devotion." In *Mary: The Complete Resource*, edited by Sarah Jane Boss, 56–73. New York: Continuum, 2004.

Ross, Loretta, and Rickie Solinger. *Reproductive Justice: An Introduction*. Berkeley: University of California Press, 2017.

Schaberg, Jane. *The Illegitimacy of Jesus: A Feminist Theological Interpretation of the Infancy Narratives*. New York: Crossroad, 1990.

Schrock, Douglas, and Michael Schwalbe. "Men, Masculinity, and Manhood Acts." *Annual Review of Sociology* 35 (2009): 277–95.

Schüssler Fiorenza, Elisabeth. *Jesus: Miriam's Child, Sophia's Prophet: Critical Issues in Feminist Christology*. New York: Continuum, 2004.

SPARK Reproductive Justice. "What Is Reproductive Justice?" Accessed March 30, 2018. http://www.sparkrj.org/about/whatisreprojustice.

Thurman, Howard. *Jesus and the Disinherited*. Nashville: Abingdon-Cokesbury, 1949.
Tronto, Joan. *Caring Democracy: Markets, Equality, and Justice*. New York: NYU Press, 2013.
US Centers for Disease Control and Prevention. *National Intimate Partner and Sexual Violence Survey: 2010 Summary Report*. Atlanta, GA: US Centers for Disease Control and Prevention, 2011. https://www.cdc.gov/violenceprevention/pdf/NISVS_Report2010-a.pdf.
Watkins, Gwynne. *Wow! A New Nativity Play for Kids*. New York: Beat by Beat Press, 2013.

Chapter Seven

Rape Culture and the Rabbinic Construction of Gender

Beatrice Lawrence

> If a virgin girl is betrothed to a man, and a man finds her in the city and lays with her, you shall bring both of them out to that city gate; you shall pelt them with stones until they die—the girl, because she did not cry out in the city, and the man because he afflicted his neighbor's wife . . . But if a man finds a betrothed girl in the field, seizes her, and lays with her, the man who laid with her, alone, shall die; but to the girl you shall do nothing. . . . For he found her in the field; the betrothed girl cried out, but there was no one to save her. (Deuteronomy 22: 23–27)

This famous biblical text addresses the question of consensual sex versus rape outside the context of a marriage. The case law contained herein concerns the status of a woman vis-à-vis a man when sex has taken place outside a sanctioned, proprietorial relationship: if a woman is married or betrothed, and another man has sex with her, what are the consequences? How do we determine her willingness in the encounter? Who has sinned, and who is a victim? What punishment is required? It is clear that the act of having sex with the woman is a sin: the man is subject to death in both cases. The sin itself, however, might be multi-layered: he has certainly committed adultery, which is itself punishable by death, but there is also reference to "affliction"; the woman has suffered in some way, and that suffering merits punishment as well.

In the verses following the text quoted here, we read that a man who seizes and has sex with a virgin who is not betrothed or married is subject to a different fate: the attacker pays her father fifty shekels and must marry her—and may never divorce her. The absence of a death penalty in this case is telling: he is subject to punishment, but it appears that the crime of taking another man's woman is seen as graver than afflicting a woman through sexual assault. His punishment, in fact, is punishment for her as well, though she is considered to have been an unwilling participant: she must spend the rest of her life with the rapist.

There is no specific term for "rape" in the Hebrew Bible.[1] It appears that the biblical writers considered, first and foremost, whether or not sex was licit; the matter of consent on the part of a woman was less frequently a point of concern. Exceptions to this pattern exist, of course: the stories of Dinah, David's daughter Tamar, and the concubine of Gibeah stand out as texts about rape, worthy of deep, ongoing analysis, and scholars focusing on these texts have contributed a great deal to our understanding of ideas about sexual assault in the biblical period.[2] But even here, in a passage that makes explicit reference to the question of consent, we lack precise language. We have to discern the values implicit in the text through reverse-engineering, and we get only a glimpse of the role of the woman's experience.

It is clear that a young woman (or girl) is in many ways "owned" by the man to whom she is betrothed (and certainly if she is married to him); in the absence of betrothal or marriage, she becomes the property of the man who raped her. However, it is not only the biblical view of sex as possessive and of female bodies as property that is evident in this text; we also see an element of what we now call rape culture: that surely, if the sex taking place were in fact rape, she would have called out and someone would have heard. Outside a populated urban environment, of course, it would not be possible for anyone to hear, and she is given the benefit of the doubt. If the act takes place in the city, however, the fact that no one heard her is seen as proof that the act was consensual. Here, we see the biblical equivalent of a contemporary trope: "Why didn't you cry for help?" or, "Why didn't you cry out *louder?*"

The impact of texts like these extends far beyond the biblical period. These texts do not exist in a vacuum, in terms of their original historical and social contexts; nor are they isolated within the centuries of their creation. These texts enjoy long afterlives. This is certainly true in the ongoing traditions of Judaism. Biblical interpretation forms the basis of Jewish thought since the late biblical period itself. Already in the later texts within the Bible, we see exegesis of earlier texts, in terms of both law and narrative. Following the biblical period, literature rooted in specific forms of interpretation flourished in Jewish communities. Rabbinic literature, dated until roughly the sixth century CE,[3] is a discrete body of texts that comprises multiple volumes. Though the medieval period brought with it new modes of exegesis, the hermeneutics of the rabbis and the texts they left behind are still used by Jewish communities today. It is impossible in a Jewish context to read and discuss the Bible without bringing the rabbis into the conversation; they remain active participants in Jewish life, serving as constant and ubiquitous conversation partners. Though they reflect the attitudes of male scholars engaged in a particular kind of discourse in late antiquity, their words are still present for Jews—as sources of normative practice, ethics, and anthropologies. These texts reflect and propagate worldviews, making them into effective tools for evaluating rape culture, revealing some constructs while decentering others. In the words of Michael Satlow, "texts are not innocuous."[4]

I have the privilege of teaching undergraduates about the Hebrew Bible and its afterlife in Judaism. My students study biblical texts as well as Talmud, Midrash, and Targums. This work falls under the general heading of "Religious Studies" in most cases because students are not only encountering the Bible, but also an entire tradition that grows out of it. Rabbinics is usually a foreign field for these students, and certainly an enjoyable one. But as conversations about rape culture make their way more and more into the undergraduate classroom, it becomes clear that it must serve as a point of analysis, and gendered lenses addressing it must come to bear on the material encountered by students and faculty alike. As such, it is my responsibility to name rape culture when we hear its resonance in rabbinic texts.

Scholarship on rabbinics and gender is a consistently growing field, including the works of Satlow, Gail Labovitz, Daniel Boyarin, Gwynn Kessler, Rachel Biale, Charlotte Fonrobert, and more.[5] However, few have engaged the question of rabbinic rape culture itself.[6] I seek to contribute to the early stages of that conversation here. Because of the limitations of space, I will be focusing on Mishnaic/Talmudic and Midrashic texts; I do not address Hellenistic Jewish texts, though they are worthy of inclusion in projects examining Jewish texts and rape culture. It is also important to note that the Jewish cultures represented by the materials discussed here were diverse, both geographically and chronologically; however, I will not be discussing redaction criticism or historical-critical analysis of these texts. I have a modest goal: to begin a conversation about how rabbinic literature presents rape, and how it supports at least two specific elements of rape culture: the belief that rape is the result of natural male sexuality, and the notion that the rape of a woman is less problematic than the rape of a man. Fortunately, one of the central elements of rabbinic hermeneutics is its dialogical nature: agreement is not the desideratum. Multivalence is assumed and celebrated.[7] In this way, the work I seek to do is well-supported by the texts themselves. I am guided by the words of Rabbi Tarfon: "It is not up to you to complete the task, nor are you free to desist from it."[8]

Chapter 7

SEXUAL ASSAULT:
THE EXPERIENCE AND THE PUNISHMENT

The rabbis of antiquity demonstrated concern about the nature of rape, and how to respond to it. Generally, the rabbis viewed the act as rooted in innate human characteristics (a natural outgrowth of sexual urges), but also recognized "the aggressive-sadistic element in rape."[9] When they turned to Deuteronomy 22, they seized upon the nature of the punishments ordained in the Bible, as well as modifications to those punishments in the case of mitigating circumstances. It appears that the rabbis were aware of the trauma that resulted from sexual assault. In a series of texts discussing the penalties applied to the seducer (Exod 22:15) versus the rapist (Deut. 22), we find reference to pain:

> The seducer gives [the father] three things, and the rapist [gives] four. The seducer gives for humiliation, degradation, and the fine. The rapist adds [to] his, as he gives [payment] for pain. . . . For what pain? Shmuel's father said: The pain that [he caused] when he slammed her onto the ground. Rabbi Zeira objects to this: But if so, [if] he slammed her onto silk, is he exempt [from payment for pain]? And if you say so, isn't it taught that Rabbi Shimon ben Yehuda says in the name of Rabbi Shimon: A rapist does not pay for the pain because she will ultimately suffer [the same pain] under her husband? They said to him: one who has intercourse against [her] will is not comparable to one who has intercourse willingly.[10]

Whereas the biblical text only prescribes payment of the bride price (and perhaps dowry) for the seducer, and a standard payment of fifty shekels for the rapist (of a non-betrothed woman), the rabbis break this payment down into segments attributed to elements of the woman's suffering, which include humiliation and degradation. In the case of rape, the rabbis see the *pain* she suffers as worthy of compensatory payment (though paid to her father, except in specific circumstances). Even as the rabbis are aware that consensual sexual intercourse can cause pain, they differentiate between that and the pain of rape; the latter is distinct.

On one hand, we see awareness of the pain experienced by a woman when she is raped. On the other hand, the rabbis address this reality not through discussion of women's experiences, but through evaluation of a legal point, concerning the appropriate punishment. This is by no means unusual. The rabbis trusted the formal legal process (*halakhah*) whereby they interpreted text to discern normative practice; they believed that if they walked through the texts carefully and closely, they would come to conclusions that would benefit all, because the *halakhic* process, after all, originated with God. But their views of the worth and dignity of women are apparent in some of their explorations of the *halakhah* of sexual assault. For example, in the

Talmudic tractate "Ketubim" pages 40a–b, the rabbis consider a woman who has been raped both vaginally and anally. Their concern is centered on the penalty the rapists should pay: are the fifty shekels ordained in Deuteronomy due from *each* rapist, or does the second rapist owe less (or nothing), since she was already no longer a virgin? Ultimately, the participants in the conversation raise the question of humiliation/degradation payments, but suggest calculating the amount based on how much her worth would change on the open market: "One considers her as though she were a servant sold [in the marketplace] . . . One estimates the difference between how much a person is willing to pay [for] a virgin servant, and [how much to pay for] a non-virgin servant to serve him."

What stands out in this discussion is the question of the woman's *worth* were she for sale as a servant/slave. Being no longer a virgin, she is apparently worth less on the open market; the rapist, responsible for her devaluation, must make up the difference. The fact that the woman in question was gang-raped and penetrated both vaginally and anally is, therefore, addressed in a point of law in relation to a woman's status as property.

When conversations about rape appear in rabbinic literature, we also find a perplexing fascination with the question of *sexual enjoyment* on the part of the victim. Two texts in particular (b. Niddah 45a and y. Sotah 4:4) raise this issue, both in the form of a woman who asks a rabbi a question, receives an answer, and then shocks the rabbi with her response. In b. Niddah 45a, we read that a woman is concerned about her ability to marry into the priesthood (an opportunity typically reserved only for virgin women):

> Our rabbis taught about a woman who came to Rabbi Akiva and said to him: "Rabbi, I was raped[11] under three years [of age]; what is [my status] concerning the priesthood?"
> He said to her, "You are acceptable for the priesthood."
> She said to him, "Rabbi, I will make a parable for you: To what is the matter comparable? To a baby whose finger is plunged into honey. The first and second times he cries about it, but the third time, he sucks it."
> He said to her, "If so, you are not fit for the priesthood."[12]

The woman surprises Rabbi Akiva by indicating that rape was initially a bad experience, but she grew to enjoy it. In the subsequent discussion between Rabbi Akiva and his students, it is revealed that Rabbi Akiva's response to the woman is a setup, providing his students with the opportunity to debate the law (which states that a girl under the age of 3, if raped, is considered to be a virgin). That point of law is significant in determining whether or not the woman may marry a *kohen*. In other words, the woman's lived experience of being raped as a young child is a tool for the rabbis to ply their trade. However, the source of shock in this tale is the idea that she grew to enjoy the experience. We cannot ascertain with certainty whether or not this conversation even took place, nor are we permitted access to more information about her experience; all we can see is that in this text, "the statement 'rape can be enjoyable' is placed in the mouth of the woman.'"[13]

RABBIS WILL BE RABBIS, OR: THE EVIL INCLINATION

An important element of rabbinic theological anthropology, which has a profound impact on constructions of gender, is rooted in a single letter. Because of the rabbinic practice of paying close attention to textual anomalies, the rabbis in both Talmud and midrash are troubled by the fact of a grammatical peculiarity in Genesis 2:7: the verb meaning "form" (יצר), describing the creation of the first human, is written with an extra letter (וייצר). A central element of rabbinic hermeneutics is the conviction that there are no "accidents" in Scripture; every sentence, every word, every letter contains meaning, and anything unusual we see in the text invites interpretation.[14] Hence, the rabbis ask, why is there an extra *yod* (י)? According to b. Berakhot 61a, each letter represents an inclination. Every human being contains two: the good inclination, which consists of mercy, kindness, love, and justice; and the evil inclination, characterized by greed, anger, pride, and lust. However, lest one be tempted to simply treat the human being as a moral binary, we see that the rabbis are not willing to vilify the evil inclination completely:

> Rabbi Nahman bar Shmu'el bar Nahman in the name of Rabbi Shmuel bar Nahman said: "Behold, it is very good." This is the good inclination. "Behold, it is very good." This is the evil inclination. Can the evil inclination be very good???[15] But without the evil inclination a man would not build a house, would not take a wife, would not procreate, and would not participate in business.[16]

The same force that can lead a person to commit an act of depravity is also responsible for central elements of survival; lust is necessary for the continuation of creation. What, therefore, constitutes sin? How can we tell the difference between good outcomes and bad outcomes, when the evil inclination is at play? It appears that sex between a husband and a wife falls into the category of "good" use of the evil inclination, and we even find that a man is obligated to satisfy his wife sexually, though she is not obligated to do that same. According to b. Ketubot 61b, a man's obligation to have sex with his wife is so serious that a schedule is established to ensure that her needs are met with regularity:

> Students may leave [their wives] to study Torah without permission for thirty days. Laborers for one week. The obligation to have sex with her is set in the Torah. Men who don't work, every day. Laborers, twice a week. Donkey

drivers, once a week. Camel drivers, once in thirty days. Sailors, once in six months. These are the words of Rabbi Eliezer.

The frequency with which a man must sexually satisfy his wife is determined by his profession, presumably because that affects his availability; sailors, for example, might be gone for long stretches of time out of necessity. Of course the rabbis (who were, themselves, Torah scholars) established these guidelines with an exemption for extended Torah study, but even that exemption is finite.[17] On one hand, this emphasis on female sexual satisfaction is, perhaps, laudable (especially in this time period), and the fact that a woman is not obligated in the reverse equates to a clear concept of marital rape: a woman must consent to every encounter (b. Eruvin 100b).[18] On the other hand, this is due in part to a construction of femininity that is profoundly passive. Moreover, that passivity is a form of punishment for the (perceived) sin Eve committed in the Garden of Eden. In the Talmud a list of curses pronounced upon Eve (and all women moving forward) includes a clause concerning sexual agency: "'And he shall rule over you' teaches that a woman desires in her heart (i.e., silently), while a man desires with his mouth (openly; he can ask for it)."[19] A woman's husband must commence sexual relations on a regular basis because she is prohibited from or incapable of doing so. In this formulation, women are meant to *receive* sexual acts, but not initiate them. In fact, a woman who is sexually aggressive with her husband is called *hatzufa* (shameless), whose children will be defective.[20] We see a trope familiar in rape culture: men are naturally aggressive, while women are—or should be—passive.

Even in the context of marital relations, we encounter the teaching that a man must curb his evil inclination to prevent the intrusion of illicit thoughts and behaviors. In b. Nedarim 20b, when Rabbi Eliezer's wife Imma Shalom was asked why her children are beautiful, she reveals a few details about her sex life with her husband:

> She said to them: "He does not speak with me [during sex] in the beginning of the night nor at the end of the night, but in the middle of the night. And when he speaks, he uncovers a handbreadth, and covers a handbreadth, and it is as if he were coerced by a demon. When I asked him, 'What is the meaning of this?' He said to me, 'So that I do not set my eyes on another woman [in my mind] and my children would come to *mamzer* status.'"[21]

According to this text, a man's lustful thoughts can corrupt even a licit sexual encounter. The evil inclination is at play even there: thoughts and deeds alike are dangerous outlets for a man's rapacious appetite. Other texts reveal a more permissive attitude towards marital sexuality, in which a couple may do what they please, and privacy is paramount. The language of those texts is, however, worth noting in the way it permits a man *using* his wife, even in ways she might not like. For example, we see an analogy of male sexual agency:

> A man may do anything he wants to do with his wife. It is analogous to meat that comes from the butcher: if he wants to eat it with salt, he may eat it; [if he wants to eat it] roasted, he may eat it; [if he wants to eat it] cooked, he may eat it; [if he wants it] boiled, he may eat it. It is the same concerning fish that come from a fisherman. . . . A woman came before Rabbi [Judah ha-Nasi] and said to him, "Rabbi, I set him a table, and he turned it over!"[22] He said to her, "My daughter, the Torah permits [him to do this to] you, so what can I do for you?" Another woman came before Rabbi said to him, "Rabbi, I set a table for him, and he turned it over!" He said to her, "How is it different from [his right to do what he wants with] a fish?"[23]

Though this text advocates for freedom in marital sexual relations, the power is decidedly one-sided: a *man* may do what he wants with his wife. Once a sexual encounter has commenced, she is to be available to him in any and every way (and hence, Rabbi Yehuda can offer no help), in the same way that a man can consume meat however he wants to. She is his meat. He may cook her however he wishes, and her view is irrelevant—just as a steak's preference for how one eats it is irrelevant.[24]

This objectification and use of the female body, here, is not a point of concern for the rabbis, but the potential for disaster concerning men's lust gone awry clearly is. The evil inclination makes a man susceptible to illicit sexual activity wherever he goes, and as such, a man needs to be protected against committing sexual violations by social constructs that prevent him from having the opportunity. B. Kiddushin 82a creates boundaries separating men from the opportunity to have illicit sex with children, women, and even animals:

> A single man may not teach children, nor may a woman teach children . . . Rabbi Yehuda says: a bachelor may not herd cattle, nor may two bachelors sleep with one blanket, but the Sages permit it. What is the reason? If we say it is because of [the risk that he might have sex with] the children, isn't it taught: They said to Rabbi Yehuda: Israel is not suspected of homosexual intercourse, nor of [intercourse with] an animal; rather, a bachelor [may not teach children] due to the mothers of the children [whom he encounters]. [Concerning] a woman [teaching children], because of the fathers of the children.[25]

The initial suggestion in this text is that a man will have sex with anyone (or anything) he can. The *baraita*[26] included here steps back from that possibility a bit, pointing out the tannaitic[27] teaching that Jews do not commit certain acts (homosexuality and bestiality). The reason Jews are not suspected of these acts is fascinating in and of itself: though the evil inclination is an integrated, elemental component of all human beings, the urge to commit these two *particular* acts was purged from Israel at Mount Sinai, when the Torah was revealed.[28] Hence we see two very different views of male sexual desire—one in which it runs rampant in relation to anything that moves and is a force that requires significant social control, and one in which acts deemed particularly offensive are no longer part of *Jewish* male sexual identity. However, a man is still at risk of having sex with any woman he can.

The issue in this particular text is more firmly in the arena of forbidden heterosexual encounters: in the case of single male or female teachers, it has to do with their access to adults with whom they might have heterosexual sex. In other words, these adults cannot be trusted to be alone with members of the opposite sex. But the anthropology behind this concept is not applied in the same way to men and women. Men are more able to serve as arbiters and protectors of each other's morality; women are more likely to give in to (though not instigate) a sexual encounter. We see this in b. Kiddushin 80b: "A man may not be alone with two women, but a woman may be alone with two men . . . What is the reason? The school of Eliyahu taught: women are simple-minded [and hence, easily seduced]." In this case, the men can prevent each other from sinning; the same passage points out that if a man is alone with two women and one of them is his wife, he is also trusted, because his wife is there. Men are in charge of the systems that keep their lustful natures in check; men have that power. They are able to respond to social structures and pressure; women are simply easy fodder for the evil inclination.

Another structure put in place to protect men from themselves is focused on regulating women's bodies, beyond matters of seclusion: the laws of modesty. Though we find within rabbinic texts teachings about modest comportment and appearance for both men and women,[29] the system of female modesty is uniquely stringent, and rooted in the notion that a woman's body is too much of a temptation for a man. The goal, according to these texts, is to cover as much of a woman's body as possible. When a sexually alluring part of a woman is uncovered, it is referred to as *ervah*, a word which references both nakedness and sexual contact. The body parts highlighted in these texts serve to mark categorical boundaries—the covering of breasts, thighs, and the like are assumed. Instead, the rabbis focus on elbows, ankles, hair, and the voice as parts of a woman's physicality that will drive a man to distraction.[30] It is best, actually, for a woman not to be seen; Sarah is lauded as an example of a modest woman because she stayed within the tent when the three angels visited Abraham (Genesis 18).[31] Though certain parts of a woman are set aside for the sole consumption of her husband (such as her hair), the rabbis also advocate modesty in the home: "Be modest before your husbands, do not eat bread before them . . . And do not evacuate in the place where your husbands evacuate."[32] The latter definition of modesty, modesty of the home, refers to the danger that a man might be disgusted by his wife's bodily needs, how much a woman eats, or by her relieving herself. The former, however, is a clear example of a concept prevalent today, one central in the constructs of rape culture: that if a woman is wearing too little, she is inviting sexual attention. If a woman is not appropriately covered up, she is deemed to be sexually permissive and brazen (*hatzufah*), and by violating the male-constructed systems to protect themselves from their evil inclinations, she is subject to their appetites. This is the rabbinic version of "Well, what were you wearing?" The fundamental male nature assumed within these texts is one of deep, barely controllable sexual urges. Male sexuality as presented here is inherently opportunistic, aggressive, and devoid of moral reasoning; a person's maleness, therefore, includes a sexual force that is destructive and easily unhinged. That nature must be controlled by external forces, and in the absence of those structures, it is simply expected that a man will take anyone—or anything—sexually, even with violence. The rabbis are not advocating rape—in fact, they are seeking to prevent it; but it is unclear if the sin they are guarding against is related to the suffering of a non-consenting victim, or about adhering to a construct of "maleness" that is marked in part by self-control.[33]

POISON IVY: WOMEN AS SEXUAL TRAPS

Men and women alike bear the evil inclination. Women's innate sexual passivity renders them unlikely perpetrators of sexual assault (as in the contemporary myth that "women don't rape"), but they are also at a disadvantage when it comes to controlling their inclination due to their natures. Their inclination runs amok, and in its most dangerous expressions results in seduction of men. The rabbinic view of female sexuality is that it is a hungry one: when women are left alone with men, when they drink, and when they subvert the control of social structures designed to protect men, they lead men into danger—not through sexual aggression, but by seduction.

The biblical book of Proverbs plays a role in the rabbinic construction of female sexuality: it presents a metaphor for the search for wisdom using two female figures: Woman Wisdom and the Dangerous Woman.[34] In rabbinic literature, the feminine figure of Wisdom is transformed into Torah: Torah was present before creation; Torah is a source of life and joy for those who cleave to her; Torah will lead you to wellbeing and safety.[35] But Torah is essentially the purview of men (as will be discussed, below); hence, this important element of what we could even term *salvation* is available only to men. This female figure is now their property. To add insult to injury, the model of the Dangerous Woman remains intact, but is projected onto *all* women. Whereas Woman Wisdom has moved into the male sphere, the Dangerous Woman has become ubiquitous outside that sphere.

The dangerous woman is identified with all women, according to Genesis Rabbah; when God created Eve, he whispered to each part of her, "be modest, be chaste"; however, the text informs us, the woman is the opposite.[36] Numbers Rabbah 9 even describes her as a sexual 'highway to Hell": "How is she more bitter than death? Because she causes him anguish in this world, for his going astray after her; and in the end, she brings him down to Gehinnom (the rabbinic conception of a realm of punishment, similar to Hell)." The Mishnah shares this view: "From this, the Sages said: Every time a man increases conversation with the woman, he causes evil to himself and neglects the words of Torah. In the end, he inherits Gehinnom."[37] When women drink, they are particularly dangerous:

> It was taught in a baraita: one cup of wine is appropriate for a woman; two cups is a disgrace; three, and she will verbally request [sexual intercourse]; four and she will even [request sex] from a donkey in the marketplace—for she is not particular [about with whom she has sexual intercourse].[38]

It is therefore not only women's nature to be lusty; they are also seduction time bombs who can lead a man to destruction with little warning.

How is the evil inclination to be contained? The role of Torah study in the lives of men as a source of control over the evil inclination is evident in several texts:

> So the Holy One, Blessed be He, said to Israel: My sons, I created the evil inclination, and I created for it Torah study as an antidote; and if you busy yourselves with Torah you will not be given into its hands . . . And if you do not busy yourselves with Torah, you will be given into its hands . . . A sage from the school of Rabbi Yishmael taught: My son, if this awful one [the evil inclination] touches you, take it into the house of study.[39]

However, while the rabbis advocate Torah study for men as a panacea, a means of controlling the evil inclination, they are divided on the question of teaching Torah to women. We find in the Mishnah a teaching advocating female Torah study, but it is rooted in a deeply misogynistic biblical text concerning the ritual trial by ordeal a woman must undergo when her husband suspects her of adultery (Num 5:12–31). Any man who suspects his wife has been unfaithful may subject her to a trial in which she is publicly shamed, and wherein she might experience a miscarriage, prolapsed uterus, or more. For the rabbis concerned about women and Torah study, this is the locus of interest: "From here Ben Azai says: A man is obligated to teach his daughter Torah, for if she drinks [as a suspected adulteress], she will know that the merit suspends it for her."[40] In other words, if a woman has studied Torah, the *Sotah* ritual will not have an impact on her. She will emerge from it unscathed. This view is certainly in the minority, however; the very next sentence expresses the opposite view, with strong language: "Rabbi Eliezer says: Whoever teaches his daughter Torah is considered as if he taught her lewdness."[41] Sifrei to Deuteronomy states: "And you shall teach them to your sons, to speak with them, and not your daughters."[42] Rabbi Eliezer even states that "the words of Torah should be burned rather than entrusted to women."[43] Though ultimately, rabbinic sentiment veered away from burning the Torah, a general ambivalence about women studying Torah prevailed.

A notable exception cited on this topic is that of Beruriah, a Torah scholar in her own right.[44] Her intellectual capacity is referenced throughout the Talmud; b. Pesachim 62b reports that she was able to learn three hundred laws in one day. She chided other scholars for their assumptions that women were weak-minded, and was not above shaming those she bested in arguments.[45] However, in the Middle Ages, the noted scholar Rashi recorded a tradition regarding the end of her life that, to an extent, undermines the significance of her role as a female Torah scholar: in commentary to b. Avodah Zarah 18b, Rashi reports that her husband went to save her sister from captivity, and arranged for his own student to seduce Beruriah while he was gone to test her, and to prove that women are, in fact, "light-minded." Though she initially refused the student's advances, she ultimately gave in. When it came to light that her husband had arranged the trap, she committed suicide. Thus, in the world of traditional Jewish interpretation, even a great scholar like Beruriah falls prey to the fact that women cannot control their own evil inclinations.

Ultimately, the rabbinic construction of the evil inclination aligns significantly with certain elements of rape culture: women are naturally passive and seductive, while men are naturally aggressive and are, by nature, going to rape if this nature is not controlled by external structures. Though the rabbis are not advocating rape, they are espousing the idea that men are naturally, innately drawn to it. In all of these discussions about the evil inclination and male sexual appetites, the rabbis do not distinguish between rape and sex with consent; the violation of female (or animal) bodies is a topic of interest because of concern about male sexual morality, not because of the suffering experienced by the victims of unwanted sexual attention.

AS LONG AS THEY DON'T RAPE MEN

In both Genesis 19 and Judges 19, the biblical text presents an underlying morality concerning sexual assault: that it is preferable that men rape women, rather than other men. The stories have similar structures: visitors to a town are offered lodging by a hospitable person and are then subject to the threat of rape by the rest of the town's men, who crowd around the house and demand that the visitors be handed over. In each case, women are offered in the place of men: virgin daughters, and, in Judges, a concubine. The message is clear: it would be better for the gang outside the house to rape women rather than men.

What does it mean for a man to be raped? Why is the violence considered to be so much greater? Rabbinic responses to this question are grouped around a few themes: that it is a shame and a risk for a man to be feminized in any way, and that it is simply in women's nature to be raped, while the rape of a man is a sin tantamount to blasphemy.

The prohibition against men having penetrative sex with one another is found in Lev. 18:22 and 20:13. Condemned with strong language, this act is considered an "abomination" and a capital crime. The rabbis of Sifra Kodashim are careful to explain why both men bear guilt:

> We heard the punishment, but we did not hear the prohibition. Scripture says: "Do not lie with a man as one lies with a woman." (Lev. 18:22). I only have a prohibition for the penetrator; where is a prohibition for the penetrated? Scripture says: "No Israelite man shall be a cult prostitute" (Deut. 23:18), and it also says: "Also there were (male) cult prostitutes in the land." (1 Kgs. 14:24) Rabbi Akiva says: "Do not lie with a man as one lies with a woman"—read here, "do not be laid."[46]

The male cult prostitutes referenced in the Bible[47] are connected by the rabbis of Sifra with the activities of the Canaanites who were dispossessed because of their sins. Hence the act of being a male prostitute is problematic not only because of its violation of Levitical sexual law, but also because of its link to idolatry. The act of male penetrative sex is equivalent to blasphemy. Men who sexually penetrated were guilty of a violation of God's divinely created order; men who were penetrated were lowered in status, humiliated, and rendered feminine. In these texts, women are, by nature, subject to penetration, which equates to a lesser status; in Genesis Rabbah, the Israelites cry out to God about the indignity they suffer at the hands of a particular enemy by saying, "Lord of the worlds, is it not enough that we are subjected to the seventy nations, but even to this one, who is penetrated like women?"[48] In fact, we find rabbinic texts that *assume* sexual abuse of women; it is simply to be expected. While describing the punishments accorded to the biblical king Yoash (2 Chr. 24:24), Rabbi Ishmael explains: "This teaches that they appointed over him cruel guards who never knew a woman and they would abuse him the way one abuses a woman."[49]

Another Talmudic story supports the assumption that rape is more naturally the experience of women, though perhaps more subtly. While describing the destruction of the Second Temple and the atrocities committed against the Jews, the Talmud reports this terrible story:

> There were four hundred boys and girls who were taken captive for the purpose of prostitution, who sensed on their own what they were expected to do. They said, if we [intentionally] drown in the sea, will we come to the life of the World to Come? "The Lord said, I will bring them back from Bashan, I will bring them back from the depths of the sea." (Ps. 68:23) . . . When the girls heard this, they all leapt and fell into the sea. The boys drew a *qal va-homer*[50] inference concerning themselves, saying: If these girls, for whom this is the natural way, do thus, how much more so should we, for whom this is not the natural way, do so. So they leapt into the sea.[51]

The children in this tale are faced with a future of sexual slavery and choose suicide instead. What stands out when examining this text as an artifact of rape culture is the way in which it frames sexual assault: the boys on the boat describe forced prostitution—not consensual sex—as "the natural way" for women. It is not, however, the natural way for men, and their use of the hermeneutical principle of *qal va-homer* reinforces that. In her study of the use of rape metaphors for rabbinic texts on destruction and colonization, Julia Watts Belser emphasizes this point:

> A rabbinic *qal va-homer* reasons that if a less serious matter warrants a strict response, then a more serious matter must also be treated with (at minimum) the same degree of strictness . . . [T]he young men claim that their violation will be more serious than that of the women . . . Through the young men's reasoning, the Bavli makes plain its profound fear of men's sexual violation. But the Bavli's terror at the prospect of male rape reinscribes *women's* sexual violation as an ordinary fact of captivity.[52]

In rabbinic laments about the destruction of the Temple and the Roman colonization, we see depictions of the people Israel (as a whole), the land, and the Temple being raped.[53] All are depicted as feminine, including the corporate identity "Israel": they are feminine, desired, and violated. Does this demonstrate a sense among the rabbis that they understand the horror of rape, that it is a deeply, subjectively violent attack? Do they have empathy for the victims of rape? Belser argues that is not the case: rather, these men are using rape as a pure metaphor, as a means of expressing their own grief and suffering, taking attention away from the lived experiences of rape victims: "These rabbinic narratives use rape and sexual assault as a way of conceptualizing *divine* woundedness and *rabbinic* lament."[54] The lived experiences of women who are raped are stripped of context and reframed as the metaphorical property of men grieving a political, national event. Even here, then, rape is assumed to be an experience that on a concrete level is relegated to women; it simply serves as a useful tool for the rabbis to explore their own suffering, which is depicted as the real tragedy.

THE RABBIS, RAPE CULTURE, AND PEDAGOGY

When my students encounter the texts discussed here, they do not often immediately detect the themes of rape culture that are inherent within the rabbis' constructions of gender and sexuality. This is due to the fact that the rabbinic dialectic is strange to them; it is also because of their own acceptance of those themes: that men are sexually rapacious and must be restrained through social constructs (even those constructs as simple as keeping women away from men); that women are irresistibly seductive and must somehow conceal their sexuality; and that the rape of a man is categorically distinct from that of a woman—it is expected that women be raped, but it is a unique kind of humiliation when it happens to a man.

The rabbis often did not agree. Thus, any thesis drawn from the texts shared here must be tempered in conversation with other scholars of rabbinic literature, who can support Daniel Boyarin's belief that "the accepted characterization of rabbinic gender discourse as monolithically misogynistic is imprecise and in serious need of nuancing."[55] But that does not mean some form of "rabbinic culture" didn't exist, or that the rabbis did not generally agree concerning women's access to Torah study or general nature. That does not mean values and constructs about gender and sexuality didn't govern their basic anthropologies and worldviews. A fundamental element of that culture—Torah study—was specifically relegated to men and was seen as a resource for distancing them from women and controlling their own rapacious natures. Within that element, they were free to build and sustain views of gender and sexuality that had—and to an extent, has—profound influence on the behaviors and expectations of both men and women. Because of the explicitly male context of this work, they were also able to *dictate* to women who they were, and what was meant to happen to them.

Whether or not women put a great deal of stock in their teachings is a matter of dispute, and it is difficult to establish.[56] But within the small world of Jews living under colonial powers in late antiquity, it is likely that the rabbis had the same kind of power of social discourse in their community that men do in male-dominated institutions do today, and as such, they enforced understandings prevalent in rape culture. According to Michael Satlow, the impact of these laws and teachings would have been significant for the women living in those contexts: "Much like modern-day 'locker-room talk' or subtle forms of sexual harassment . . . these texts would have been one factor in the promotion of a societal outlook that would have indirectly discouraged women from unsanctioned sexual behavior."[57] Satlow's understanding of the power of these texts over women is warranted; however, what he and others writing on gender in rabbinics have not yet done is address rabbinic rape culture, which would have certainly shaped both men's and women's self-understanding and behavior and, within Jewish contexts, still does so today.

NOTES

1. For an examination of the language in the Hebrew Bible surrounding non-consensual sex, see Sandie Gravett, "Reading 'Rape' in the Hebrew Bible: A Consideration of Language," *Journal for the Study of the Old Testament* 28:3 (2004), 279–99.
2. See, for example, Frank Yamada, *Configurations of Rape in the Hebrew Bible: A Literary Analysis of Three Rape Narratives* (New York: Peter Lang, 2008); Caroline Blyth, *The Narrative of Rape in Genesis 34: Interpreting Dinah's Silence* (New York: Oxford University Press, 2010); Susanne Scholz, *Sacred Witness: Rape in the Hebrew Bible* (Minneapolis: Augsburg Fortress, 2014).
3. Hermann L. Strack and Gunter Stemberger, *Introduction to the Talmud and Midrash* (Edinburgh: T & T Clark, 1991), 1–7.
4. Michael Satlow, "'Texts of Terror': Rabbinic Texts, Speech Acts, and the Control of Mores," *AJS Review* 21:2 (1996), 293.
5. Satlow, "'Try to be a Man': the Rabbinic Construction of Masculinity," *Harvard Theological Review* 89 (1996), 19–40; "'The Abused Him Like a Woman': Homoeroticism, Gender Blurring, and the Rabbis in Late Antiquity," *Journal of the History of Sexuality* 5 (1994), 1–25. Gail Labovitz, *Marriage and Metaphor: Constructions of Gender in Rabbinic Literature* (Lantham: Lexington, 2009). Daniel Boyarin, *Carnal Israel: Reading Sex in Talmudic Culture* (Berkeley: University of California, 1993); *Unheroic Conduct: The Rise of Heterosexuality and the Invention of the Jewish Man* (Berkeley: University of California Press, 1997). Gwynn Kessler, "Let's Cross that Body When We Get to It: Gender and Ethnicity in Rabbinic Literature," *Journal of the American Academy of Religion* 73:2 (2005), 329–59. Rachel Biale, *Women and Jewish Law: The Essential Texts, Their History, and Their Relevance for Today* (New York: Schocken Books, 1995). Charlotte Fonrobert, "Regulating the Human Body: Rabbinic Legal Discourse and the Making of Jewish Gender," in *The Cambridge Companion to the Talmud and Rabbinic Literature*, ed. Charlotte E. Fonrobert and Martini S. Jaffee, 270–94. Cambridge: Cambridge University Press, 2007; "Gender Identity in Halakhic Discourse," in "Jewish Women: A Comprehensive Historical Encyclopedia," March 1, 2009. Jewish Women's Archive. https://jwa.org/encyclopedia/article/gender-identity-in-halakhic-discourse.
6. An exception to this lacuna in rabbinic scholarship on gender is Gavi S. Ruit's "Rabbinic Commentaries on Genesis 34 and the Construction of Rape Myths," *Journal of Jewish Ethics* 3:2 (2017), 247–66.
7. See discussion of this phenomenon throughout Boyarin, *Intertextuality and the Reading of Midrash* (Bloomington: Indiana University Press, 1994); also Satlow, *Creating Judaism: History, Tradition, Practice* (New York: Columbia University Press: 2006), chs. 4 and 5.
8. m. Avot 2:16.
9. Biale, *Women and Jewish Law*, 239.
10. b. Ketubot 39a; payment for pain is also discussed in b. Baba Kama 83b–84a. It is standard citation method to indicate a source from the Talmud as, for example, b. Keutbot 40a–b. Further Talmudic citations will match this method.
11. The word translated here as "rape" is נבעלתי, which carries the meaning of being mastered, controlled, or dominated. The word itself bears a sense of what it means to be raped.
12. A similar story appears in y. Sotah 4:4, in which a woman reports she was raped, and Rabbi Yohanan asks her if she enjoyed it by the end.
13. Satlow, "Texts of Terror," 284.
14. Satlow, *Creating Judaism*, ch. 4; Yitzhak Heinemann, דרכי האגדה (Jerusalem: Hebrew University, 1954).
15. The use of three ? marks here is to indicate the element of shock and surprise evident in the language of the text itself.
16. Genesis Rabbah 9:7.

17. There is a notable narrative exception to this rule: According to b. Nedarim 50a, Rabbi Akiva left home to study Torah, with his wife's permission and support. When he returned 12 years later and approached their house, he heard her being chastised for allowing her husband to leave for so long; she replied, "If he listens to me, he should (go for) another 12 years." Without greeting her, he turned and left to study for 12 more years.

18. See Mari Rethelyi, "Rabbinic Understandings of Marital Rape in the Talmud," in *Rape Culture, Gender Violence, and Religion: Interdisciplinary Perspectives,* ed. Caroline Blyth, Emily Colgan, and Katie B. Edwards (New York: Palgrave Macmillan, 2018), 195–212.

19. b. Eruvin 100b.

20. See b. Nedarim 20b, in which the rabbis record lists of offspring who are negatively affected by the actions of their parents (usually, though not always, the mother). This includes babies conceived by a brazen (openly sexual) woman, or in the context of inappropriate sexual behaviors, or in the act of marital rape.

21. A *mamzer* is a child resulting from an illicit union, whose status is permanently affected by their origin in terms of community roles and marriage.

22. This is a euphemism: the woman prepared herself for sex with him, and he turned her onto her stomach, penetrating her from behind.

23. b. Nedarim 20b.

24. A fascinating correlation between masculine sexuality and meat can be explored in Carol J. Adams, *The Sexual Politics of Meat: A Feminist Vegetarian Critical Theory* (New York: Bloomsbury, 1995).

25. See also t. Kiddushin 5:9–10.

26. A *baraita* is a text from the Mishnaic period that is not found in the Mishnah.

27. The tannaitic period refers to the first to third centuries CE. This was a time of formation for rabbinic texts, of flowering in the hermeneutics that characterize these texts, and of collection of teachings that might have been lost to time and exile. Because tannaitic views are among the oldest in the rabbinic collections, they hold a great deal of authority. See discussion throughout Michael Berger, *Rabbinic Authority* (Oxford: Oxford University Press), 1998.

28. b. Avodah Zarah 22b.

29. See b. Yoma 35b, b. Shabbat 113a and 114a.

30. b. Nedarim 20a, b. Berakhot 24a.

31. b. Baba Metzia 87a.

32. b. Shabbat 140b.

33. "Self-restraint, like war, is constructed as a masculine activity." Satlow, "Try to Be a Man," 27.

34. In the case of the latter character, the Dangerous Woman, translations vary: "strange woman," "loose woman," "forbidden woman," and "adulterous woman." For analysis of this character and the language describing her, see: Daniel J. Estes, "What Makes the Strange Woman of Proverbs 1–9 Strange?" in *Ethical and Unethical in the Old Testament: God and Humans in Dialogue,* ed. Katharine J. Dell (London: T & T Clark, 2010), 151–69; Gale Yee, "'I Have Perfumed by Bed with Myrrh': The Foreign Woman ('iššâ zārâh) in Proverbs 1–9," *Journal for the Study of the Old Testament* 13:43 (1989), 53–68; Matthew J. Goff, "Hellish Females: The Strange Woman of Septuagint Proverbs and 4QWiles of the Wicked Woman," *Journal for the Study of Judaism in the Persian, Hellenistic, and Roman Period* 39:1 (2008), 20–45.

35. Michael Satlow, "'And on the Earth You Shall Sleep': *Talmud Torah* and Rabbinic Asceticism," *The Journal of Religion* 83:2 (2003), 204–25. This concept is evident even in a component of the liturgy drawn from Proverbs 3:18: "She (Torah, for the rabbis) is a tree of life for all who hold fast to her."

36. Genesis Rabbah 18:2.

37. m. Avot 1:5.

38. b. Ketubot 65a.

39. b. Kiddushin 30b.

40. m. Sotah 3:4; b. Sotah 21b.

41. Also b. Sotah 21b, in which the rabbis link the study of Torah with the development of "cunning," implying that it would be dangerous for a woman to gain that characteristic.

42. Sifrei Deuternomy 46:1.
43. Y. Sotah 3:4, 19a.
44. Boyarin, *Carnal Israel,* 182–96.
45. b. Berakhot 10a, b. Eruv 53b–54a, bin. Eruvin 53b.
46. Sifra Kedoshim 9:14, b. Sanhedrin 54b.
47. Though the idea that there were male cult prostitutes is now rejected, the rabbis believed they had existed and their commentaries are therefore based on that view. For a contemporary analysis, see Ken Stone, "The Hermeneutics of Abomination: On Gay Men, Canaanites, and Biblical Interpretation," *Biblical Theology Bulletin: Journal of Bible and Culture* 27:2 (1997), 36–41.
48. Genesis Rabbah 63:10.
49. y. Kiddushin 1:7, 61a.
50. From lesser to greater, an *ad fortiori* argument.
51. b. Gittin 57b.
52. Belser, 19–20.
53. This is particularly evident throughout b. Gittin.
54. Belser, 6.
55. Boyarin, *Carnal Israel,* 77.
56. For analysis of this question, see Judith Hauptman, "A New View of Women and Torah study in the Talmudic Period," *Jewish Studies, an Internet Journal* 9 (2010); Gail Labovitz, "Rabbis and 'Guerilla Girls': A Bavli Motif of the Female (Counter) Voice in the Rabbinic Legal System," *Women in Judaism* 10:2 (2013).
57. Satlow, "Texts of Terror," 294.

BIBLIOGRAPHY

Adams, Carol J. *The Sexual Politics of Meat: A Feminist Vegetarian Critical Theory.* New York: Bloomsbury, 1995.

Belser, Julia Watts. "Sex in the Shadow of Rome: Sexual Violence and Theological Lament in Talmudic Disaster Tales." *Journal of Feminist Studies in Religion* 30, no. 1(2014): 5–24.

Biale, Rachel. *Women and Jewish Law: The Essential Texts, Their History, and Their Relevance for Today.* New York: Schocken Books, 1995.

Blyth, Caroline. *The Narrative of Rape in Genesis 34: Interpreting Dinah's Silence.* New York: Oxford University Press, 2010.

Boyarin, Daniel. *Carnal Israel: Reading Sex in Talmudic Culture.* Berkeley: University of California, 1993.

———. *Intertextuality and the Reading of Midrash.* Bloomington: Indiana University Press, 1994.

———. *Unheroic Conduct: The Rise of Heterosexuality and the Invention of the Jewish Man.* Berkeley: University of California Press, 1997.

Estes, Daniel J. "What Makes the Strange Woman of Proverbs 1–9 Strange?" In *Ethical and Unethical in the Old Testament: God and Humans in Dialogue,* edited by Katharine J. Dell, 151–169. London: T & T Clark, 2010.

Fonrobert, Charlotte. "Regulating the Human Body: Rabbinic Legal Discourse and the Making of Jewish Gender." In *The Cambridge Companion to the Talmud and Rabbinic Literature,* edited by Charlotte E. Fonrobert and Martin S. Jaffee, 270–294. Cambridge: Cambridge University Press, 2007.

———. "Gender Identity in Halakhic Discourse." In "Jewish Women: A Comprehensive Historical Encyclopedia," March 1, 2009. Jewish Women's Archive. https://jwa.org/encyclopedia/article/gender-identity-in-halakhic-discourse.

Goff, Matthew J. "Hellish Females: The Strange Woman of Septuagint Proverbs and 4QWiles of the Wicked Woman." *Journal for the Study of Judaism in the Persian, Hellenistic, and Roman Period* 39, no. 1 (2008): 20–45.

Gravett, Sandie. "Reading 'Rape' in the Hebrew Bible: a Consideration of Language." *Journal for the Study of the Old Testament* 28, no. 3 (2004): 279–99.

Hauptman, Judith. "A New View of Women and Torah study in the Talmudic Period." *Jewish Studies, an Internet Journal* 9 (2010).
Heinemann, Yitzhak. דרכי האגדה. Jerusalem: Hebrew University, 1954.
Kessler, Gwynn. "Let's Cross that Body When We Get to It: Gender and Ethnicity in Rabbinic Literature." *Journal of the American Academy of Religion* 73, no. 2 (2005): 329–359.
Labovitz, Gail. *Marriage and Metaphor: Constructions of Gender in Rabbinic Literature.* Lantham: Lexington, 2009.
_____. "Rabbis and 'Guerilla Girls': A Bavli Motif of the Female (Counter) Voice in the Rabbinic Legal System." *Women in Judaism* 10, no. 2 (2013): 1–35.
Rethelyi, Mari. "Rabbinic Understandings of Marital Rape in the Talmud." In *Rape Culture, Gender Violence, and Religion: Interdisciplinary Perspectives*, edited by Caroline Blyth, Emily Colgan, and Katie B. Edwards, 195–212. New York: Palgrave Macmillan, 2018.
Ruit, Gavi S. "Rabbinic Commentaries on Genesis 34 and the Construction of Rape Myths." *Journal of Jewish Ethics* 3, no. 2 (2017): 247–66.
Satlow, Michael. "'The Abused Him Like a Woman': Homoeroticism, Gender Blurring, and the Rabbis in Late Antiquity." *Journal of the History of Sexuality* 5 (1994):1–25.
_____. "'Texts of Terror': Rabbinic Texts, Speech Acts, and the Control of Mores." *AJS Review* 21, no. 2 (1996): 273–97.
_____. "'Try to be a Man': the Rabbinic Construction of Masculinity." *Harvard Theological Review* 89 (1996): 19–40.
_____. "'And on the Earth You Shall Sleep': *Talmud Torah* and Rabbinic Asceticism." *The Journal of Religion* 83, no. 2 (2003): 204–25.
_____. *Creating Judaism: History, Tradition, Practice.* New York: Columbia University Press, 2006.
Scholz, Susanne. *Sacred Witness: Rape in the Hebrew Bible.* Minneapolis: Augsburg Fortress, 2014.
Stone, Ken. "The Hermeneutics of Abomination: On Gay Men, Canaanites, and Biblical Interpretation." *Biblical Theology Bulletin: Journal of Bible and Culture* 27, no. 2 (1997): 36–41.
Strack, Hermann L. and Gunter Stemberger. *Introduction to the Talmud and Midrash.* Edinburgh: T & T Clark, 1991.
Yamada, Frank. *Configurations of Rape in the Hebrew Bible: A Literary Analysis of Three Rape Narratives.* New York: Peter Lang, 2008.
Yee, Gale. "'I Have Perfumed by Bed with Myrrh': The Foreign Woman ('iššâ zārâh) in Proverbs 1–9." *Journal for the Study of the Old Testament* 13, no. 43 (1989): 53–68.

Chapter Eight

Sex and Alien Encounter

Rethinking Consent as a Rape Prevention Strategy

Meredith Minister

Guided by President Obama's White House Task Force to Protect Students from Sexual Assault and organizations such as RAINN (The Rape, Abuse and Incest National Network), many programs on college campuses have attempted to respond to the crisis of sexual assault by teaching affirmative consent, or affirmative, conscious, and voluntary agreement as a contractual basis for engaging in sex.[1] Although the Department of Education under the leadership of Betsy DeVos no longer supports the Obama-era guidance on Title IX, many of the strategies colleges and universities implemented following the 2011 guidance remains in place. Moreover, many state legislatures formed laws that remain on the books. California, New York, and Illinois, for example, have legislated affirmative consent, requiring colleges and universities to evaluate disciplinary charges of sexual assault using a standard of affirmative consent. Many students have embraced this notion of consent as a prerequisite for sexual activity.

In a 2015 White House PSA, the actors offer this common narrative, "There's one thing you can never have sex without. It's not something you buy. It's not something you take. In fact, there's only one way to get it. It has to be given to you, freely. It's consent. Because sex without it isn't sex; it's rape."[2] RAINN similarly argues that consent be the baseline for determining whether or not sexual assault has occurred.[3] In these arguments for consent, a narrow definition of consent functions to identify proper sex through the exclusion of any improper sex, defined as rape.

Rather than embrace consent as a means of rape prevention, I am interested in exploring the histories and assumptions of consent and how and why we might imagine alternatives to the dominance of consent as a rape preventative. In this chapter, I explore the histories and assumptions of our contemporary models of consent before considering how consent operates in three examples of human-alien encounters in Octavia Butler's speculative fiction. In particular, I explore Butler's *Xenogenesis* novels, her short story "Amnesty," and her novelette "Bloodchild." Through this investigation, I argue that considering alternatives to consent creates space for a more robust horizon for the possibilities of sexuality outside of the hegemony of rape culture.

CONSENT: HISTORY AND ASSUMPTIONS

In education toward rape prevention, consent is often assumed as an obvious alternative to the sublimation of another's agency that occurs in rape. The apparently obvious contrast between consensual sex and rape, however, ignores the specific histories and assumptions of contemporary understandings of consent in order to position consensual sex as the good alternative to the bad of rape. In this framing, consensual sex and rape form a binary that consumes all sexual encounters.

Such a framing avoids contextualizing consent. In lieu of contextualization, the ideal of consent sublimates context in order to become the hero of contemporary sexual expression. Any sexual encounter that is consensual is supposed to be good. What part of consensual sexual encounters are not good? Moreover, how did consent become the sole criteria by which good sex is defined? By considering the histories and assumptions of consent, this section challenges the ideal of consent as the cure-all for rape.

Histories of Consent

When and under what political conditions did consent become the foundation for social relationships? Moreover, how does understanding the history of consent's use in contemporary social institutions challenge the use of consent as a rape preventative? Carole Pateman, Charles Mills, Wendy Brown, Pamela Haag, Joseph Fischel, and others have drawn on histories of the use of consent in order to critique consent as a foundation for social relations.[4]

Because consent functions as the means by which parties may enter into a contract, the history of the rise of consent is connected to the development and rise of the social contract. This ideal contract, with theoretical foundations in Locke and Rousseau, assumes the equality of potentially contractually-bound parties. Pateman and Mills reveal the white male assumptions in the supposedly neutral social contract. Pateman reveals these assumptions by exposing the gendered logics of contracts. Mills exposes the assumptions in the social contract through an exploration of racial logics. In *Contract and Domination*, Pateman and Mills bring their gendered and racial analyses together in order to reveal the intersection of race and gender in the social contract. Mills states, "If the sexual contract establishes patriarchy, and the racial contract establishes white supremacy, the racial-sexual contract establishes the white-supremacist patriarchal polity."[5] According to Mills, the social contract is dependent upon assumptions of racial and gender superiority. Although contemporary institutions continue to be governed by contracts, the analysis of Pateman and Mills reveals the fundamental inequality that shapes those contracts. The history of the social contract undermines the notion of consent as an equality producing panacea insofar as the rise of consent depends on the rise of the contract as an organizer of social relationships.

Drawing on the link between consent and contract, Pamela Haag argues that contractual relationships, and, thus, relationships governed by consent, often function to maintain coercive inequalities. The failure to understand how coercive inequalities functioned in the apparently equal relationships governed by contract created a situation in which social reformers viewed contract and consent as a cure to redress social inequalities. This understanding of consent as a cure for social inequality developed in contrast to understandings of consent as a tool that maintained those social inequalities. The labor contract, for example, does not adequately protect the rights of the laborer because the conditions of the contract are dependent upon the employer. Haag states, "Middle class reformers [Elizabeth Cady Stanton and Susan B. Anthony], arguably, struggled to visualize the working woman as virtuous because they approached contract as a *cure for* rather than an *instrument of* power."[6] While Haag is specifically referencing Stanton and Anthony's approach to sex work, her analysis suggests how contract and consent continue to be seen as a cure for rather than an instrument of power in contemporary discourses around consent as a rape preventative. Following this trajectory, consent education is the new middle/upper-class white feminism.

Understanding the link between contract and consent historicizes consent, a move that challenges its dominant power for ordering sexual relations. Wendy Brown complicates Mills and Pateman's clear link between contract and consent by distinguishing between contract, which she argues is a civil act that presumes equality, and consent, which she argues is an intimate act that presumes inequality. In consent, one person makes a proposition which another party receives and, at least in theory, may either accept or reject. Even in intimate contexts, the terms are set by the proposer. Brown's distinction helps us understand how consent became disassociated from political and civil relationships and came to govern intimate relationships. Within these relationships, Brown contends, "Consent marks the subordinate status of the consenting party."[7] Even as it takes new shape in the context of intimate relationships, consent does not function to enter into an equal relationship, as is so often presumed in attempts to draw on consent as a rape preventative. Rather, for Brown, consent still functions as a means of submitting to power.

Finally, Joseph Fischel historicizes consent by exploring how consent replaced heterosexuality as the form of privileged sexuality in the United States. This move, Fischel contends, draws on the construction of the child and the sex offender to shift sexual deviance from people who pursue sex outside of heteronormative frames to people who pursue sex outside of consensual frames. Fischel argues that this shift forecloses the possibility of a more capacious understanding of sex, one that tolerates ambiguity. Fischel states, "Consent cannot do the kind of things we want it to do, cannot divide good sex from bad, harm from freedom, or respond to the kinds of sexual/ sexualized inequalities and injustices that pervade late modern life in the United States."[8] Consensual sex cannot be equated with good sex. Some consensual sex is good; some consensual sex is bad. This is true both morally and physically.

By contextualizing consent, each of these theorists (whether implicitly or explicitly) challenges the use of consent as a rape prevention strategy. These histories reveal the linkage between consent and liberal formations of the social and political order, formations that assume equality while depending on gendered and racial difference. Questioning these histories of theories of consent does not mean that it is suddenly ok to have sex with someone who has rejected advances or someone who is unconscious. Consent has served as a (sometimes) useful stop gap in the wake of alarmingly high rates of sexual violence. Normalizing sexual violence is not the point of questioning the history and assumptions of consent. Rather, I contend that when we use consent to demarcate good sex from bad sex, we fail to account for the particularities of social and historical context that make it easier for some to make a proposition and for others to accept or reject a proposition. The following section takes up this argument by exploring the assumptions that ground contemporary understandings of consent.

Assumptions in Theories of Consent

Affirmative consent assumes that bodies are owned and exchanged via speech acts and that bodies are autonomous and unrelated until they are forced (via consensual agreement or violence) into relation with others. These assumptions belie the relational constitution of personhood, exchanging it for the myth of bodily autonomy.[9] Moreover, affirmative consent fetishizes self-control, verbal communication, and the boundary between public and private.

Appeals to consent fetishize self-control by suggesting that, in order to be suitable for sexual activity, one must be fully in control of oneself and that, if one is not fully in control, one cannot really consent. Such a notion of consent assumes that human beings are autonomous individuals with a range of physical and emotional capacities that can maintain this individual autonomy. Such an understanding of the individual belies theories that implicate individuals in webs of connection and constraint in ways that compromise individual consent. Robert McRuer explains, "The hegemonic mode, then, to put forward a rather straightforward (Gramscian) definition, elicits consent to the dominant economic and political ideologies of a particular historical context."[10] That is, consent is something that can be forced based on a particular context. Consent, McRuer implies, can be implicitly coerced (even before overt badgering takes place). This is to say that the pressure to follow social agreements compromises an individual's agency and ability to freely consent. If the hegemonic mode can elicit consent, appeals to consent cannot be a panacea that will end sexual assault.

The fetishization of self-control in appeals to consent can also be seen in the focus on verbal communication, a focus that attempts to foreclose non-verbal methods of communication. Alison Kafer draws on Amanda Baggs's "In My Language," a video Baggs made to explain how people with autism communicate, to describe that language is not always verbal. In her interpretation of Baggs, Kafer states, "In foregrounding this mutual interaction between fingers and water, between self and stream, Baggs pushes us to expand our conceptions of both language and nature; indeed, the two are intimately related. Language is about interaction with our environments, a mutual interaction that does not, cannot, occur only in spoken words or written text."[11] Kafer's consideration of non-verbal models of communication can be used to highlight how limiting sexual expression to the realm of verbal consent depends on compulsory able-bodiedness. In particular, appeals to verbal consent foreclose the possibility that anyone who cannot express consent verbally can participate in legitimate sex acts. While this argument does not legitimate perpetrator excuses such as "her lips said no but her eyes said yes," it does suggest the limitations of excluding non-verbal communication for expressing sexual desire.

The supposedly clear delineation of legitimate sex from illegitimate sex maintains a privileged public/private boundary by suggesting that individuals can control when, how, and by whom they are accessed. In other words, the appeal to consent implies that individuals make a conscious decision to express their sexualities and then pick and choose which parts of themselves to make available for sexual expression. The verbal act of consent, in this framing, becomes the gate between a public self, one available for dissemination, and a private self, one accessible by invitation only. Sexual expression, as a result, is assumed to be an entirely private encounter. Feminist, queer, crip, and disability theorists including McRuer, Siebers, Kafer, and Erevelles challenge the understanding of sexual expression as something that occurs on the private side of a clearly demarcated boundary between public and private.

In particular, they show how privacy is linked to normativity and, as such, is denied to anyone understood to be disabled. This denial of privacy reveals the privilege behind the assumption that individuals choose when to be public and when to be private. Calling attention to the denial of privacy to some reveals how the public/private boundary denies selfhood to persons deemed socially unworthy or unfit. In this challenge, they implicitly challenge an understanding of the self in which private and public selves are clearly demarcated via verbal speech acts.

Appeals to consent education as a rape prevention strategy have created a binary between rape and consensual sex. This binary not only assumes social inequality by functionalizing consent to create equality; it also fetishizes self-control and bodily autonomy. The binary between rape and consensual sex limits sex to those with privileged social positions where the myths of self-control and bodily autonomy can be upheld. Thinking from contexts where sex occurs outside of the binary of rape and consensual sex creates possibilities for desirable sexual encounters in contexts where free consent is impossible. In what follows, my analysis draws on Octavia Butler's fictional worlds in order to imagine alternatives to the reliance on affirmative consent as a rape prevention strategy.

CONSENT IN OCTAVIA BUTLER'S *ALIEN ENCOUNTERS*

Octavia Butler (1947–2006) was a speculative fiction writer born in the United States. Her novels and short stories create worlds in which humans have to survive in extreme circumstances including alien invasion after nuclear war and severe climate change. Through these fictional contexts, Butler offers social commentary on racism, sexism, and environmental degradation. Her writing is enjoying a cultural moment as Ava DuVernay is currently adapting Butler's *Xenogenesis* novels for television and her Parable books, in which she describes a Presidential candidate with the slogan "Make America Great Again," have been called prescient.[12]

The human-alien encounters in Butler's fiction reveal the limitations of affirmative consent and imagine erotic possibilities outside of the sexual binary of affirmative consent and rape. While "Amnesty" focuses on the fraught and failed processes of communication after alien ships have landed on earth, "Bloodchild" and the *Xenogenesis* trilogy explore the continuation of species in the midst of interspecies encounter. In both "Bloodchild" and the *Xenogenesis* series, reproduction sublimates sex. The stories are, therefore, primarily about survival via reproductive futurity and not about erotic pleasure.[13] Despite this focus, both stories invite a reconsideration of consent via the conditions under which sexual encounter does occur. "Amnesty," "Bloodchild," and the *Xenogenesis* novels reveal the limitations of affirmative consent by exploring the limits of language and communication (both across and within species), the bounds of the self, individual autonomy, and an idealized equality within relationships. In this section, I offer a brief note about each of the stories before exploring how these stories reveal the limitations of affirmative consent and create the conditions for imagining new paths toward pleasure.

The short story "Amnesty" describes the attempts of aliens to form a symbiotic relationship with human beings after landing on earth in a not-distant future. The narrative develops from the perspective of an abductee who was tortured by the U.S. government after being released by the aliens and who decided to return to work for the aliens. The attempt of the aliens to communicate with humans is constantly thwarted because the communities communicate via non-speech patterns. "Amnesty" also takes up the themes of fear, violence, and misunderstanding as the central character is tortured, first and accidentally, by the aliens as they attempt to learn how to communicate with humans and, second and intentionally, by humans after she is released from the alien ship and assumed to have information that cannot be given or received through the techniques of interview.

In the novelette "Bloodchild," Butler describes a world in which humans live on a preserve on which they are protected by benevolent aliens (the Tlic) from those in their species that would enslave humans. On this preserve, Tlic and human families merge and the bodies of humans, the only animals that will not kill Tlic eggs upon implantation, gestate Tlic young. While Tlic may impregnate either men or women, they tend to choose men in order to free women for human reproduction.

In the more developed *Xenogenesis* trilogy, which has been published under the name Lilith's Brood and contains the novels *Dawn*, *Adulthood Rites*, and *Imago*, Butler imagines an earth decimated by nuclear war and leaves the fate of humanity in the hands of gene-trading aliens, the Oankali, who have saved some humans from the earth in the hopes of producing fruitful gene trades between humans and Oankali. While the most promising genetic trade is based on a cancer-causing gene that the Oankali have repurposed toward being able to make themselves more like the beings they encounter, *Xenogenesis* focuses on the reproductive merging of human and Oankali to create a new hybrid being.

Across her work, Butler imagines humans in contexts that clearly constrain human agency. While the hegemonic orders that compromise consent in everyday encounters have ways of appearing to be invisible and, thus, making it appear that our choices are our own, Butler imagines situations that clearly constrain individual choice. Because her worlds elide the possibility of unconstrained consent, Butler's fiction creates possibilities for rethinking consent as a strategy for rape prevention. In the following sections, I explore how Butler's stories help us investigate the limits of language and communication (both across and within species), the bounds of the self and individual autonomy, and how power differentials shape relationships.

Language and Communication

Butler imagines aliens outside of humanoid boundaries, including speech-dominated communication patterns. The communication patterns exhibited by Butler's aliens challenge expectations that sex is preconditioned on verbal exchanges and create ways of imagining meaningful nonverbal methods of communication. Thinking with Butler's aliens, therefore, can expand our imagination for non-verbal forms of communication.

In the *Xenogenesis* series, the aliens communicate primarily through touch but they have adapted to communicate with humans aurally. In "Amnesty," the aliens communicate primarily through visual electrical displays but they, together with humans they have abducted, create a shared language of touch and gesture by which they can communicate with humans. In Bloodchild, the aliens appear to communicate verbally but this could be because Bloodchild focuses on the interactions of humans with Tlic and we rarely see the Tlic interacting with one another. This section focuses on alien-human communication in *Xenogenesis* and in "Amnesty."

In the *Xenogenesis* series, the Oankali communicate via a meeting of "sensory organs." These organs look like hair but, unlike the cells of human hair, which hang between the life and death of the body, these sensory organs connect to the central systems of the Oankali. As the protagonist of *Dawn*, the first book in the *Xenogenesis* series, describes, "Some of the 'hair' writhed independently, a nest of snakes startled, driven in all directions . . . 'They're not separate animals,' he said. 'They're sensory organs. They're no more dangerous than your nose or eyes. It's natural for them to move in response to my wishes or emotions not to outside stimuli. We have them on our bodies as well. We need them in the same way you need your ears, nose, and eyes."[14] Because the Oankali communicate with these sensory organs, they have adapted themselves in order to communicate with humans verbally and aurally. In spite of this adaptation, most Oankali continue to prefer communicating via touch, as Butler describes, "They spoke aloud very little, but there was much touching of tentacles to flesh or tentacles to other tentacles."[15] These bodily interactions are not predicated on verbal agreements. Rather, these non-verbal connections are understood as primary, in spite of the potential to communicate verbally and aurally.

The aliens in "Amnesty" communicate visually, via electrical displays of light. As Butler describes,

> The stranger-Community focused its attention on Noah, electricity flaring and zigzagging, making a visible display within the dark vastness of its body. She

knew that the electrical display was speech, although she could not read what was said. The Communities spoke in this way between themselves and within themselves, but the light they produced moved far too quickly for her to even begin to learn the language. The fact that she saw the display, though, meant that the communications entities of the stranger-Community were addressing her. Communities used their momentarily inactive organisms to shield communication from anyone outside themselves who was not being addressed.[16]

Unlike the Oankali, who must touch in order to communicate, the aliens in "Amnesty" prefer to communicate among themselves using visual cues and energy.

Although visual cues are the primary mode of communication among the alien communities, because humans cannot communicate via these visual electrical displays, the humans and communities develop a common shared language of touch. It is through this common shared language that the communities begin to interact with humans and that Noah, the central character in the story, develops a shared language with the communities. As Noah describes to a group of humans looking to be employed by the communities, "They can read English, and even write it—with difficulty. But since they can't hear at all, they never developed a spoken language of any kind. They can only converse with us in the gesture and touch language that some of us and some of them have developed. It takes some getting used to since they have no limbs in common with us."[17] The common "gesture and touch" language to which Noah refers requires humans to be completely enfolded by the alien community so that the community can feel the signs expressed by the human body.

This enfolding requires humans to be completely subject to the alien community as the community may harm the human if the human's response is undesirable to the community. Butler uses Noah to describe this harm, "She was hit with a sudden electrical shock that convulsed her. It drove the breath out of her in a hoarse scream. It made her see flashes of light even with her eyes tightly closed. It stimulated her muscles into abrupt, agonizing contortions."[18] In this exchange, the community uses power to elicit agreement from Noah. The precondition for communication in these circumstances is a willingness to submit entirely to the alien community, a submission that may result in injury.

Communication between humans and aliens is, in Butler's worlds, always compromised: first, by the power differentials that exist between humans and aliens in both "Amnesty" and the *Xenogenesis* series, both of which are initially set on alien ships where humans are entirely in the control of the aliens and, second, by bodily differences in how the humans and aliens communicate. Yet, in both stories, humans and aliens learn to communicate with one another even as those communications remain fraught. Moreover, these mismatched communication patterns do not foreclose the possibility of mutual pleasure. Through these encounters where consent is compromised yet pleasure achieved, we might be able to imagine sexual possibilities outside of the binary of consent and rape.

Autonomy and the Bounds of the Self

These ways of communicating that prioritize touch and visual cues reveal that Butler does not assume that the bounds of individual selves work in alien communities as they do in human ones. If touch is required for a message to be passed between alien entities, then one cannot verbally assent prior to being touched as touch becomes the means of negotiating and establishing relationships.

Because Butler's alien selves are not bounded in the way of individual humans, there are not individual bodies or entities to decide or defend. This is particularly in the case in "Amnesty," where Butler describes the aliens as "communities" because they are composed of multiple intelligences. "Each community contains several hundred individuals—an intelligent multitude," Noah explains to the group of humans who are potential employees of the aliens, "But that's wrong too, really. The individuals can't really survive independently, but they can leave one community and move temporarily or permanently to another."[19] The bounds of these alien communities are fluid, amorphous, and constantly changing. The fluidity of these boundaries reveals the connectedness of the alien life forms and the limitations of individual autonomy and consent.

In "Bloodchild," the bounds of the self are clearer but these boundaries still do not result in clear individual autonomy. While both the humans in the story and the Tlic aliens have clearly distinguishable, individual bodies, the processes of reproduction described in the story challenge these boundaries as the humans gestate the Tlic young until the point at which the Tlic young require more food to survive than the human body can offer without death. At this point, the Tlic young are surgically removed and placed into an animal carcass where they can feed and continue to grow. The feeding practices of the young "grubs," as they are described, reveal the dependency of the Tlic on other life forms. While it is possible for Tlic to gestate in other beings, humans provide the best known hosts for Tlic young. Butler compares two Tlic, T'Khotgif Teh and T'Gatoi, in order to illustrate the superiority of humans as hosts, "She [T'Khotgif Teh] was paler and smaller than T'Gatoi—probably born from the body of an animal. Tlic from Terran [human] bodies were always larger as well as more numerous."[20] Because Tlic gestated in humans are larger and because the yield is higher, humans have become the preferred host. The novelette does not explain how the Tlic came to be unable to reproduce intra-species but it does make apparent their dependence upon other life forms.

Like in "Bloodchild," the Oankali of the *Xenogenesis* series have clearer boundaries than the alien communities in "Amnesty," but these clear boundaries do not result in clear autonomy. Like the Tlic, the Oankali are dependent upon other species for their continuation. With humans, they have found a way to manipulate cancer cells to change their appearance. Through their work with these cells, they have figured out how to remove cancer from human bodies and have cured the main character of the series. The Oankali, like the Tlic, require other species to continue their own. "We do what you would call genetic engineering. We know you had begun to do it yourselves a little, but it's foreign to you. We do it naturally. We *must* do it. It renews us, enables us to survive as an evolving species instead of specializing ourselves into extinction of stagnation," Jdahya, one of the Oankali, explains to Lilith, the human protagonist, "We are powerfully acquisitive. We acquire new life—seek it, investigate it, manipulate it, sort it, use it."[21] These acquisitions allow the Oankali to perpetuate their existence instead of, as Jdahya explains, specializing themselves into stagnation.

While human bodies make it possible to develop and maintain theories of disconnectedness, Butler's aliens consistently remind us that lifeforms, including humans, are interdependent. This interdependency reveals the limitations of idealistic notions about individual autonomy that undergird consent. Consent assumes that bodies exist in a relatively disconnected state that then have the possibility of being connected via a verbal agreement. Rather than presume the disconnection that underlies consent, Butler's alien forms reveal the complex ways in which bodies are connected and interdependent, whether we like it or not. This is not to say that we do not have choices about how we relate to one another. Rather, it suggests that our choices are more circumscribed than most theories of consent allow. Unless theories of consent can account for these complexities, they will continue to fail to be an adequate response to sexual violence.

Compromised Pleasure

Liberal formations of consent undergird the use of consent education on college campuses. These liberal formations mitigate power differentials at play in sexual relationships. Butler's worlds, on the other hand, describe contexts that clearly circumscribe the choices of the main characters. Power remains a constant theme in Butler's works and her characters are often choosing between undesirable options. Butler's descriptions of sexual and erotic pleasure within these contexts reveal possibilities for sexual pleasure that occurs in relationships characterized by inequality.

In the encounters between humans and Oankali, sex and erotic pleasure are compromised but not impossible. Butler refuses legal abstractions based on non-existent ideals, instead opting for finding pleasure in the midst of circumstances that are not ideal. In spite of the ways in which consent is compromised, the *Xenogenesis* series includes scenes of erotic pleasure, particularly between two human partners as mediated by the Oankali third gender ooloi. The ooloi is a member of the Oankali who can become a third party in a human sexual encounter in order to amplify the pleasure of the two humans (always a male and a female as described by Butler). Butler describes one of these early encounters between Lilith, her human lover Joseph, and an Oankali ooloi Nikanj:

> Nikanj focused on the intensity of their attraction, their union. It left Lilith no other sensation. It seemed, itself, to vanish. She sensed only Joseph, felt that he was aware only of her. Now their delight in one another ignited and burned. They moved together, sustaining an impossible intensity, both of them tireless, perfectly matched, ablaze in sensation, lost in one another. They seemed to rush upward. A long time later, they seemed to drift down slowly, gradually, savoring a few more moments wholly together.[22]

In this encounter, the Oankali ooloi increases the pleasure of the human encounter, making it possible for Joseph and Lilith to feel each other with more intensity than if their encounter were unmediated by Nikanj.

Feminist scholars have debated how to categorize the human-Oankali sex that is required for the *Xenogenesis*. Meghan Riley interprets the sexual encounters in the series as examples of the violation of consent through force, coercion, and use of drugs.[23] Riley does not mince words: the Oankali rape humans. Employing Kant's Formula of the End in Itself, in which deceit and consent are mutually exclusive, Riley argues that the Oankali act as rapists.[24] Riley states, "What is clear is that the humans in the two novels do not have the right to choose, any more than do rape victims, women coerced into initiating or sustaining a pregnancy, and many medical patients. They are not respected as ends in themselves and as such, cannot give consent."[25] In this statement, Riley assumes a stable subject that has to be the foundation of consent. Moreover, Riley draws on an abstract notion of consent that fails to understand the concrete contexts in which consent is always constrained. The question of whether the sex between humans and Oankali is consensual depends on an idea of consent that has developed under the assumption that human beings are autonomous and self-directed.

Rather than work with a pre-existing understanding of consent that I apply to Butler's novels, I propose drawing on Butler's novels to rethink our assumptions about consent. Catharine MacKinnon famously (or infamously, depending on your perspective) argued that all heterosexual sex that takes place within patriarchal contexts is rape. MacKinnon's argument recognizes that consent is always compromised within contexts governed by power imbalances.[26] While some take MacKinnon's argument to foreclose sexual possibilities ("sex negative"), it is possible to interpret MacKinnon's argument as outside of the binary of consensual and non-consensual sex. Butler's fiction explores sex outside of this binary. Rather than creating a clear picture of rape, as Riley argues, Butler offers the possibility for erotic pleasure even in the midst of coercive contexts.

"Amnesty" does not describe sexual pleasure but it does depict an erotic, physical pleasure that occurs when humans are enfolded by the alien communities,

> She was at once touched, stroked, messaged, compressed in the strangely comfortable, peaceful way that she had come to look forward to whenever she was employed. She was turned and handled as though she weighed nothing. In fact, after a few moments, she felt weightless. She had lost all sense of direction, yet she felt totally secure, clasped by entities that had nothing resembling human limbs. Why this was pleasurable, she had never understood, but for twelve years of captivity, it had been her only dependable comfort. It had happened often enough to enable her to endure everything else that was done to her. Fortunately, the Communities also found it comforting—even more than she did.[27]

This is not an encounter where Noah feels betrayed by her body in a way that her body seems to respond to something she does not want. Rather, Noah finds pleasure in the midst of a circumstance that is not ideal, one that circumscribes her autonomy and makes her dependent upon the communities. The mutual pleasure derived from this interspecies interaction is, like the interspecies interactions Butler describes in *Xenogenesis*, not an encounter based on consent. Neither is it an encounter where consent is clearly violated. The context of interspecies alien encounter makes unconstrained consent impossible in both "Amnesty" and the *Xenogenesis* series. In spite of this impossibility, erotic pleasure remains a possibility outside of the bounds of consent.

Like *Xenogenesis*, the depictions of alien-human encounter in Bloodchild are mediated with a drug that causes mild sedation. In both contexts, the aliens provide the humans with the drugs. In *Xenogenesis*, the drugs mediate sexual encounter while, in Bloodchild, the drugs mediate the process in which the Tlic aliens inseminate the humans, called Terrans. Bloodchild begins, "My last night of childhood began with a visit home. T'Gatoi's sister had given us two sterile eggs. T'Gatoi gave one to my mother, brother, and sisters. She insisted that I eat the other one alone. It didn't matter. There was still enough to leave everyone feeling good."[28] Told from the perspective of Gan, a Terran chosen for implantation, this beginning sets up an evening in which Gan watches and assists in a birth gone awry before being implanted with Tlic young.

"Bloodchild" focuses on Gan's decision of whether or not to be implanted. And it is a kind of choice that the Tlic, T'Gatoi, gives him, but Gan knows that, if he refuses, T'Gatoi will implant his sister, Hoa. While the focus of the narrative is on reproduction, there are moments of erotic pleasure in which Gan is enfolded in T'Gatoi's limbs. In a conversation between T'Gatoi and Gan just prior to implantation, Butler describes, "'But you came to me . . . to save Hoa.' 'Yes.' I leaned my forehead against her. She was cool velvet, deceptively soft. 'And to keep you for myself,' I said it. It was so. I didn't understand it, but it was so. She made a soft hum of contentment."[29] Here, a compromised mutual pleasure.

Butler argues that "Bloodchild" is not, as some have interpreted, a story about slavery but, rather, both an interspecies love story and a coming-of-age story.[30] While Gan chose implantation, perhaps for love, as Butler suggests, it was not a choice that was uncompromised, as many appeals to consent demand. Gan's choice, if consent at all, is a constrained consent. And, yet, in spite of this constraint, a pleasurable erotic exchange occurs. "Bloodchild," thus offers another Butlerian example of compromised pleasure.[31]

The word consensual cannot describe the human-alien encounters in the *Xenogenesis* series, "Bloodchild," or "Amnesty." Butler, however, does consistently describe these encounters as pleasurable. And the pleasure of these encounters between humans and aliens often exceeds the pleasures of sexual encounters between humans. While the compromised nature of communication and the lack of clearly definable individual boundaries do not excuse the overt forms of violence sometimes exerted by the aliens against the humans, it can help explain why the encounters between the humans and aliens can be described as both coercive and pleasurable. There is, Butler's stories seem to suggest, a crossing between pain and pleasure.

While Butler's stories may seem outlandishly removed from our present social context, the clear ways in which Butler describes humans as dependent and not autonomous creates space to see the ways in which humans are dependent even under present conditions (minus alien encounter). Appeals to consent as a response to sexual violence depend on the equality of the parties agreeing to sex. Rather than relying on responses that require a theoretical vacuum to work, we should develop responses to sexual violence that attend to pervasive existing inequalities—including the inequalities that make some people in some places more susceptible to sexual violence than others.

TEACHING ABOUT SEX: FROM CRITICAL TO PEDAGOGICAL ENGAGEMENTS

Appeals to consent skirt the complicated questions about sex raised in Butler's novels. At their worst, they masquerade as sex education, offering prescriptions for sex that circumvent the important questions raised in and around sexual encounters. Rather than supporting this dogmatic approach, classrooms might create space to be open to questions about sexual encounter. Teaching about sex also creates horizons for sex outside of the binary of rape and consent. Because sexual encounters occur in contexts that are compromised according to complicated power differentials (the patriarchal power of rape culture is only the beginning[32]), sex rarely achieves the purity of non-coercion demanded by consent education. Rather than call this sex rape, sex education might help students engage in the questions raised by compromised sexual encounters. While the questions raised by and around sexual encounters are many, we might use Butler's novels as a starting point to engage questions around language and communication, the bounds of the self and individual autonomy, and the nature of pleasure.

First, appeals to consent assume that communication is predominantly verbal and foreclose the multivalent possibilities of communication present not only in Butler's alien bodies but also in human bodies. Drawing on Butler's imaginary worlds, we might begin to ask how we communicate with one another using spoken and written words, images, and the parts of human bodies from eyebrows to posture that are so often reduced to "body language." Bodies do not only enter into language but are themselves/ourselves language. How does thinking about language differently help us think about sexual encounter, particularly sexual encounter in the midst of inequality? We can also ask how communication patterns shift around social media and what it means to meet someone in a bar versus on tinder. These questions encourage students to consider sex within the context of communication patterns and assumptions about communication in, around, and beyond sexual encounters.

Second, appeals to consent assume that individual selves are bounded and autonomous. This assumption forecloses questions around the relations not only of human bodies but also of animal, plant, and material bodies. What does it mean to live as beings that are not related according to consensual agreements but according to messy, happenstance collisions that drive us together? Elsewhere, I have argued for fragility to replace notions of autonomy in how we think about sexual encounters, including rape. Butler's descriptions of mutual pleasure that occurs between humans and aliens in the midst of coercive contexts reveal the fragile mutuality that constitutes human beings. Through these stories, Butler's novels encourage pedagogical engagements that challenge assumptions of autonomy.

Finally, appeals to consent continue a tradition of sexual education in which the isolation of sex prevents conversations about the structural power dynamics of the contexts in which sex occurs. These power dynamics include, but are not limited to, the misogyny of rape culture. Butler's novels, on the other hand, offer possibilities for erotic pleasure in the midst of coercive contexts. Teaching with her stories, therefore, creates the potential to explore sex and pleasure in the midst of structural power dynamics that make equal exchanges impossible.

Raising these questions moves students away from cordoning off sex as a discreet activity and encourages an educational approach to sex in which sex taps into questions that are fundamental to humanities classrooms. Creating space for discussions about communication, relationships, and power offers a better rape prevention strategy than simple consent education, even if the strategy requires more time and resources. Butler's fictional worlds cannot offer a clear alternative to notions of consent. They can, however, spark our imaginations to rethink assumptions about sex that go unquestioned in appeals to consent and other forms of dogmatic sex education.

NOTES

1. United States White House Task Force to Protect Students from Sexual Assault, "Not Alone: The First Report of the White House Task Force to Protect Students from Sexual Assault," Task Force Report, Washington D.C.: The White House, April 2014, http://www.changingourcampus.org/resources/not-alone/WH_Task_Force_First_Report.pdf.

2. Tyler Kingkade, "New White House PSA Is A Reminder: Sex Without Consent Is Rape," *The Huffington Post*, September 1, 2015, http://www.huffingtonpost.com/entry/new-its-on-us-psa_55e59e1ae4b0c818f61904e8.

3. Rape, Abuse and Incest National Network, "What Consent Looks Like," accessed December 8, 2015, https://rainn.org/get-information/sexual-assault-prevention/what-is-consent.

4. Carole Pateman, and Charles W. Mills, *Contract and Domination* (Malden, MA: Polity Press, 2007); Wendy Brown, *States of Injury: Power and Freedom in Late Modernity* (Princeton, NJ: Princeton University Press, 1995); Pamela Haag, *Consent: Sexual Rights and the Transformation of American Liberalism* (Ithaca and London: Cornell University Press, 1999); and Joseph J. Fischel, *Sex and Harm in the Age of Consent* (Minneapolis and London: University of Minnesota Press, 2016).

5. Mills, *Contract and Domination*, 173.

6. Haag, *Consent*, 43, emphasis in original.

7. Brown, *States of Injury*, 163.

8. Fischel, *Sex and Harm*, 7.

9. Disability theorists offer one example on bodily autonomy as a myth. See, for example, Tobin Siebers, *Disability Theory* (Ann Arbor: University of Michigan, 2008), 93.

10. Robert McRuer, *Crip Theory* (New York and London: New York University Press, 2006), 192.

11. Alison Kafer, *Feminist, Queer, Crip* (Bloomington, Indiana: Indiana University Press, 2013), 145.

12. The Xenogesis series is made up of three novels *Dawn* (1987), *Adulthood Rites* (1988), and *Imago* (1989). These novels are published together in Octavia Butler, *Lilith's Brood: The Complete Xenogenesis Series* (New York: Warner Books, 1989). *Parable of the Sower* (New York: Warner Books, 1993) and *Parable of the Talents* (New York: Warner Books, 1998) make up the two-novel Parable Series (Butler was working on a third but abandoned it). For the prescience of her novels, see Abby Aguirre, "Octavia Butler's Prescient Vision of Zealot Elected to 'Make America Great Again'" *The New Yorker*, July 26, 2017, https://www.newyorker.com/books/second-read/octavia-butlers-prescient-vision-of-a-zealot-elected-to-make-america-great-again.

13. Perhaps this focus on reproductive futurity is one of the reasons why Donna Haraway argues, "*Dawn* [the first novel of the *Xenogenesis* trilogy] fails in its promise to tell another story, about another birth, a xenogenesis. Too much of the sacred image of the same is left

intact." Donna Haraway, *Primate Visions: Gender, Race, and Nature in the World of Modern Science* (London and New York: Routledge, 1989), 380.
   14. Butler, *Lilith's Brood*, 13–14.
   15. Butler, *Lilith's Brood*, 57.
   16. Butler, "Amnesty" in *Bloodchild and Other Stories*, second edition (New York: Seven Stories Press, 1996, 2005), 150.
   17. Butler, "Amnesty," 177.
   18. Butler, "Amnesty," 154.
   19. Butler, "Amnesty," 162.
   20. Butler, "Bloodchild" in *Bloodchild and Other Stories*, 18.
   21. Butler, "Bloodchild," 40.
   22. Butler, *Lilith's Brood*, 162.
   23. Meghan K. Riley "'Your Body Has Made a Different Choice': Cognition, Coercion, and the Ethics of Consent in Octavia E. Butler's Lilith's Brood and Fledgling" *Journal of Cognition and Neuroethics* 3:3 (October 2015): 129.
   24. Riley, 131.
   25. Riley, 134.
   26. Catharine A. MacKinnon, *Toward a Feminist Theory of the State* (London and Cambridge, MA: Harvard University Press, 1989), 172.
   27. Butler, "Amnesty," 151–52.
   28. Butler, "Bloodchild," 3.
   29. Butler, "Bloodchild," 28.
   30. Butler, *Bloodchild and Other Stories*, 30.
   31. Lewis Call differentiates between consent in the liberal state and desiring consent, or the kind of consent that enables erotic exchanges of power. (Lewis Call, "Structures of Desire: Postanarchist Kink in the Speculative Fiction of Octavia Butler and Samuel Delany" in J. Heckert and R. Cleminson (eds.) *Anarchism and Sexuality: Ethics, Relationships, and Power* (New York: Routledge, 2011), 131–53.)
   Unlike the stable subject assumed in liberal and economic understandings of consent, desiring consent and the postanarchist kink it facilitates recognizes that power relations and identities are fluid. According to Call, desiring consent contains the potential to subvert power by creating an alternative symbolic order. Call turns to Octavia Butler's Patternist series to explore desiring consent in the reappropriation of the master-slave dynamic toward an erotic exchange of power. Bodies in the Patternist series are flexible; two of the main characters have, on the one hand, the ability to jump bodies and, on the other hand, the power to shape-shift. This material malleability reveals the myth of a stable subject and creates, according to Call, new forms of consent based on the fluidity of power and identity.
   32. Meredith Minister, *Rape Culture on Campus* (Lanham, MD: Lexington, 2018), see, in particular, 1–48.

BIBLIOGRAPHY

Aguirre, Abbey. "Octavia Butler's Prescient Vision of Zealot Elected to 'Make America Great Again.'" *The New Yorker*, July 26, 2017. https://www.newyorker.com/books/second-read/octavia-butlers-prescient-vision-of-a-zealot-elected-to-make-america-great-again.
Brown, Wendy. *States of Injury: Power and Freedom in Late Modernity*. Princeton, NJ: Princeton University Press, 1995.
Butler, Octavia. *Bloodchild and Other Stories*. Second edition. New York: Seven Stories Press, 1996, 2005.
———. *Lilith's Brood: The Complete Xenogenesis Series*. New York: Warner Books, 1989.
———. *Parable of the Sower*. New York: Warner Books, 1993.
———. *Parable of the Talents*. New York: Warner Books, 1998.
Call, Lewis. "Structures of Desire: Postanarchist Kink in the Speculative Fiction of Octavia Butler and Samuel Delany" in *Anarchism and Sexuality: Ethics, Relationships, and Power*, edited by J. Heckert and R. Cleminson, 131–53. New York: Routledge, 2011.

Fischel, Joseph J. *Sex and Harm in the Age of Consent*. Minneapolis and London: University of Minnesota Press, 2016.

Haag, Pamela. *Consent: Sexual Rights and the Transformation of American Liberalism*. Ithaca and London: Cornell University Press, 1999.

Haraway, Donna. *Primate Visions: Gender, Race, and Nature in the World of Modern Science*. London and New York: Routledge, 1989.

Kafer, Alison. *Feminist, Queer, Crip*. Bloomington, Indiana: Indiana University Press, 2013.

Kingkade, Tyler. "New White House PSA Is A Reminder: Sex Without Consent Is Rape." *The Huffington Post*, September 1, 2015. http://www.huffingtonpost.com/entry/new-its-on-us-psa_55e59e1ae4b0c818f61904e8.

MacKinnon, Catharine A. *Toward a Feminist Theory of the State*. London and Cambridge, MA: Harvard University Press, 1989.

McRuer, Robert. *Crip Theory*. New York and London: New York University Press, 2006.

Minister, Meredith. *Rape Culture on Campus*. Lanham, MD: Lexington, 2018.

Pateman, Carole and Charles W. Mills. *Contract and Domination*. Malden, MA: Polity Press, 2007.

Rape, Abuse and Incest National Network. "What Consent Looks Like." https://rainn.org/get-information/sexual-assault-prevention/what-is-consent. Accessed December 8, 2015.

Riley, Meghan K. "'Your Body Has Made a Different Choice': Cognition, Coercion, and the Ethics of Consent in Octavia E. Butler's Lilith's Brood and Fledgling." *Journal of Cognition and Neuroethics* 3, no. 3 (October 2015): 114–37.

Siebers, Tobin. *Disability Theory*. Ann Arbor: University of Michigan, 2008.

United States White House Task Force to Protect Students from Sexual Assault. "Not Alone: The First Report of the White House Task Force to Protect Students from Sexual Assault." Task Force Report. Washington D.C.: The White House, April 2014. http://www.changingourcampus.org/resources/not-alone/WH_Task_Force_First_Report.pdf.

Chapter Nine

Good Intentions are Not Enough

Rhiannon Graybill

In thinking about responding to sexual violence and rape culture on campus, I have found myself drawn to the phrase "good intentions are not enough." This phrase is useful because it acknowledges the good intentions that motivate much activism, while also gesturing at the limits of those good intentions. Wishing to do good does not guarantee that good is actually done. There is often a gap between intentions and actions; New Years' resolutions and pledges to *start going to the gym* offer an easy reminder of this. Or good intentions may lead to something worse; after all, as another familiar saying has it, "the road to hell is paved with good intentions."

My goal in writing this essay is to complicate pedagogical responses to rape culture, particularly as they play out in the religious studies classroom. I discuss four concerns: the shifting meanings of "harm," the significance of race and racialized histories of violence, the question (borrowed from postcolonial feminism) of whether women "really need saving," and the matter of pleasure. The issues I identify are not new issues in and of themselves, but they have not been sufficiently addressed in relation to the religious studies classroom and the other roles that religious studies plays in the academy.

Most of the theoretical work I draw on comes from beyond the discipline of religious studies as ordinarily construed. Thus the work of this essay is as much translation across disciplinary boundaries as it is the construction of something new. In critiquing "harm," I join an ongoing conversation that has mostly taken place outside religious studies, though with significant implications, I will suggest, for both our pedagogy and our discipline. The critique of race and carceral feminism is also one that is mostly articulated outside the discipline of religious studies, though with notable exceptions.[1] In contrast, issues of postcolonial critique and gender are no doubt familiar to many religious studies professionals, especially those who teach about religious practices or nonwestern religions. Pleasure also makes appearances in religious studies classrooms and conversations, though it is often held at a distance from sexual violence. The essay thus invites religious studies teachers and practitioners to listen in on and to engage with ongoing conversations about, in, and around feminist theory and to use them to rethink how we teach and talk about sexual violence in our own discipline.

I also aim to demonstrate that the discipline of religious studies has something useful and important to offer to ongoing conversations about sexual violence and rape culture in and around college and university communities. The anxiety, discomfort, and even controversy that bubble up in many religious studies classrooms provide a model for how to address difficult topics, including those involving sexual violence. Insofar as religious traditions and religious practices are centered on the body, our discipline has developed relatively sophisticated ways of talking and teaching about embodiment. Given the ways rape culture centers the body, this is a useful resource. At the same time, such pedagogical practices as careful listening, suspending easy judgment, and balancing critique with empathetic observation all represent strategies in engaging sexual violence in texts, in traditions, and on campus. This essay also suggests the possibility for coalition building across traditional disciplinary boundaries. Engaging with feminist critique and critical inquiry only strengthens this process.

Good intentions are an important part of both college teaching and campus activism, but on their own, they are not enough. While feminist teachers and scholars are often called—with the best of intentions—to be "first responders" in campus conversations (or clashes) over sexual violence and sexual cultures, I want to insist that we are *scholars* as much as we are *teachers*, and part of our scholarly work is the work of critique. This essay contributes to the project of critique while also setting forth the frameworks in which critical concerns can continue to be articulated and debated.

WHAT IS HARM, AND WHO IS BEING HARMED?

The idea of harm is omnipresent when it comes to talking about sexual violence and rape culture on campus. Rape, sexual violence, and sexual harassment are all clear forms of harm. But "harm" is also used in other ways. Institutional efforts at prevention frame sexual violence as "a harm to our community," as much as to individual victims/survivors. Students increasingly use the language of harm to describe not simply specific acts of violence, but broader issues of culture, language, and "campus climate." Conversations about trigger warnings are in many ways conversations about harm: the goal of a trigger warning is to reduce harm to vulnerable students; trigger warnings themselves are sometimes seen as bringing harm to academic freedom or to the free exchange of ideas. Furthermore, those who introduce difficult conversations on campus—whether raising the problem of sexual assault (e.g., Emma Sulkowicz, who became widely known for their senior thesis art project at Columbia University, entitled "Mattress Performance (Carry That Weight)"[2]) or problematizing institutional responses to this problem (most dramatically, feminist provocateur Laura Kipnis,[3] though also, e.g., feminist scholar Jennifer Doyle[4])—are framed as agents of harm.

Harm thus names multiple related but distinct phenomena that occur under rape culture. It describes the effect of violence, assault, or harassment on victims. It describes the consequences of this personal harm on the larger community. It provides a convenient way to name issues of "climate" and broader cultural forces circulating in and around campus. It is used to describe the effects of being "triggered," and to advocate against these policies. And it is employed to reproach those who challenge dominant scripts, whether in the classroom, in scholarship, or in activism.

While these phenomena are clearly related—indeed, the term "rape culture" was coined to name such broad and complex cultural configurations of actions, discourses, and affects—we would do well to be wary about overreliance on a single category of harm. Constructing broad categories can be strategic for activist purposes, as the success of the #MeToo hashtag shows. However, the same strategic elision of nuance can be, and often is, redirected against feminist and queer scholars and teachers. My thinking about the harm of sexual violence is influenced greatly by Sarah Schulman's work on violence and harm in *Conflict is Not Abuse: Overstating Harm, Community Responsibility, and the Duty of Repair*.[5] The sentence in the title, "conflict is not abuse," insists on the importance of distinguishing between different forms of suffering, offense, and trauma. As Schulman demonstrates throughout the book, to treat all "conflict" or harm as "abuse" is to commit a category error with serious consequences. Misreading conflict as abuse, whether in the case of a disagreement with a friend, a flirtation gone awry, a domestic altercation, or the criminalization of HIV, has serious consequences that shut down the possibility of resolution while ultimately shoring up the power of the state.[6]

One problem with the lack of clarity surrounding the use of the language of "harm" is that it is frequently used against feminist and queer thinkers. Lisa Duggan notes that queer studies scholars are often caught in the dragnet of sexual misconduct policies aimed at addressing sexual harassment or sexual assault.[7] Duggan notes that "teaching 'improper' materials in class" can be grounds for a complaint of sexual misconduct; the institutional systems that respond to such complaints often lack the nuance to determine whether the accusation of impropriety is in fact a cover for homophobia, misogyny, or personal discomfort. Teaching what are often referred to as "difficult topics" (such as sexuality, gender, or race) thus becomes a professional risk as well as a pedagogical one. Furthermore, choosing to study such topics may also be turned against the scholar. Jennifer Doyle, a professor of English at UC Riverside who writes on feminist and queer topics, describes a similar experience in her own Title IX case, which began when she was harassed by a student:

> My situation would become even stranger when, in a university hearing, my scholarship (which is feminist, queer, and about sexual politics) was treated by faculty as evidence of sexual impropriety. Writing about *Moby Dick* and *Jude the Obscure*, a syllabus from a queer theory class, and essays on abortion and promiscuity supported the committee's conclusion that I was not, in fact, being harassed.[8]

Thus the content of Doyle's own teaching and research was used against her, specifically to deny her experience of harassment. Doyle's situation is hardly exceptional and indeed aligns with the dynamics Duggan describes. Both Duggan and Schulman further offer critiques of the current rallying cry of "Believe women!," noting the ways it ignores both structures of power and the complex ambivalences of desire and selfhood.

The academic study of religion may also run up against these same institutional policies targeting harm and bias. Teaching about religion can be a troubling business; students are as likely to be offended by descriptions of religious traditions (their own or others) as by discussions of sexual violence or critiques thereof. The critical study of religion, as much as the critical theorization of sex and gender, can be experienced by students as a cause of harm in the classroom. There is thus an important parallel between the feminist politics of sexuality and religious studies' disciplinary commitments to understanding religious difference without assimilating it to dominant liberal values. In this way, both a feminist critique of rape culture as purity culture and a religious studies critique of secularism as crypto-Protestantism threaten students' closely held beliefs and may even be understood as doing harm to them.

This is a good example of the difficulty of "good intentions." It is considered an ethical and pedagogical "good" to respect students' religious backgrounds; it is also "good" to teach students seriously and critically about religious traditions. And yet not infrequently, these two goals come into conflict. So too with the assumptions about sex, sexuality, and sexual violence that students bring with them into the college or university classroom. In both cases (religion and sexual violence), the very structure of the pedagogical encounter means there is no way to do good without also doing harm; the question is whether to preserve students' preexisting faith/assumptions/ truths, or the integrity of the pedagogical process.

A second problem with the expansion of the discourse of harm is the way it supports the neoliberalization of the university. Universities often use the "harm" of sexual violence, broadly construed, to justify administrative innovations that expand their own power. As Doyle describes, the figure of the "very young girl"[9] or the "endangered girl" becomes a driving force in the increased securitization of the campus, which combines an amplification of surveillance and disciplinary apparatuses with a neoliberal turn to the market for solutions. What Laura Kipnis terms the "industrialization of sexual assault," including bystander intervention trainings, consent apps, and inspirational campus speakers—all of which command a much higher market price than that old standby of campus protection, the pocket rape whistle.[10] This shift to the market and to crisis management brings with it all the familiar harms of the neoliberalization of higher education.

The neoliberalization of the university is threatening for many reasons; the arguments have already been effectively articulated elsewhere, so I will provide only a cursory overview. Feminist and queer critiques illustrate the ways in which the neoliberal university works in the service of traditional values, including sexual values. Reflecting upon academia, scholars in the humanities and social sciences have offered scathing critiques of neoliberalization.[11] The discipline of religious studies has contributed to this project.[12] While neoliberalism may increase university profits, it is hardly in the best interest of either feminists or religious studies scholars. Resistance to this process, meanwhile, may provide an occasion for new coalition-building and activism, including between religious studies and feminist and queer theory.

Returning to the "harm reduction" strategies of the neoliberal university, it is important to recognize the damage that harm mitigation policies frequently inflict on the very people they are intended to help. Doyle warns that "people victimized by assault will find themselves obliterated by the idea of the 'rape victim.'"[13] Similarly, Rachel Hall describes "the imaginary figure of woman as victim" who "bear[s] the brunt of representing the problem of sexual violence to the American public":

> Never mind that woman-as-victim is an abstraction. Her emptiness renders her more appropriate for the task at hand: we fill her up with cultural ideals of feminine suffering, so that she comes to embody suffering as female. Woman as victim is: a fantasy, a nightmare, a cultural transfer point, a container to be filled, a signifier beneath which chains of complementary and contradictory signifieds endlessly slip.[14]

Thus, specific efforts to reduce harm may, instead, end up perpetuating it. The abstraction of woman-as-victim, even as it summons discourses of harm, does real harm to real women. As religious studies professionals, we are adept at deconstructing such overgeneralizing abstractions. Thus as we teach, with sensitivity, about sexual violence, we must also work to avoid creating figures and stereotypes of the "victim" or "endangered young girl" (whether "endangered" by rape, by religious fundamentalism, or by late capitalist modernity).

RACE, SEXUALITY, AND INTERSECTIONALITY

One of the problems with the expansion of the category of "harm" is the way it neglects or even encourages the glossing over of specific historical harms. In the American context, one of these is the historical—and ongoing—entanglement of sexual violence and race.[15] Central to the idea of the "endangered young girl" or the model victim is the idea of whiteness. The victim of sexual assault is imagined as a white woman; rape is figured as a threat not just to women, but to whiteness. In this way, representations of rape offer another iteration of cultural narratives protecting (and policing) white womanhood, such as panic over "white slavery" and sex trafficking of white women. The whiteness of the imagined rape victim has been chronicled by numerous feminist scholars.[16] Furthermore, the imagined whiteness of the ideal rape victim is bound up with the implied blackness of the imagined rapist. Protecting (white) women from rape means protecting them from (black) men. Already in the nineteenth century, Ida B. Wells described the ways in which the fear of rape of white women was used to justify the lynching of black men.[17]

Added to this racial history is the myth of black sexual appetite, particularly black male sexual appetite, which is also deployed to justify violence.[18] During Reconstruction and afterward, these same myths were used to justify the lynching of black men and to dismiss claims of rape by black women, even as rape was used as a "weapon of terror" against both black men and women. Danielle L. McGuire summarizes,

> When African Americans tested their freedom during Reconstruction, former slaveholders and their sympathizers used rape as a 'weapon of terror' to dominate the bodies and minds of African-American men and women. Interracial rape was not only used to uphold white patriarchal power but was also deployed as a justification for lynching black men who challenged the Southern status quo. In addition to the immediate physical danger African Americans faced, sexual and racial violence functioned as a tool of coercion, control, and harassment.[19]

The patterns McGuire describes—the use of rape as a weapon against black Americans, white paranoia about the raping of white women by black men, the strategic exploitation of the fear of rape to justify discrimination and violence against black Americans, especially black men—all continue long beyond Reconstruction, into our present moment. There are similar stories to be found when we look, for example, at the experiences of Native

Americans, undocumented migrants, and numerous other disenfranchised groups. Here we have another example of good intentions—reducing sexual violence—being insufficient to prevent another social harm—racism and racialized terror.

It is not only in the modern American context that both rape and anxiety over rape are used as weapons of terror and social control. The Hebrew Bible, the focus of my own research, is filled with stories about rape as a practice of power and domination; this is supported by reference to other ancient Near Eastern materials, such as the records of Assyrian practices toward prisoners of war. In teaching this material, I have found it useful to connect the use of rape in the text to contemporary political contexts. Thus the threat of sexual violence that we find in the Hebrew prophets—leveled mostly against foreign enemies, though also, occasionally, against the Israelites and Judeans themselves—is not simply an idle threat. Instead, it is substantiated by a lengthy literature, both ancient and modern, of rape as a weapon of war. Alice Bach, for example, has read the rape of the Shiloh women (Judg. 21) through the recent historical example of mass rape in Bosnia during the war.[20] Emma England has similarly linked the book of Judith to the recent experience of sexual humiliation and torture of Iraqi prisoners of war by American soldiers at Abu Ghraib.[21] Upon reading these works, students find the parallels disturbing—more disturbing by far than the original violence described in the biblical text. However, teaching these parallels forces students to take seriously the complex interrelations of sexual violence, power, and empire.

Another useful biblical story for reflecting on the entanglements of rape and race, with particular attention to the representations of black male sexuality, is the story of the curse of Ham (Gen. 9:18–27). In this brief story, which follows immediately after the flood, Noah plants a vineyard, makes wine, and then passes out drunk. His son Ham "sees his nakedness" (a phrase that encompasses a range of possible meanings from literally seeing a naked body to rape); when Noah finds out, he curses Ham's son, Canaan:

> [25]"Cursed be Canaan;
>   lowest of slaves shall he be to his brothers."
> [26]He also said,
> "Blessed by the Lord my God be Shem;
>   and let Canaan be his slave.
> [27]May God make space for Japheth,
>   and let him live in the tents of Shem;
>   and let Canaan be his slave." (Gen. 9:25–27; NRSV)

On one level, Noah's curse of Canaan justifies the conquest of Israel; the land, after all, is also known as Canaan. But because Ham is the purported ancestor of the Africans, the text has a racialized legacy at well; in the United States, it was used to justify the slavery of black Americans as biblically commanded.[22] Teaching this story means reckoning not just with the intersections of alcohol and sexual abuse (Noah is intoxicated) and of homosexuality and sexual transgression (the rape, if rape occurs, is a homosexual one), but also the racialized deployment of this story in the American context (race, slavery, and white terror over black male sexuality). There is no easy answer here—especially when teaching in the southern United States, where the legacy of the curse of Ham was especially strong. Still, drawing these connections, I would suggest, is an important task in teaching about rape and rape culture.[23]

Untangling racism from rape also requires feminists to take seriously the consequences of what Elizabeth Bernstein has termed "carceral feminism." Carceral feminism names the way in which feminism and feminist activism collaborate with state systems of power—yet another example of "good intentions are not enough." Much of Bernstein's work focuses on antitrafficking activism, which brings together feminists and Christian evangelicals who share a "commitment to carceral paradigms of social, and in particular gender, justice . . . and to militarized humanitarianism as the pre-eminent mode of engagement by the state."[24] Such carceral feminism seeks to aid women through a turn to the disciplinary apparatus of the state.[25] While Bernstein's work emphasizes the international anti-trafficking movement, carceral feminisms emerge elsewhere as well, including in the U.S. criminal justice system where, in Bernstein's words, "recent feminist activism around questions of sexual violence has been a crucial enabler of the late-capitalist carceral turn."[26] Marie Gottschalk, whose work Bernstein cites, suggests that the carceral term in feminism bears responsibility for mass incarceration in America. Gottschalk draws attention to the ways feminist advocacy against rape and domestic violence collaborated with prosecutors and the carceral system; she concludes that the "contemporary women's movement in the United States helped facilitate the carceral state."[27] Bernstein traces similar patterns in other national contexts, including anti-immigrant sentiment in France.

The critique of carceral feminism is highly relevant, I would suggest, to teaching religious studies. First, religion plays a key role in the emergence of carceral feminism. As Bernstein and Janet R. Jakobsen demonstrate, antitrafficking activism represents a collaboration between feminists, including radical feminists, and Christian evangelicals.[28] It thus provides a teachable moment about religion and globalization that also connects the global (human trafficking) to the local (mass incarceration in America). In the context of Christian ethics, Letitia M. Campbell and Yvonne C. Zimmerman provide a progressive critique of anti-trafficking activism that also introduces questions of queerness and sexual ethics.[29] The concept of "carceral feminism" also suggests a way to connect conversations about religion and globalization, including the global sex trade, to critiques of mass incarceration. Religion is complicit in the crafting of many of these structures, from white supremacy to carceral feminism. This means that religious studies is uniquely positioned to critique and deconstruct these cultural formations.

DO WOMEN REALLY NEED SAVING?

The third critical issue is informed by postcolonial feminist critique. Readers versed in contemporary conversations about Islam will recognize that the question *Do women really need saving?* is a variant of Lila Abu-Lughod's "Do Muslim Women Really Need Saving?," published first as an essay in *American Anthropologist*, then as volume entitled *Do Muslim Women Need Saving?*[30] Interestingly, the "really" that drops when the article becomes a book title is also the word that most clearly signals the argument: *really*, in fact, Muslim women do *not* need saving, certainly not by the forces of Western imperialism and colonialism that Abu-Lughod singles out for critique. Abu-Lhugod writes,

> It is deeply problematic to construct the Afghan woman as someone in need of saving. When you save someone, you imply that you are saving her from something. You are also saving her to something. What violences are entailed in this transformation, and what presumptions are being made about the superiority of that to which you are saving her? Projects of saving other women depend on and reinforce a sense of superiority by Westerners, a form of arrogance that deserves to be challenged.[31]

Abu-Lughod's immediate concern is with American action in Afghanistan and the supposed "plight of Afghan women," which is mobilized to sell American military imperialism abroad. Importantly, the discourse of "saving women" does not have to be employed disingenuously to be a problem. Many actors in U.S. colonial endeavor in Afghanistan believed, in good faith, that their actions were right and justified, that women truly needed "saving." But as Abu-Lughod points out, these good intentions are not enough—the project is at a minimum arrogant and more likely harmful as well. Indeed, Chandra Talpade Mohanty identifies any Western feminist concern with "third world women" as potentially colonialist.[32]

The question of "saving women" is also bound up with sex and sexuality. As in the case of racialized rape hysteria discussed above, the desire to save women frequently extends to a compulsion to protect women's "purity," especially from brown and black men. Rape, sexual exploitation, and sexism have all been used to justify the colonial project; in Gayatri Chakravorty Spivak's famous formulation, colonialism is "white men saving brown women from brown men."[33] Thus the desire to save women also has significance in the context of discussing, and critiquing, rape and rape culture, particularly given the Orientalist history of the disciplines of "Comparative Religion," *Orientalische Wissenschaft*, and even the field at present.[34]

Thus, concerns with "saving" women, including saving them from sexual violence, cannot be dissociated from militarization and imperialism. Even well-intentioned projects are implicated in colonialism. And religious studies, and the religious studies classroom, is not immune. Both contemporary and historical religious texts and traditions are vulnerable to the appeal to "save the women!" In the case of Islam, the work of Abu-Lughod, Spivak, Saba Mahmood, and a host of others has already clearly established the tacit—and explicit—colonialism of religious studies projects that aim to "save" women, particularly in the context of gender, sexuality, and bodily autonomy. Saba Mahmood writes,

> I am making a rather straightforward and familiar point here: No discursive object occupies a simple relation to the reality it purportedly denotes . . . Consequently, contemporary concern for Muslim women in Euro-American public debate cannot be dissociated from the war declared by European and American governments on the Muslim world (which includes Muslim immigrant populations residing in Europe and America.)[35]

As Mahmood's quote already indicates, this critique has been fully and persuasively articulated by these scholars; it is incumbent that religious studies teachers who take up the issue of rape as well as female circumcision, marriage laws, or even the veil address the postcolonial feminist critique. Often, this means guiding students, eager to jump to conclusions and animated by the moral (over)clarity of the young, toward a deeper understanding and hear the critique before rejecting it with a simple appeal to universals or "human rights." Of course, it is not only in the teaching of Islam that this is an issue. Instead, it extends to a wide range of religious texts and traditions (though the specificity of colonial contexts is also something we should attend to, without, e.g., collapsing Iran into Yemen or Arkansas purity balls into Afghan marriage practices. Context matters.)

This critique is also relevant, I would suggest, for those of us whose teaching is outside of "living religions" or is confined to texts. The desire to "save women" who are not living beings but simply characters in religious texts may seem less pernicious—"*no real women were harmed in the making of this slightly imperialist argument.*" I have traced this tendency at length with reference to scholarship on Jephthah's daughter (Judges 11), who is sacrificed by her father to fulfill a foolhardy vow. While an older generation of critics is mostly interested in what the story tells us about Yahweh's character, the structure of vows, or the narrative threads and themes of the book of Judges, a number of feminist critics have set forth to "hear the voice" of Jephthah's daughter and to save her from the patriarchal machinations of the text. As I document in my own work on Jephthah's daughter, this critical response, while inarguably motivated by feminist "good intentions," also traffics in nasty colonialist and racist stereotypes. The desire to save women, even ancient fictional ones, becomes a foothold for paternalism, Orientalism, and imperialism.[36] That these concepts are smuggled in under the auspices of feminism makes them all the more difficult to expose and root out, especially to students in the thralls of their first feminist awakening. One pedagogical task is to help readers, especially feminist readers, recognize the urge to "save" Jephthah's daughter and to explore what resisting this urge might look like.

This does not mean we should not talk about rape or gendered violence in ancient texts or modern contexts. Instead, these conversations can and should occur, but with an awareness of history of colonialism and imperialism, and in particular the ways in which feminism has been used by these cultural forces. This, in turn, opens feminist questions of who gets to do feminist work for whom, as well as what our obligations are for communities other from ourselves. This is especially a concern when the work of dismantling rape culture becomes a work not just of assessment and diagnosis, but of reconfiguring the sacred or reimagining the tradition. Before saving religious others "from themselves," it is necessary to reckon with the colonialist implications of such a position.

THE PROBLEM OF PLEASURE

The concern for women as victims has not always been matched by an interest in women as agents, especially sexual agents. Sexual pleasure has often proved a problem for feminist theory, particularly feminist responses to sexual violence. In directing attention to the ways in which sex and sexual organizations of power exploit women, feminist theories have often left little space for theorizing or even acknowledging pleasure. This issue lay at the heart of the so-called feminist "sex wars" in the 1980s—including the controversial 1982 Barnard conference "Toward a Politics of Sexuality"—and it has returned in a new way in recent conversations about sexual violence, particularly in the campus context. Alice Echols, one of the participants at the 1982 Barnard conference, has reflected,

> Today, there is arguably more danger—both concrete and imagined—than at the height of the sex wars. No doubt these are dangerous times for women in many, many places across the globe. Meanwhile, closer to home, those of us who teach college are witnessing a sea change on our campuses as students mobilize for greater protection from all manner of danger, sometimes including our own dangerous ideas. Yet if some younger women are feeling imperiled, others are searching for unabashed sexual fulfillment, demanding more

pleasure, as evidenced most obviously by SlutWalks and a still-thriving hook-up culture.[37]

As Echols goes on to note, this increased sense of harm and danger has been mobilized *against* feminist ideas and practices, including in many of the ways discussed above. The central concern of her essay, however, is the ways in which sexuality is "tangled up in pleasure and danger," a formulation introduced by Carole Vance at the 1982 Barnard conference and the cause of much debate then and since. Of Vance's work, Echols writes,

> It was designed to recalibrate feminist discussions of sexuality so that there might again be room within the women's movement for frank discussions about women's sexual pleasure. Vance took aim at movement shibboleths, particularly easy generalizations about women's soft, gauzy eroticism and men's rock-hard, predatory sexuality. Her address was both an invitation to begin talking honestly about sex and a substantial intervention in the feminist discourse about pornography, which at the time was dominated by the antipornography movement.[38]

On one level, this is simply a reflection on the paper Carole Vance presented at the Barnard conference in 1982.[39] But it is also, I would suggest, a keen diagnosis of our own moment. While the antipornography movement, once dominant in feminist theory and activism, has faltered, campus movements against sexual violence have risen to take its place. The "movement shibboleths" that Echols attributes to 1980s feminism have returned, in new forms, in the new campus activism; what is largely missing is a conversation that accounts for ambiguity, difficulty and ambivalence that often surround sex and sexual pleasure, particularly as they are articulated under pervasive purity culture.[40] In *Conflict is Not Abuse*, Schulman takes up the complexity that surrounds "no," including "No Means No!" and calls for nuance, adding "People do not always know what they feel."[41] Our feelings are not always straightforward or transparent; we do not always understand what we are feeling or why. Sara Ahmed makes a similar argument about the ambiguities of consent in *Willful Subjects*.[42] And Rebecca Traister, in an article in New York magazine entitled, "Why Sex That's Consensual Can Still Be Bad. And Why We're Not Talking About It" concludes,

> One thing that's clear is that feminists need to raise the bar for women's sex lives way, way higher. "Sure, teaching consent to college freshmen may be necessary in a culture in which kids are graduating from high school thinking it's okay to have sex with someone who is unconscious," says [Maya] Dusenbery. "But I don't want us to ever lose sight of the fact that consent is not the goal. Seriously, God help us if the best we can say about the sex we have is that it was consensual."[43]

These arguments reveal two issues: the complexity and ambiguity of speaking about sexual pleasure, which is often erased in slogans and the strategic essentializing of much campus sexual activism, and the ways in which this erasure leaves no space for pleasure.

The question becomes: how do we resist rape and teach about rape culture without killing pleasure? Is it possible to describe and speak against rape culture while still leaving a space for sexual enjoyment and eroticism?[44] In a classic essay entitled "Thinking Sex" that remains relevant today, Gayle Rubin suggests that feminist theory is not, alone, sufficient to the task:

> Feminist conceptual tools were developed to detect and analyse gender-based hierarchies. To the extent that these overlap with erotic stratifications, feminist theory has some explanatory power. But as issues become less those of gender and more those of sexuality, feminist analysis becomes misleading and often irrelevant. Feminist thought simply lacks angles of vision which can fully encompass the social organization of sexuality. The criteria of relevance in feminist thought do not allow it to see or assess critical power relations in the area of sexuality. In the long run, feminism's critique of gender hierarchy must be incorporated into a radical theory of sex, and the critique of sexual oppression should enrich feminism. But an autonomous theory and politics specific to sexuality must be developed."[45]

Thus teaching about sex and sexuality in a time of rape culture requires not just feminist frameworks, but a close engagement with theories of sexuality, including queer theories of religion.

In the religious studies classroom, this means that feminist approaches are at once necessary and insufficient. Teaching about sexual violence responsibly means, as well, holding open a space for sexual pleasure. It also means opening spaces in the classroom and in conversations about texts and practices for queer or otherwise non-heteronormative practices of sexuality. This requires us to model thinking about sex, power, pleasure, and (non)consent without an easy recourse to rape culture clichés.

CONCLUDING REFLECTIONS

This essay has outlined four difficulties for teaching about sexual violence, rape, and rape culture, with a particular emphasis on issues that arise in religious studies classrooms. Discourses surrounding sexual violence, sexual harassment, sexual assault, and rape culture make frequent use of the language of harm. This includes the question of who is harmed, the issue of who or what can inflict harm (a person, a body, a text, a classroom comment, a look), and what it means to harmed in the larger context of sexual violence. Institutional responses to sexual violence often center on "harm reduction," rather than other ways of working through pain, discomfort, trauma, or violence. Often, this extends to instructions concerning the classroom or professor as well. As religious studies teachers operate in this environment, it is crucial to think critically about the problem of harm, as well as to attend to the increasing number of feminist and queer critiques of this discourse.

The second problem involves the historical—and ongoing—relationship between race and sexual violence (particularly in the U.S. context). Feminist activism against sexual violence has an unpleasant history of collaborating with state structures of authority, such as the police and "tough on crime" lawmakers, with racist consequences. Discourses of the endangered white woman, threatened by the hypersexualized black man, emerge in new figurations as part of the metaphorics of sexual violence prevention. The problem is thus both administrative and symbolic. Feminism, including feminist advocacy on campus and in the classroom, must acknowledge its own complicity in racist discourses and policies, which play off of fears of the vulnerable white woman. This is of particular relevance to religious studies pedagogy insofar as teaching about religion requires that we address the histories of race.

The third problem borrows from postcolonial critique to ask whether women "really need saving." In its original postcolonial context, this question concerns liberal feminist attempts to "save" women, especially in the global south, from various harms (including the threat of male sexual predation). In the context of sexual violence on campus, this question highlights—again following the groundbreaking work of postcolonial feminist critique—the problematics of starting from the assumption of women as victims or potential victims. In the context of the largely secular religious studies department or classroom, this question assumes particular urgency.

The fourth and final problem is pleasure. If we are to teach and research responsibly about sexual violence, then this responsibility extends to an accounting for pleasure—or its absence. If critique eliminates all space for pleasure then, I suggest, the critique must be altered. There is also the risk that well-intentioned but strident critique will ignore or erase the ambiguity or ambivalence that surrounds so much of desire, while reducing its complexities to a reductive binary of consensual/nonconsensual.

I began with the claim "good intentions are not enough"; I want to end by returning to it. Good intentions on their own are not enough to avoid perpetuating racist, queerphobic, or colonialist notions as we teach about religion; this is particularly true in the case of religion and sexual violence. Good intentions are not enough to negotiate the shifting meanings of the term "harm" and the risky consequences of its conceptual dilution. And good intentions are not enough to hold onto pleasure in the face of fear, sloganeering, and a desire for conceptual clarity that erases all space for ambiguity and ambivalence. Thus if we hope to be ethical teachers—not just in representing our source material, but in reaching our students—we must take seriously the complexity of issues that surround any conversation about rape and rape culture.

NOTES

1. For example, Kelly Brown Douglas, *Stand Your Ground: Black Bodies and the Justice of God* (Maryknoll, NY: Orbis Books, 2015); Vincent W. Lloyd and Andrew Prevot, eds., *Anti-Blackness and Christian Ethics* (Maryknoll, NY: Orbis Books, 2017).
2. Sulcowicz alleged that they had been sexually assaulted by a male student and that the University had failed to respond appropriately; they pledged to carry a mattress (representing the location where the assault occurred) until either resolution or graduation. The accused student has strenuously denied the accusations.
3. Laura Kipnis is a cultural critic and professor of Media Studies at Northwestern University and the author of *Unwanted Advances: Sexual Paranoia Comes to Campus*, which argues that efforts to mitigate sexual violence on campus have exceeded reasonable limits while failing to achive their goals, with highly negative consequences for both academic freedom and feminism. Two years prior, in 2015, Kipnis published an article in the Chronicle of Higher Education entitled "Sexual Paranoia Strikes Academe," which discussed Title IX and accusations of sexual misconduct at Northwestern. Kipnis was subsequently subjected to a Title IX investigation of her own and cleared of wrongdoing. Following the publication of *Unwanted Advances*, Kipnis faced another Title IX complaint. Laura Kipnis, *Unwanted Advances: Sexual Paranoia Comes to Campus* (HarperCollins, 2017); Laura Kipnis, "Sexual Paranoia Strikes Academe," *The Chronicle of Higher Education*, February 27, 2015, https://www.chronicle.com/article/Sexual-Paranoia-Strikes/190351; Laura Kipnis, "My Title IX Inquisition," *The Chronicle of Higher Education*, May 29, 2015, https://www.chronicle.com/article/My-Title-IX-Inquisition/230489; Robin Wilson, "A Professor, a Graduate Student, and 2 Careers Derailed," *The Chronicle of Higher Education*, June 19, 2015, https://www.chronicle.com/article/A-Professor-a-Graduate/231007; Andy Thomason, "Laura Kipnis Says She Faced Another Title IX Investigation, This Time for Her Book," *The Chronicle of Higher Education Blogs: The Ticker* (blog), September 20, 2017, https://www.chronicle.com/blogs/ticker/laura-kipnis-says-she-faced-another-title-ix-investigation-this-time-for-her-book/120210; Jeannie Suk Gersen, "Laura Kipnis's Endless Trial by Title IX," *The New Yorker*, September 20, 2017, https://www.newyorker.com/news/news-desk/laura-kipniss-endless-trial-by-title-ix.
4. Jennifer Doyle, *Campus Sex, Campus Security* (South Pasadena, CA: Semiotext(e), 2015). I discuss Doyle's case in what follows.
5. Sarah Schulman, *Conflict Is Not Abuse: Overstating Harm, Community Responsibility, and the Duty of Repair* (Vancouver, BC: Arsenal Pulp Press, 2016).
6. As Schulman writes, "Ultimately, when groups bond over shunning or hurting or blaming another person, it is the state's power that is enhanced. Because the state doesn't want to understand causes, because the state doesn't want things to get better, it doesn't want people to understand each other. State apparatuses are there to maintain the power of those in control and punish those who contest that power; that is what bad families do, and that is what bad friends do. And nothing disrupts dehumanization more quickly than inviting someone over, looking into their eyes, hearing their voice, and listening" (*Conflict is Not Abuse*, 279-280).
7. Lisa Duggan, "Rapture and Risk on Campus in the Age of the Sexual Security State | Bully Bloggers," Bully Bloggers, June 6, 2017, https://bullybloggers.wordpress.com/2017/06/06/rapture-and-risk-on-campus-in-the-age-of-the-sexual-security-state/.
8. Doyle, *Campus Sex, Campus Security*, 9.
9. *Very Young Girls* is also the name of a documentary about teenage prostitution discussed by Elizabeth Bernstein in "Militarized Humanitarianism Meets Carceral Feminism: The Politics of Sex, Rights, and Freedom in Contemporary Antitrafficking Campaigns." *Signs* 36, no. 1 (2010): 45–71.
10. Kipnis, *Unwanted Advances*, 247 note.

11. e.g. Doyle, *Campus Sex, Campus Security*; Henry A. Giroux, "The Terror of Neoliberalism: Rethinking the Significance of Cultural Politics," *College Literature* 32, no. 1 (2005): 1–19; Bill Readings, *The University in Ruins* (Cambridge, Mass.: Harvard University Press, 1996); Elizabeth Freeman, "Monsters, Inc.: Notes on the Neoliberal Arts Education," *New Literary History* 36, no. 1 (April 11, 2005): 83–95; Fuyuki Kurasawa, "The State of Intellectual Play: A Generational Manifesto for Neoliberal Times," *TOPIA: Canadian Journal of Cultural Studies* 0, no. 18 (September 1, 2008): 11.

12. Banu Gökariksel and Katharyne Mitchell, "Veiling, Secularism, and the Neoliberal Subject: National Narratives and Supranational Desires in Turkey and France," *Global Networks* 5, no. 2 (April 1, 2005): 147–65; Amelie Barras, *Refashioning Secularisms in France and Turkey: The Case of the Headscarf Ban* (New York: Routledge, 2014); Keri Day, *Religious Resistance to Neoliberalism: Womanist and Black Feminist Perspectives* (Basingstoke: Palgrave Macmillan, 2016; Christine M. Jacobsen, "Veiled Nannies and Secular Futures in France," *Ethnos* 0, no. 0 (April 21, 2017): 1–21.

13. Doyle, *Campus Sex, Campus Security*, 36.

14. Rachel Hall, "'It Can Happen to You': Rape Prevention in the Age of Risk Management," *Hypatia* 19, no. 3 (August 1, 2004): 1–18, p. 12).

15. I will speak only to the U.S. context here, but similar examples may be found in many other national contexts. Similarly, while my focus is on the experience of black Americans, there are related arguments to be made about other racial minorities in the United States.

16. See e.g., Maria Bevacqua, *Rape on the Public Agenda: Feminism and the Politics of Sexual Assault* (Boston: Northeastern University Press, 2000); Lisa Lindquist Dorr, *White Women, Rape, and the Power of Race in Virginia, 1900–1960* (Chapel Hill: University of North Carolina Press, 2005); Crystal Nicole Feimster, *Southern Horrors: Women and the Politics of Rape and Lynching* (Cambridge, Mass.: Harvard University Press, 2009); Danielle L. McGuire, *At the Dark End of the Street: Black Women, Rape, and Resistance: a New History of the Civil Rights Movement from Rosa Parks to the Rise of Black Power* (New York: Vintage Books, 2011).

17. Ida B. Wells-Barnett, *On Lynchings* (Mineola, New York: Dover, 2014); originally published as *Southern Horrors: Lynch Law in All Its Phases* (New York: New York Age Print, 1892); *A Red Record: Tabulated Statistics and Alleged Causes of Lynchings in the United States 1892–1893–1894* (Chicago: Donohue & Henneberry, 1895); *Mob Rule in New Orleans: Robert Charles and His Fight to the Death* (Chicago: Ida B. Wells, 1900).

18. Valerie Smith, *Not Just Race, Not Just Gender: Black Feminist Readings* (New York: Routledge, 2013), 1.

19. McGuire, *At the Dark End of the Street*, xviii.

20. Alice Bach, "Rereading the Body Politic: Women and Violence in Judges 21," *Biblical Interpretation* 6, no. 1 (1998): 1–19.

21. Emma England, "Violent Superwomen: Super Heroes or Super Villains? Judith, Wonder Woman and Lynndie England," in *A Feminist Companion to Tobit and Judith*, ed. Athalya Brenner-Idan and Helen Efthimiadis-Keith (Bloomsbury T&T Clark, 2015), 242–58.

22. See Stephen R. Haynes, *Noah's Curse: The Biblical Justification of American Slavery* (New York: Oxford University Press, 2002).

23. There is another trajectory of interpretation that involves the possibility that Ham raped Noah's wife (that is, that seeing his father's nakedness refers to having sex with his father's wife). While I do not have time to take up this interpretation here, it suggests additional avenues for thinking about Genesis 9 in and through rape culture. I am grateful to Beatrice Lawrence for reminding me of this interpretation.

24. Elizabeth Bernstein, "Militarized Humanitarianism Meets Carceral Feminism," 47.

25. See Bernstein, "Carceral Politics as Gender Justice? The 'Traffic in Women' and Neoliberal Circuits of Crime, Sex, and Rights," *Theory and Society* 41, no. 3 (2012), p. 53; Janet E. Halley, *Split Decisions: How and Why to Take a Break from Feminism* (Princeton University Press, 2006), 21–22. In this way, it resembles what Janet Halley has termed "governmental feminism."

26. Bernstein, "Carceral Politics as Gender Justice?," 241.

27. Marie Gottschalk, *The Prison and the Gallows: The Politics of Mass Incarceration in America* (New York; Cambridge: Cambridge University Press, 2006), 115.
28. Elizabeth Bernstein and Janet R. Jakobsen, "Sex, Secularism and Religious Influence in US Politics," *Third World Quarterly 31*, no. 6 (September 1, 2010): 1023–39.
29. Letitia M. Campbell and Yvonne C. Zimmerman, "Christian Ethics and Human Trafficking Activism: Progressive Christianity and Social Critique," *Journal of the Society of Christian Ethics* 34, no. 1 (2014): 145–72.
30. Lila Abu-Lughod, "Do Muslim Women Really Need Saving? Anthropological Reflections on Cultural Relativism and Its Others," *American Anthropologist* 104, no. 3 (2002): 783–90; Lila Abu-Lughod, *Do Muslim Women Need Saving?* (Cambridge, MA: Harvard University Press, 2013).
31. Abu-Lughod, "Do Muslim Women Really Need Saving?" 788–89.
32. Chandra Talpade Mohanty, "Under Western Eyes: Feminist Scholarship and Colonial Discourses," *Boundary* 2 12/13 (1984): 351.
33. Gayatri Chakravorty Spivak, "Can the Subaltern Speak?" in *Colonial Discourse and Postcolonial Theory: A Reader*, ed. Patrick Williams and Laura Chrisman (New York: Columbia University Press), 93; reprinted from C. Nelson and L. Grossberg (eds.), *Marxism and the Interpretation of Culture* (Macmillan Education: Basingstoke, 1988, 271–313.
34. Tomoko Masuzawa, *The Invention of World Religions: Or, How European Universalism Was Preserved in the Language of Pluralism* (University of Chicago Press, 2005).
35. Saba Mahmood, "Retooling Democracy and Feminism in the Service of the New Empire," *Qui Parle* 16, no. 1 (2006): 130.
36. Rhiannon Graybill, "No Child Left Behind: Reading Jephthah's Daughter with The Babylon Complex," *The Bible & Critical Theory* 11, no. 2 (2015): 36–50.
37. Alice Echols, "Retrospective: Tangled Up in Pleasure and Danger," *Signs: Journal of Women in Culture and Society* 42, no. 1 (September 1, 2016): 11–22, 19.
38. Echols, "Retrospective: Tangled up in Pleasure and Danger," 11.
39. See also Carole Vance, ed., *Pleasure and Danger: Exploring Female Sexuality.* Boston: Routledge & Kegan Paul, 1984.
40. Jessica Valenti, *The Purity Myth: How America's Obsession with Virginity Is Hurting Young Women, First Trade Paper Edition* (Berkeley, CA: Seal Press, 2009).
41. Schulman, *Conflict Is Not Abuse,* 49.
42. Sara Ahmed, *Willful Subjects* (Durham, NC: Duke University Press, 2014), 55; see Rhiannon Graybill, "Critiquing the Discourse of Consent," *Journal of Feminist Studies in Religion* 33, no. 1 (April 12, 2017): 175–76, 175.
43. Rebecca Traister, "Why Sex That's Consensual Can Still Be Bad. And Why We're Not Talking About It.," *The Cut,* October 20, 2015, http://www.thecut.com/2015/10/why-consensual-sex-can-still-be-bad.html ; accessed Dec. 2, 12017.
44. Here, the debate over "affirmative consent" offers a parallel. While many feminist groups and scholars have flocked to affirmative consent ("Yes Means Yes") policies as a way of fighting rape, other feminist critics have noted that such policies are fundamentally conservative and opposed to feminist principles. See Janet Halley, "The Move to Affirmative Consent," *Signs: Journal of Women in Culture and Society* 42, no. 1 (September 1, 2016): 257–79. We might also think about how the emphasis on consent sets a disturbingly low bar for sexual encounters—the baseline for sex is not "good," but rather "consensual."
45. Gayle S. Rubin, "Thinking Sex: Notes for a Radical Theory of the Politics of Sexuality," *The Lesbian and Gay Studies Reader*, ed. Henry Abelove, Michèle Aina Barale, and David M. Halperin (New York: Routledge, 1993): 3–44, 34. Originally published in Carole S. Vance, ed., *Pleasure and Danger: Exploring Female Sexuality* (1984).

BIBLIOGRAPHY

Abu-Lughod, Lila. *Do Muslim Women Need Saving?* Cambridge, MA: Harvard University Press, 2013.

———. "Do Muslim Women Really Need Saving? Anthropological Reflections on Cultural Relativism and Its Others." *American Anthropologist* 104, no. 3 (2002): 783–90.
Ahmed, Sara. *Willful Subjects.* Durham: Duke University Press Books, 2014.
Bach, Alice. "Rereading the Body Politic: Women and Violence in Judges 21." *Biblical Interpretation* 6, no. 1 (1998): 1–19.
Barras, Amelie. *Refashioning Secularisms in France and Turkey: The Case of the Headscarf Ban.* New York: Routledge, 2014.
Bernstein, Elizabeth. "Carceral Politics as Gender Justice? The 'Traffic in Women' and Neoliberal Circuits of Crime, Sex, and Rights." *Theory and Society* 41, no. 3 (2012): 233–59.
———. "Militarized Humanitarianism Meets Carceral Feminism: The Politics of Sex, Rights, and Freedom in Contemporary Antitrafficking Campaigns." *Signs* 36, no. 1 (2010): 45–71.
Bernstein, Elizabeth, and Janet R. Jakobsen, "Sex, Secularism and Religious Influence in US Politics." *Third World Quarterly* 31, no. 6 (September 1, 2010): 1023–39.
Bevacqua, Maria. *Rape on the Public Agenda: Feminism and the Politics of Sexual Assault.* Boston: Northeastern University Press, 2000.
Campbell, Letitia M., and Yvonne C. Zimmerman. "Christian Ethics and Human Trafficking Activism: Progressive Christianity and Social Critique." *Journal of the Society of Christian Ethics* 34, no. 1 (2014): 145–72.
Day, Keri. *Religious Resistance to Neoliberalism: Womanist and Black Feminist Perspectives.* Basingstoke: Palgrave Macmillan, 2016.
Dorr, Lisa Lindquist. *White Women, Rape, and the Power of Race in Virginia, 1900–1960.* Chapel Hill: Univ. of North Carolina Press, 2005.
Douglas, Kelly Brown. *Stand Your Ground: Black Bodies and the Justice of God.* Maryknoll, NY: Orbis Books, 2015.
Doyle, Jennifer. *Campus Sex, Campus Security.* South Pasadena, CA: Semiotext(e), 2015.
Duggan, Lisa. "Rapture and Risk on Campus in the Age of the Sexual Security State." *Bully Bloggers* (blog), June 6, 2017. https://bullybloggers.wordpress.com/2017/06/06/rapture-and-risk-on-campus-in-the-age-of-the-sexual-security-state/.
Echols, Alice. "Retrospective: Tangled Up in Pleasure and Danger." *Signs: Journal of Women in Culture and Society* 42, no. 1 (September 1, 2016): 11–22.
England, Emma. "Violent Superwomen: Super Heroes or Super Villains? Judith, Wonder Woman and Lynndie England." In *A Feminist Companion to Tobit and Judith,* ed. Athalya Brenner-Idan and Helen Efthimiadis-Keith, 242–58. London: Bloomsbury T&T Clark, 2015.
Feimster, Crystal Nicole. *Southern Horrors: Women and the Politics of Rape and Lynching.* Harvard University Press, 2009.
Freeman, Elizabeth. "Monsters, Inc.: Notes on the Neoliberal Arts Education." *New Literary History* 36, no. 1 (April 11, 2005): 83–95.
Gersen, Jeannie Suk. "Laura Kipnis's Endless Trial by Title IX." *The New Yorker*, September 20, 2017. https://www.newyorker.com/news/news-desk/laura-kipniss-endless-trial-by-title-ix.
Giroux, Henry A. "The Terror of Neoliberalism: Rethinking the Significance of Cultural Politics." *College Literature* 32, no. 1 (2005): 1–19.
Gökariksel, Banu, and Katharyne Mitchell. "Veiling, Secularism, and the Neoliberal Subject: National Narratives and Supranational Desires in Turkey and France." *Global Networks* 5, no. 2 (April 1, 2005): 147–65.
Gottschalk, Marie. *The Prison and the Gallows: The Politics of Mass Incarceration in America.* New York; Cambridge: Cambridge University Press, 2006.
Graybill, Rhiannon. "Critiquing the Discourse of Consent." *Journal of Feminist Studies in Religion* 33, no. 1 (April 12, 2017): 175–76.
———. "No Child Left Behind: Reading Jephthah's Daughter with The Babylon Complex." *The Bible & Critical Theory* 11, no. 2 (2015): 36–50.
Graybill, Rhiannon, Meredith Minister, and Beatrice Lawrence. "Sexual Violence in and around the Classroom." *Teaching Theology & Religion* 20, no. 1 (2017): 70–88.
Hall, Rachel. "'It Can Happen to You': Rape Prevention in the Age of Risk Management." *Hypatia* 19, no. 3 (August 1, 2004): 1–18.

Halley, Janet E. *Split Decisions: How and Why to Take a Break from Feminism.* Princeton University Press, 2006.
Halley, Janet. "The Move to Affirmative Consent." *Signs: Journal of Women in Culture and Society* 42, no. 1 (September 1, 2016): 257–79.
Haynes, Stephen R. *Noah's Curse: The Biblical Justification of American Slavery.* New York: Oxford University Press, 2002.
Jacobsen, Christine M. "Veiled Nannies and Secular Futures in France." *Ethnos* 0, no. 0 (April 21, 2017): 1–21.
Kipnis, Laura. "My Title IX Inquisition." *The Chronicle of Higher Education*, May 29, 2015. https://www.chronicle.com/article/My-Title-IX-Inquisition/230489.
———. "Sexual Paranoia Strikes Academe." *The Chronicle of Higher Education*, February 27, 2015. https://www.chronicle.com/article/Sexual-Paranoia-Strikes/190351.
———. *Unwanted Advances: Sexual Paranoia Comes to Campus.* HarperCollins, 2017.
Kurasawa, Fuyuki. "The State of Intellectual Play: A Generational Manifesto for Neoliberal Times." *TOPIA: Canadian Journal of Cultural Studies* 0, no. 18 (September 1, 2008): 11.
Lloyd, Vincent W., and Andrew Prevot, eds. *Anti-Blackness and Christian Ethics.* Maryknoll, NY: Orbis Books, 2017.
Mahmood, Saba. "Retooling Democracy and Feminism in the Service of the New Empire," Qui Parle 16, no. 1 (2006).
Masuzawa, Tomoko. *The Invention of World Religions: Or, How European Universalism Was Preserved in the Language of Pluralism.* Chicago: University of Chicago Press, 2005.
Mohanty, Chandra Talpade. "Under Western Eyes: Feminist Scholarship and Colonial Discourses." *Boundary* 2 12/13 (1984).
Readings, Bill. *The University in Ruins.* Cambridge, MA: Harvard University Press, 1996.
Rubin, Gayle S. "Thinking Sex: Notes for a Radical Theory of the Politics of Sexuality." *The Lesbian and Gay Studies Reader*, ed. Henry Abelove, Michèle Aina Barale, and David M. Halperin. New York: Routledge, 1993, 3–44.
Schulman, Sarah. *Conflict Is Not Abuse: Overstating Harm, Community Responsibility, and the Duty of Repair.* Vancouver, BC: Arsenal Pulp Press, 2016.
Smith, Valerie. *Not Just Race, Not Just Gender: Black Feminist Readings.* New York: Routledge, 2013.
Spivak, Gayatri Chakravorty. "Can the Subaltern Speak?" in *Colonial Discourse and Postcolonial Theory: A Reader*, ed. Patrick Williams and Laura Chrisman. New York: Columbia University Press, 1994.
Thomason, Andy. "Laura Kipnis Says She Faced Another Title IX Investigation, This Time for Her Book." *The Chronicle of Higher Education Blogs: The Ticker* (blog), September 20, 2017. https://www.chronicle.com/blogs/ticker/laura-kipnis-says-she-faced-another-title-ix-investigation-this-time-for-her-book/120210.
Traister, Rebecca. "Why Sex That's Consensual Can Still Be Bad. And Why We're Not Talking About It." *The Cut*, October 20, 2015. http://www.thecut.com/2015/10/why-consensual-sex-can-still-be-bad.html.
Valenti, Jessica. *The Purity Myth: How America's Obsession with Virginity Is Hurting Young Women.* First Trade Paper Edition. Berkeley, CA: Seal Press, 2009.
Vance, Carole, ed., *Pleasure and Danger: Exploring Female Sexuality.* Boston: Routledge & Kegan Paul, 1984.
Wells-Barnett, Ida B. *On Lynchings.* Mineola, NY: Dover, 2014, 1892.
Wilson, Robin. "A Professor, a Graduate Student, and 2 Careers Derailed." *The Chronicle of Higher Education*, June 19, 2015. https://www.chronicle.com/article/A-Professor-a-Graduate/231.

Index

abjection, 103–105
Abu-Lughod, Lila, 81, 86, 183, 184
activism, 2, 5, 26; antitrafficking, 182; good intentions motivating, 175, 176, 177, 179, 182, 186, 187, 188; pedagogical, 10, 14, 47–50, 55, 67
Adetiba, Elizabeth, 3
Advent, 128
affirmative consent: assumptions of, 160; limitations of, 162–163, 191n44; rethinking, 11, 15, 157, 160, 162, 162–163, 191n44
Afghanistan war, 83, 183
Against Our Will (Brownmiller), 11
agency: constrained, 163; disregard for, 68n7; in Judges, 96, 98, 101, 107; of Mary, 118, 119, 132n31; sexual, 143, 144, 158; of students, 58, 66
Ahmed, Leila, 83, 86
Ahmed, Sara, 186
Akiva, Rabbi, 141, 153n17
alien encounters: in "Amnesty," 158, 162–163, 164, 164–165, 166, 167, 169, 170; in "Bloodchild," 158, 162, 163, 164, 166–167, 169–170; in *Xenogenesis*, 158, 162, 163, 164, 165, 167, 168, 169, 170, 172n12–172n13
"Amnesty" (Butler): alien encounters in, 158, 162–163, 164, 164–165, 166, 167, 169, 170; autonomy and bounds of self in, 166, 167; communication in, 164, 164–165; compromised pleasure in, 169, 170
Anderson, Cheryl, 95
animals, in Bible, 57, 66, 70n32
Annunciation, 117–118, 129
Ansari, Aziz, 73–74, 74, 87
antipornography movement, 186
antitrafficking activism, 182
Apne Aap Women Worldwide, 49, 50
AR app. *See* augmented reality app
Asian Communities for Reproductive Justice, 121
Assumption, of Mary, 129, 133n46
augmented reality (AR) app, 48
autonomy, in consent, 166–167, 171
Azam, Hina, 7, 8

Bach, Alice, 181
Bagge Laustsen, Carsten, 104
Baggs, Amanda, 161
Bal, Mieke, 95
#BalanceTonPorc, 77, 88n14
Bapu, Asaram, 39
baraita, 144, 153n26
Barnard conference, on politics of sexuality, 185–186
Behr-Sigel, Elisabeth, 116
Belser, Julia Watts, 150
Bernstein, Elizabeth, 182, 189n9
Beruriah, 148

195

bhakti (devotion of a deity), 43–44, 44–45, 51
Biale, Rachel, 139
Bible: academic study of, 57–58; animals in, 57, 66, 70n32; cop-out hermeneutics and, 23–31, 32; culture influenced by, 56–57, 61, 67; genocide in, 14, 55–57, 59, 60–61, 62–63, 64, 65, 66–67, 70n25; hierarchical binaries in, 57, 67, 70n32, 70n37; New Testament, 6–7, 56; patriarchy in, 27, 69n17, 70n35, 114; rape culture in, 6–7, 14, 22, 23, 23–25, 25–26, 30–31, 55–62, 66–67, 93–107, 138–139, 140, 146, 147, 148, 149–150, 181–182; reproductive justice and, 122–123; slavery in, 6, 14, 55–63, 65, 66–67, 67n1, 68n15, 69n17; "strangeness" of, 58, 60, 66. *See also* Hebrew Bible/Old Testament
"Biblical Interpretation as Violence" (Anderson), 95
Biden, Joe, 2
Biele, Nancy, 5
Black Lives Matter, 55
Blasey-Ford, Christine, 77
"Bloodchild" (Butler): alien encounters in, 158, 162, 163, 164, 166–167, 169–170; autonomy and bounds of self in, 166–167; communication in, 164; compromised pleasure in, 169–170; slavery in, 170
Blyth, Caroline, 10
body language, 171
Boyarin, Daniel, 139, 151
brahminical Hinduism, 38
Brinkema, Eugenie, 93
Brock, Rita Nakashima, 125
Broken Princess: as *Dead or Alive* spinoff, 97, 109n20; Judges 19 and, 15, 97–101, 103–104; as Non-Con, 15, 97–101, 103–104, 109n20, 109n24; sequel to, 99, 109n24
Brown, Wendy, 158, 159–160
Brownmiller, Susan, 4–5, 11
Buchwald, Emilie, 5, 11
Buddhism, 7–8
Buhay, Hilda, 116
Burke, Tarana: critiques by, 3, 76; #MeToo founded by, 3, 3–4, 4, 5–6, 75, 76

Bush, Laura, 81
Butler, Octavia: "Amnesty," 158, 162–163, 164, 164–165, 166, 167, 169, 170; "Bloodchild," 158, 162, 163, 164, 166–167, 169–170; consent and, 15, 162–170, 173n31; Patternist series, 173n31; *Xenogenesis* series, 158, 162, 163, 164, 165, 167, 168, 169, 170, 172n12–172n13

Cahill, Ann, 4–5
Call, Lewis, 173n31
Campbell, Letitia M., 182
Campus Sex, Campus Security (Doyle), 12
Canaan, 65, 67, 181
carceral feminism, 15, 175, 182–183
Card, Claudia, 63, 70n25
Cardijn, Joseph, 115
"The Case for Reparations" (Coates), 55
Catholics, Mary and, 127, 129, 132n31–132n32, 133n46
Chapman, Jean, 38
Cheng, Patrick, 96
children, parents influencing negatively, 143, 153n20–153n21
Christa/Community, 125–126
Christianity: evangelical, 26, 28, 182; Jesus in, 113–114, 117, 118, 122, 124, 125–126, 128, 128–129, 133n43; liberationist, 115; purity culture, 7; rape culture in, 6–7, 22, 26, 116; Right of, 28–29. *See also* Bible; Mary
Christmas, 117, 128–129
christological sexual and reproductive coercion, 118–119, 124–125, 129–130, 131n20, 132n35
Coates, Ta-Nehisi, 55
coercion: christological sexual and reproductive, 118–119, 124–125, 129–130, 131n20, 132n35; defined, 131n21; inequality in, 159
Colgan, Emily, 10
college campuses: good intentions on, 15–16, 175–177, 178, 185, 186, 187, 188; neoliberalization of, 178–179; sexual violence on, 2, 10, 13, 16n2, 18n25, 189n3; Title IX and, 13, 14, 21–22, 23, 25, 26, 31, 55, 157, 178, 189n3

Index

colonial feminism, 83, 84, 185
comic book, *Priya's Shakti* as, 42, 45
communication: non-verbal, 161, 164, 164–165, 171; verbal, 161, 164–166, 171
companion species, 66
Conflict is Not Abuse (Schulman), 177, 186
consent: affirmative, 11, 15, 157, 160, 162, 162–163, 191n44; assumptions of, 157, 160–162, 168; autonomy in, 166–167, 171; Butler and, 15, 162–170, 173n31; complexity of, 74; constrained, 163, 168, 169, 170; education, 162, 167, 171, 172; gender roles and, 74; histories of, 157–160; Judaism and, 137, 138, 140, 143, 148, 150; in Judges, 98, 107; lack of, 17n16, 61, 62; liberal formations of, 160, 167, 173n31; of Mary, 117–119, 124, 125, 128, 129, 130; #MeToo and, 73, 74–75, 77, 82, 83–84, 86–87; Non-Con and, 15, 97–101, 102, 103–105, 107, 108n14, 109n20, 109n24; non-verbal communication in, 161, 164, 164–165, 171; norms, 74; patriarchy and, 168, 171; pedagogy, 74, 170–172; as rape prevention strategy, 157–158, 158, 159, 160, 162, 163, 172; sexual pleasure and, 15, 158, 160, 166, 167–170, 171, 186, 187, 188, 191n44; verbal communication in, 161, 164–166, 171
contract, social, 158–159
Contract and Domination (Pateman and Mills), 158–159
cop-out hermeneutics: Bible and, 23–31, 32; defined, 23; movement beyond, 25–31
Crenshaw, Kimberlé, 10
culture: Bible influencing, 56–57, 61, 67; sexual violence in makings of, 101–103

dangerous women, 146–147, 153n34
Dead or Alive (*DOA*), 97, 109n20
death: physical, 63, 70n32; social, 63–64, 69n19–69n21
Deuteronomy: punishment in, 137–138, 140, 141; rape culture in, 14, 56, 58–66, 69n24, 137–138, 140, 141, 148, 149

Devineni, Ram: AR app of, 48; *Priya's Mirror*, 40, 44, 45, 47, 50; *Priya's Shakti*, 14, 39–51
DeVos, Betsy, 13, 21, 22, 157
devotion of a deity (*bhakti*), 43–44, 44–45, 51
Diken, Bülent, 104
Dikshit, Sheila, 37
disability, 3, 161–162, 172n9
DOA. See *Dead or Alive*
"Do Muslim Women Really Need Saving?" (Abu-Lughod), 81, 183
Doniger, Wendy, 45
double bind, 81, 82
Doyle, Jennifer, 12, 177, 178, 179
Duggan, Lisa, 177, 178
Durga (goddess), 45, 49
Dutta, Debolina, 38
DuVernay, Ava, 162
Dworkin, Andrea, 5

Echols, Alice, 185–186
Edwards, Katie, 10
Eliezer, Rabbi, 143, 148
Eltahawy, Mona, 77–79, 79, 80, 81
England, Emma, 181
ervah (nakedness), 145
essentialism, 25, 27–29
evangelical Christianity, 26, 28, 182
Eve, 143, 147
evil inclination, 142–146, 147–148
Exodus, 62, 68n15, 69n17, 70n31
Exum, Cheryl, 95, 108n16
Ezekiel, 67

fantasy: as genre, 103; rape, 15, 97–98, 101, 102–103, 105, 107, 108n14, 108n16
fatal objecthood, resisting, 93, 103–106, 107
female power (*shakti*), 40, 45–46, 49
feminism: carceral, 15, 175, 182–183; colonial, 83, 84, 185; exegetical path, 31–32; hermeneutics and, 22, 23, 25–28, 29–32; methodologies, 30; race and, 23, 76, 119, 159, 175–176; scholarship, 4–5; sex wars in, 185
Fetterly, Judith, 98
Fischel, Joseph, 158, 160

Fletcher, Pamela, 5, 11
Fonrobert, Charlotte, 139
formal legal process (*halakha*), 140
Formula of the End in Itself, 168
fragility, autonomy and, 171
Fuchs, Esther, 29
Fundamental Marian Dogma, 15, 122, 126–130
"The Game is Rigged" (Traister), 186

GBV. *See* gender based violence
gender: essentialism, 25, 27–29; rabbis constructing, 15, 139, 142, 151; roles, 5, 74; social contract and, 158–159; third, in *Xenogenesis*, 168
gender based violence (GBV), 38, 39–41, 46, 47, 48, 49, 50–51
genealogies, in Hebrew Bible, 65
Genesis: genealogies in, 65; rape culture in, 6, 102, 148, 181–182, 190n23
genocide: animals and, 57, 66; in Bible, 14, 55–57, 59, 60–61, 62–63, 64, 65, 66–67, 70n25; holocaust, 70n25; social death and, 63; women and, 64
Gil, Rosa, 116
Goldman, Dan: AR app of, 48; *Priya's Mirror*, 40, 44, 45, 47, 50; *Priya's Shakti*, 14, 39–51
good intentions: in activism, 175, 176, 177, 179, 182, 186, 187, 188; on campus, 15–16, 175–177, 178, 185, 186, 187, 188; difficulty of, 178; harm and, 175, 176–180, 181, 186, 187–188; limitations of, 175–189; pedagogy and, 175–176, 178, 185, 187–188; in Religious Studies, 175–176, 178, 179, 182–183, 184, 187, 187–188; trigger warnings and, 176–177
Gordon, Avery, 69n20
Gottschalk, Marie, 182
Greek literature, 8

Haag, Pamela, 158, 159
Hajj pilgrimage, 78–79
halakha (formal legal process), 140
Halberstam, Jack, 12
Hall, Rachel, 179
Ham, curse of, 181–182, 190n23
Haraway, Donna, 172n13

Harding, James, 96
harm: critique of, 15, 175, 176–180, 181, 186, 187–188; intersectionality and, 180–183; reduction, 179, 187; in Religious Studies, 178
Headscarves and Hymens (Eltahawy), 78
Hebrew Bible/Old Testament: Deuteronomy, 14, 56, 58–66, 69n24, 137–138, 140, 141, 148, 149; Exodus, 62, 68n15, 69n17, 70n31; Ezekiel, 67; genealogies in, 65; Genesis, 6, 65, 102, 148, 181–182, 190n23; Leviticus, 149; Proverbs, 146; rape culture in, 6, 56–62, 66–67, 138–139, 140, 146, 147, 148, 149–150, 181–182; slavery in, 6, 14, 56–62, 66–67, 67n1, 68n15, 69n17; Torah, 142–143, 145, 146–148, 151, 153n17, 153n41. *See also* Judges
Heidegger, Martin, 106
Herman, Dianne F., 11
hermeneutics, feminism and, 22, 23, 25–28, 29–32
Hernandez, Patricia, 98
hidden transcript, 95
hierarchical binaries, in Bible, 57, 67, 70n32, 70n37
Hindu American Foundation, 46–47
Hinduism: *bhakti* in, 43–44, 44–45, 51; brahminical, 38; Durga in, 45, 49; GBV and, 38, 39–41, 46, 47, 48, 49, 50–51; Pandey and, 14, 37–39, 40, 45, 48, 51; Parvati in, 40, 43, 44, 46, 47, 49, 51; patriarchy and, 39, 50; *Priya's Shakti* and, 14, 39–51; Purana in, 14, 41–47, 51; rape culture and, 14, 37–41, 45–46, 46, 47, 48–49, 50–51, 51; Shiva in, 40, 44, 46
holocaust, 70n25
homosexuality, 149
The Hunting Ground, 2, 55

India's Daughter, 38
individualism, 5, 24
initah, 60, 68n6
"In My Language," 161
intersectionality: defined, 10; harm and, 180–183; of #MosqueMeToo, 84; rape culture and, 5, 10, 24, 29, 84, 180–183
Iraq War, 81

Ishmael, Rabbi, 149
Islam: Hajj in, 78–79; Muhammad in, 7; Qur'an in, 7, 77; rape culture in, 7, 8; "saving" of women and, 81, 183–185. *See also* Muslim #MeToo
Islamophobia, 80–81
"It's on Us," 2, 5

Jackson, Candice, 21
Jacob, Sharon, 132n33
Jakobsen, Janet R., 182
Jephthah, daughter of, 99, 184–185
Jesus: birth of, 113–114, 117, 118, 128–129; community forming, 125–126; Mary and, 113–114, 117, 118, 122, 124, 125–126, 128, 128–129, 133n43; virginity of, 117
Johnson, Elizabeth, 115, 116, 117
Jones-Warsaw, Koala, 96
Joseph, 125, 132n38
Judaism: consent and, 137, 138, 140, 143, 148, 150; evil inclination in, 142–146, 147–148; rape culture in, 6, 22, 26, 137–139, 140, 142–146, 147–148, 150, 151–152. *See also* Hebrew Bible/Old Testament; rabbis
Judd, Ashley, 3
Judges: agency in, 96, 98, 101, 107; *Broken Princess* and, 15, 97–101, 103–104; consent in, 98, 107; daughter of Jephthah in, 99, 184–185; fatal objecthood in, 93, 103–106, 107; makings of culture and, 101–103; Non-Con and, 97–100, 102, 103–105, 107; pedagogy and, 93–95, 96–98, 105–106, 107, 108n14; questioning text of, 95–101; rape culture in, 15, 93–107, 108n14, 108n16, 148–149; toxic masculinity in, 103, 106
Justice Verma Committee, 38–39

Kafer, Alison, 161
Kahn, Madeleine, 8
Kalmanofsky, Amy, 10
Kandiyoti, Deniz, 86
Kant, Immanuel, 104, 168
Kavanaugh, Brett, 77
Kawashima, Robert S., 17n16, 69n17
Keefe, Alice A., 96, 102

Kessler, Gwynn, 139
Khalid, Maryam, 86
Khan, Sabica, 78–79, 80
Kindig, Jessie, 4
Kipnis, Laura, 12, 177, 178, 189n3
Krakauer, Jon, 2, 16n2
Kristeva, Julia, 103
Kuja, Ryan, 100, 101
Kunoichi. See Broken Princess
kyriarchy: defined, 32n7; rape culture and, 22, 23, 25, 25–26, 28, 31, 32n7

labor contract, 159
Labovitz, Gail, 139
Lacan, Jacques, 94, 104
Lakshman rekha (moral limits), 39, 41
language: body, 171; communication and, 161, 164–166, 171
Lasine, Stuart, 99, 104
Lauer, Matt, 1, 73
Lazarus, Margaret, 11
Lemos, T.M., 69n18, 69n24
Lettini, Gabriella, 124
Leviticus, 149
liberationist Christianity, 115
Lipka, Hilary B., 23–25
liturgical practices, 128–129

MacKinnon, Catharine, 4–5, 168
Mahmood, Saba, 184
Marian Dogma, 15, 122, 126–130
marriage: laws, 62; rape and, 137, 138, 143–144; slavery and, 61, 62, 63–64, 69n17
Marshall, John W., 6
Mary: agency of, 118, 119, 132n31; Annunciation and, 117–118, 129; Assumption of, 129, 133n46; Catholics and, 127, 129, 132n31–132n32, 133n46; consent of, 117–119, 124, 125, 128, 129, 130; education about, 128; in Fundamental Marian Dogma, 15, 122, 126–130; Jesus and, 113–114, 117, 118, 122, 124, 125–126, 128, 128–129, 133n43; Joseph and, 125, 132n38; in liturgical practices, 128–129; as mother, 114, 116, 117, 122, 127, 131n9, 132n32; obedience of, 116, 117, 122, 125, 131n9; patriarchy and, 114, 116,

117, 123, 132n38; Protestants and, 113, 127, 132n31–132n32, 133n43; rape culture and, 15, 114–119, 120, 122, 124, 126–128, 129, 130n4, 131n20; reproductive justice of, 15, 114, 115, 119–123, 124–125, 126–130, 130n4, 132n31, 132n33, 133n46; self-determination of, 120, 121, 123, 127, 132n38; teaching about, 115–119, 122–126, 127–128, 130n6, 130n8, 131n15; toxic masculinity and, 115, 120, 130; virginity of, 114, 116–117, 122, 127–128, 133n44
#Masaktach, 77
Masenya, Madipoane, 100
"Mattress Performance (Carry That Weight)," 177, 189n2
Mbembe, Achille, 103
McEwan, Melissa, 11
McGuire, Danielle L., 180
McRuer, Robert, 161
Meijer, Maaike, 98
men: as prostitutes, 149, 154n47; rape of, 139, 148–150
Mernissa, Fatima, 86
Messina-Dysert, Gina, 10
Metamorphoses (Ovid), 8
#MeToo: #BalanceTonPorc, 77, 88n14; blurred lines in, 87, 90n49; Burke founding, 3, 3–4, 4, 5–6, 75, 76; complexity of, 73–75; consent and, 73, 74–75, 77, 82, 83–84, 86–87; critiques of, 3–4, 76, 82–83; goals of, 74, 76, 82; introduction to, 1–6; Muslim #MeToo, 14, 75, 76–87; patriarchy and, 73, 76, 79, 81, 83; success of, 31, 177; "Time's Up" and, 17n6
Midrash, 15, 139, 142
Milano, Alyssa, 3, 75
Miller, Peggy, 5
Mills, Charles, 158–159
Milne, Pamela J., 30
Minister, Meredith, 10, 12, 69n21
Mir-Hosseini, Ziba, 86
Mishnah, 147, 153n26
Missoula (Krakauer), 2, 16n2
modesty, laws of, 145–146
Mohanty, Chandra Talpade, 183
moral limits (*Lakshman rekha*), 39, 41

moral logic, 104
#MosqueMeToo: consent and, 75, 77, 82, 83–84, 86–87; Eltahawy starting, 77–79; importance of, 81; intersectionality of, 84; Khan in, 78–79, 80; #MeToo and, 75, 77–87; in Muslim #MeToo, 14, 75, 77–87; pedagogy and, 84–86, 87
mother, Mary as, 114, 116, 117, 122, 127, 131n9, 132n32
Muhammad (prophet), 7
Murtad, Aisha, 79
Muslim #MeToo: critique of, 83; episodes, 76–81; #Masaktach in, 77; #MosqueMeToo, 14, 75, 77–87; Muslim women seen in, 81–84, 84–85, 86, 87
mythical norm, 95

Nair, Yasmin, 12
nakedness (*ervah*), 145
nativity plays, 113–114
New Testament, 6–7, 56
Non-Con (non-consensual) pornography: *Broken Princess*, 15, 97–101, 103–104, 109n20, 109n24; defined, 97; Judges and, 97–100, 102, 103–105, 107; pedagogy and, 108n14
non-Israelites, as slaves, 62, 65
non-verbal communication, 161, 164, 164–165, 171

Obama administration: "It's On Us" campaign, 2, 5; Title IX and, 13, 22, 23, 157; White House Task Force to Protect Students from Sexual Assault of, 157
obedience, of Mary, 116, 117, 122, 125, 131n9
objecthood, resisting, 93, 103–106, 107
O'Donnell, Christopher, 131n9
Old Testament. *See* Hebrew Bible/Old Testament
Orientalism (Said), 86
Ovid, 8

Pandey, Jyoti Singh, 14, 37–39, 40, 45, 48, 51
Parvati (goddess): in *Priya's Mirror*, 44; in *Priya's Shakti*, 40, 43, 44, 46, 47, 49,

51
pastoral cycle, 115
Pateman, Carole, 158–159
patriarchy: in Bible, 27, 69n17, 70n35, 114; consent and, 168, 171; Hinduism and, 39, 50; Mary and, 114, 116, 117, 123, 132n38; in *Metamorphoses*, 8; #MeToo and, 73, 76, 79, 81, 83; social contract and, 159
Patternist series (Butler), 173n31
Patterson, Orlando, 63
Paul (saint), 6
pedagogy: activism in, 10, 14, 47–50, 55, 67; on consent, 74, 170–172; good intentions and, 175–176, 178, 185, 187–188; Judges and, 93–95, 96–98, 105–106, 107, 108n14; #MosqueMeToo and, 84–86, 87; Non-Con and, 108n14; *Priya's Shakti* and, 41, 47–50; rabbis and, 151–152; rape culture and, 2, 8–11, 55–62, 66–67, 151–152
Peskowitz, Miriam, 75
Peters, Rebecca Todd, 125
pornography: movement against, 186; Non-Con, 15, 97–101, 102, 103–105, 107, 108n14, 109n20, 109n24; Vance and, 186
postcolonial critique, 15, 175, 183–184, 188
power: rape culture in contexts of, 4, 6, 171–172, 173n31; *shakti*, 40, 45–46, 49; state, 177, 189n6
Priya's Mirror (Devineni, Goldman, and Vohra), 40, 44, 45, 47, 50
Priya's Shakti (Devineni and Goldman): as comic book, 42, 45; Hinduism and, 14, 39–51; Pandey and, 39; Parvati in, 40, 43, 44, 46, 47, 49, 51; pedagogy and, 41, 47–50; as Purana, 14, 41–47, 51; story of, 40–41
property, women as, 62, 63, 64, 65, 67, 69n17–69n18, 138, 141
prostitutes, male, 149, 154n47
Protestants, Mary and, 113, 127, 132n31–132n32, 133n43
Proverbs, 146
punishment, 137–138, 140–142, 149
Purana, 14, 41–47, 51

purity culture, Christian, 7

queer studies, 177, 179
Qur'an, 7, 77

rabbis: Akiva, 141, 153n17; Eliezer, 143, 148; evil inclination and, 142–146, 147–148; gender constructed by, 15, 139, 142, 151; Ishmael, 149; Midrash and, 139, 142; Mishnah and, 147, 153n26; modesty and, 145–146; pedagogy and, 151–152; rape culture and, 15, 139–142, 143, 146, 148, 150, 151–152; in Religious Studies, 139; sexual pleasure and, 141–142, 143; Talmud and, 15, 139, 141, 142, 143, 148, 149; Tarfon, 139; Targums and, 139; on women as sexual traps, 146–148; Yehuda, 144
race: critique of, 175; feminism and, 23, 76, 119, 159, 175–176; harm and, 180–183; in rape culture, 3, 4, 5, 23, 76, 82, 83, 119, 180–183, 188; reproductive justice and, 119; social contract and, 158–159
RAINN. *See* Rape, Abuse and Incest National Network
Ramadan, Tariq, 76–77
Ramayana, 39
Rape, Abuse and Incest National Network (RAINN), 157
rape culture: defined, 11–12, 177; thinking with and beyond, 11–13. *See also specific topics*
Rape Culture, 11
"The Rape Culture" (Herman), 11
rape-narrative, 94, 99–100, 102
rape prevention: consent as strategy for, 157–158, 158, 159, 160, 162, 163, 172; education toward, 158, 162, 167; harm reduction and, 179, 187
Rashi, 148
real rape, 97–99, 108n16
Religious Studies: applied, 114–115; discipline of, 2; value of, 176. *See also specific topics*
reparations, 55, 61
representation: fantasy in, 101; rape and, 93, 94–95, 96–101, 103–106

reproductive justice: defined, 119–120; of Mary, 15, 114, 115, 119–123, 124–125, 126–130, 130n4, 132n31, 132n33, 133n46; as practical theology, 126–130
resistance: to fatal objecthood, 93, 103–106, 107; Trump administration and, 32
Resisting Reader (Fetterly), 98
Rethinking Rape (Cahill), 5
revenge, 102
Right, Christian, 28–29
Riley, Meghan, 168, 169
Rodrigues, Hillary, 43
Roman literature, 8
Rose, Charlie, 1, 4
Roth, Martha, 5, 11
Rubin, Gayle, 187

Sadean maxim, 104
Said, Edward, 86
St. Anthony's College, 76–77
Satlow, Michael, 139, 151
Scholz, Susanne, 6, 96, 102
Schulman, Sarah, 177, 178, 186, 189n6
Schüssler Fiorenza, Elisabeth, 23, 27–28, 29, 32n7
Schwartz, Regina, 57
science fiction. *See* Butler, Octavia
scientific positivism, 23–25
"see-judge-act" model, 115
self, bounds of, 166–167, 171
self-control, fetishization of, 160–161
self-determination, 120, 121, 123, 127, 132n38
sex education, 170–172
sexual agency, 143, 144, 158
sexuality, harm and, 180–183
sexual pleasure: compromised, 167–170; consent and, 15, 158, 160, 166, 167–170, 171, 186, 187, 188, 191n44; problem of, 15, 175, 176, 185–187, 188; rabbis and, 141–142, 143
Sexual Transgression in the Hebrew Bible (Lipka), 23–25
sex wars, 185
Shakir, Imam Zaid, 77
shakti (female power), 40, 45–46, 49
Shambhala community, 7–8
Shelley, Carter, 98

Shiva (god), 40, 44, 46
shruti literature, 41
Siebers, Tobin, 161
Sircar, Oishik, 38
situatedness, 58, 68n4
slavery: in Bible, 6, 14, 55–63, 65, 66–67, 67n1, 68n15, 69n17; in "Bloodchild," 170; curse of Ham and, 182; marriage and, 61, 62, 63–64, 69n17; of non-Israelites, 62, 65; reparations for, 55, 61; slaves as property, 62, 69n17; social death in, 63–64, 69n19; white, 180
smriti literature, 41
social contract, 158–159
social death, 63–64, 69n19–69n21
social location, 58, 68n4
social media, 171
social reproduction, 121, 125, 126
Spacey, Kevin, 1, 73
Spivak, Gayatri, 183–184
St. Anthony's College, 76–77
state, power of, 177, 189n6
Stone, Ken, 96–97, 100
street art, 49–50
structural violence, 61
students: agency of, 58, 66; *Metamorphoses* and, 8; in Religious Studies classroom, 8–11
Studio FOW, 97–98, 103
Sulkowicz, Emma, 177, 189n2
Swarthmore College, 55

Take Back the Night, 5
Talmud, 15, 139, 141, 142, 143, 148, 149
tannaitic period, 144, 153n27
Tarfon, Rabbi, 139
Targums, 139
tawaf, 78
"Thinking Sex" (Rubin), 187
"Time's Up" movement, 17n6
Title IX: Obama administration and, 13, 22, 23, 157; rape culture and, 13, 14, 21–22, 23, 25, 26, 31, 55, 157, 178, 189n3; Trump administration and, 13, 21–22, 23, 157
Torah: revealed, 145; study of, 142–143, 146–148, 151, 153n17, 153n41
"Toward a Politics of Sexuality" conference, 185–186

toxic masculinity: defined, 120; in Judges 19, 103, 106; Mary and, 115, 120, 130
Traister, Rebecca, 186
Transforming a Rape Culture (Buchwald, Fletcher, and Roth), 5, 11
Trible, Phyllis, 95, 101, 106
trigger warnings, 176–177
Tronto, Joan, 132n29
Trump administration: DeVos in, 13, 21, 22, 157; feminist resistance and, 32; rape culture and, 13, 21–22, 23, 27, 31, 32, 157; Title IX and, 13, 21–22, 23, 157

Union, Gabrielle, 3, 16n4
Unwanted Advances (Kipnis), 12, 189n3

Vance, Carole, 186
Vazquez, Carmen, 116
verbal communication, 161, 164–166, 171
victims, women as, 179–180
Vijayvargiya, Kailash, 39
"Violence against Women in Democratic India" (Chapman), 38
virginity: of Jesus, 117; of Mary, 114, 116–117, 122, 127–128, 133n44
Vohra, Paromita, 40, 44, 45, 47, 50

Weinstein, Harvey, 1, 3, 3–4, 73, 75, 88n14
Wells, Ida B., 4, 5, 180
West, Gerald, 94
Where Freedom Starts (Kindig), 4
white feminism, 23, 119, 159
White House Task Force to Protect Students from Sexual Assault, 157

white slavery, 180
Why are We reading Ovid's Handbook on Rape? (Kahn), 8
Willful Subjects (Ahmed, S.), 186
wisdom, women as, 146
women: dangerous, 146–147, 153n34; genocide and, 64; Muslim, seen, 81–84, 84–85, 86, 87; passivity of, 143, 148; as property, 62, 63, 64, 65, 67, 69n17–69n18, 138, 141; rape of men and, 139, 148–150; "saving" of, 15, 81, 183–185, 188; as sexual traps, 146–148; social death of, 63, 69n19, 69n21; as surviving object, 106; Torah study and, 142–143, 146–148, 151, 153n17, 153n41; as victims, 179–180; visibility of, 94, 100; as wisdom, 146; worth of, 141
Women and Gender in Islam (Ahmed, L.), 83
Wunderlick, Renner, 11

Xenogenesis series (Butler): alien encounters in, 158, 162, 163, 164, 165, 167, 168, 169, 170, 172n12–172n13; autonomy and bounds of self in, 165, 167; communication in, 164, 165; compromised pleasure in, 168, 169, 170

Yehuda, Rabbi, 144

Zed, Rajan, 46–47, 52n29
Zeroth Marian Dogma, 15, 122, 126–130
Zimmerman, Yvonne C., 182

About the Contributors

Kirsten Boles is a PhD candidate in Women's Studies in Religion at Claremont Graduate University. She studies transnational feminist and queer theory, gender and sexuality in Islam, religion in popular culture, feminist theology, and women in world religions. She has taught at Santa Ana College and the University of Redlands. She also writes for the AAR's *Reading Religion* series.

T. Nicole Goulet is Assistant Professor of Religious Studies at Indiana University of Pennsylvania. She studies Hinduism, with a focus on colonial India. At the heart of Goulet's research interests is identifying the role and interplay of race, class, and gender as it relates to religion in general, and Hinduism specifically. These interests inform her current projects, including a collaborative effort on women, religion, and clothing, which is in its initial stages in development. These interests have also influenced how Goulet approaches and understands the study of religion in contemporary society.

Rhiannon Graybill is W.J. Millard Professor of Religion and Associate Professor of Religious Studies at Rhodes College in Memphis, TN. At Rhodes, she also serves as Director of the Gender and Sexuality Studies Program. She is the author of *Are We Not Men?: Unstable Masculinity in the Hebrew Prophets* (Oxford, 2016) and multiple articles on gender, sexuality, and biblical texts. Her second book, *Texts after Terror*, explores how queer feminist critique troubles narratives of sexualized violence in the Hebrew Bible. She is also co-authoring a commentary on the book of Jonah.

Gwynn Kessler is Associate Professor of Religion at Swarthmore College. Her teaching interests and experience encompass classes on the Hebrew

Bible, Midrash, Talmud, Judaism and Gender, Feminist and Queer Theology, Queer and Transgender Bibilical Interpretation, Race and Gender in the Bible, and Method and Theory in Religious Studies. She is author of *Conceiving Israel: The Fetus in Rabbinic Narratives* (UPenn Press, July 2009), which explores rabbinic traditions about the fetus for the purpose of examining rabbinic constructions of gender, ethnicity, and theology. She is currently working on a monograph about Queer Theory and Rabbinic Literature.

Minenhle Nomalungelo Khumalo is an American based, South African PhD Candidate in the Bible and Cultures Program at Drew University. Her research interests include readings of the (Hebrew) Bible that are informed by critical understandings of popular cultural productions of narrative—with a special focus on gender, sexuality, race, and ethnicity. Her recent work consists of readings of biblical texts using hermeneutics informed by Afro-Marxism and Afro-pessimism; literary theories concerning representation, recognition, and the epistemic functions of violence in literature; as well as critical pedagogies for collective psychosocial resistance.

Beatrice Lawrence is Associate Professor of Hebrew Bible at Seattle University in Seattle, WA, where she teaches courses in biblical studies as well as Jewish studies. She has published on rabbinic hermeneutics, Jewish-Christian dialogue, and rape culture in sacred text (and in the teaching of those texts). In addition, she serves as a lay leader for Jewish communities in Idaho and Washington.

Meredith Minister is Assistant Professor of Religion at Shenandoah University in Winchester, VA. She is the author of *Rape Culture on Campus* (Lexington, 2018) and *Trinitarian Theology and Power Relations: God Embodied* (Palgrave, 2014) and the coeditor (with Sarah Bloesch) of *Cultural Approaches to Studying Religion: An Introduction to Theories and Methods* (Bloomsbury, 2018) and *The Bloomsbury Reader in Cultural Approaches to the Study of Religion* (Bloomsbury, 2018).

Jeremy Posadas is Chair and Associate Professor of Religious Studies at Austin College (on the Texas-Oklahoma border). He holds the John F. Anderson Chair of Christian Thought and is a core faculty member in the gender studies program. In addition, he chairs the Class, Religion, and Theology unit of the American Academy of Religion. As a social ethicist and constructive theologian, his writing is rooted in Christian traditions that struggle for the liberation of all people, along with the Earth, from injustice in its multivalent forms. His scholarship engages working class studies, social reproduction theory, queer studies, and anti-work theory, among other critical discourses. He is also the creator of the "United Regions of America Map," a county based regionalization of the United States that calibrates natural landscapes, dominant industries, and local perceptions.

Susanne Scholz is Professor of Old Testament at SMU Perkins School of Theology in Dallas, Texas, USA. As a diasporic German, naturalized U.S.-American, post-Holocaust, and feminist scholar, she researches, writes, and works in the area of sacred text studies, with an emphasis on cultural studies, historiography, and hermeneutics. Among her recent books are *The Bible as Political Artifact: On the Feminist Study of the Hebrew Bible* (Fortress, 2017), *Introducing the Women's Hebrew Bible: Feminism, Gender Justice, and the Study of the Old Testament* (2nd rev. edn; Bloomsbury T&T Clark, 2017), and *Sacred Witness: Rape in the Hebrew Bible* (Fortress, 2010).

www.ingramcontent.com/pod-product-compliance
Lightning Source LLC
Chambersburg PA
CBHW020119010526
44115CB00008B/894